Contemporary Issues in Individual, Couple, and Family Lives and Treatment

Florence W. Kaslow
Editor

Contemporary Issues in Individual, Couple, and Family Lives and Treatment

Springer

Editor
Florence W. Kaslow
Kaslow Associates
Palm Beach Gardens, FL, USA

ISBN 978-3-031-90005-1 ISBN 978-3-031-90006-8 (eBook)
https://doi.org/10.1007/978-3-031-90006-8

This Springer imprint is published by the registered company Springer Nature Switzerland AG
The registered company address is: Gewerbestrasse 11, 6330 Cham, Switzerland

Preface

Foreword

The purpose of this book is to highlight current and emerging issues that impact couples and families and the practice of family psychology/therapy. It is intended to be utilized as a textbook, for university and other courses, a handbook for practitioners, and a book for readers interested in this subject and the multitude of contemporary issues elaborated.

In Chap. 1, Dr. Friedland covers how contemporary families have changed in the past few decades with higher divorce rates, more children being raised in single parent families, fewer close connections to their families of origin, and many more people experiencing more of a sense of loneliness and isolation. She also highlights the positives that characterize healthy families and how to help create them, sometimes with the guidance of a competent therapist.

In Chap. 2, Dr. Groveman discusses the use of psychedelic drugs in couples therapy to help the couple relax and enjoy each other and their sexuality together. He emphasizes the importance of the therapist being specifically trained in this area, following all the legal and therapeutic pharmacological guidelines, and being certified for this practice where necessary. He reports good to excellent results and much client satisfaction when they use the psychedelic drugs properly and they can evolve a more loving relationship.

Chapter 3, which I wrote, presents a current overview of the four and five generation families, in which the oldest members can be over 90 years of age and the youngest are still in their infancy. It tackles where seniors live, especially if widowed and retired, what they may want and need, and which family members and/or retirement facilities can provide, as well as the financial issues to cover living expenses and aides, if needed, and often the feeling of being unloved and unwanted. It offers numerous suggestions for enhancing life in the senior years and recommends younger family members consider what they will want in their future and see if they can help provide it for their grandparents and/or parents in the present. It also mentions the dearth of affordable, suitable, low cost or government supported retirement housing and stresses the need for this to be provided.

In Chap. 4, Dr. Harway elaborates the issues involved in post-partum depression, a topic not often discussed in the couples/family literature, but rather tossed off because "this too shall pass." She highlights how this condition affects the mother; the father who may be torn between taking off from a job that doesn't allow "paternity leave" to help care for his wife and baby; and the infant who needs constant care when neither the mom nor dad is very available and when there are no relatives nearby to come and help care for the baby. Many of these mothers/couples cannot afford a live-in baby nurse and often the obstetrician is uninvolved except when she/they visit their office. Dr. Harway presents a touching, vivid portrait of this situation and some ideas on how it might be handled.

Next, in Chap. 5, Dr. Rothman, a Concierge Physician, provides an overview of contemporary changes in primary care medical practice, including the emergence of Concierge Practices that charge an annual fee of anywhere from $2,500 to $40,000, depending on such factors as clientele served and geographical locale. She indicates that concierge physicians usually have between 400-600 members on their panel whereas other primary care physicians may have several thousand. This permits them to provide same- or next-day appointments; long virtual or phone sessions and when needed, as during the COVID-19 pandemic; and make house calls if need be. She also indicates many concierge physicians do not have hospital privileges and if they need to hospitalize a patient they collaborate with the hospitalist on duty. The reader may feel like they are accompanying her for a day in the office as they peruse this very timely, informative chapter.

Chapter 6, by Dr. Leon and Ms. Cedeño, delves into a very new and still somewhat unusual practice—the utilization of neuropsychological evaluations to determine the suitability of a patient for neurosurgery when working in conjunction with a neurosurgeon. Their model also highly recommends meeting with significant family members to ascertain their thoughts about such a serious procedure, how the outcome might affect the patients' life, and their lives and the relationship. This is a relatively recent development in the fields of neurosurgery and neuropsychology. As of now, they are only aware of this approach being used in three Florida hospitals. It seems that this is a significant contribution to the domain of neurosurgery and (that they wish) hopefully will be adopted by more neurosurgery departments and that more neuropsychologists are trained in how to do such evaluations.

Chapter 7, by Dr. Sirkin, shifts the book's attention to family businesses. He highlights the dynamics of the family business and factors which contribute to its longevity over four and five generations vs. those that end after two or three generations. As in many of the other chapters, family dynamics, loyalties, resentments, and hidden agendas must be taken into account by the family business consultant and may need to be interpreted to the leadership of the business. Sometimes if a member of the family wants a career outside of the business, this is construed as rejection. The consultant may need to bring several people together to help the key players understand and accept the different scripts and motivations and not feel rejected or excluded. His discussion of family businesses, which are a major part of the economy in the United States and elsewhere, is very illuminating.

A tumultuous, relatively new dilemma is highlighted in Chap. 8, by Drs. Nadine Kaslow, Hunnicut-Ferguson, and Patton. They magnify the horrific difficulties some couples and families are having "navigating across the political spectrum" when the couples and perhaps their children, strongly and sometimes explosively, disagree about political issues and/or candidates for office. They discuss how these disagreements can become so challenging, almost to the point of destroying relationships. They tactfully elaborate how these opposite views, which have led to serious clashes within the couple can be dealt with in couples and/or family therapy and provide a fascinating case example. This is an extremely provocative case in an absorbing chapter. This chapter may provide guidance to professors and practitioners of psychotherapy who are encountering this relatively recent kind of strife in previously satisfying relationships.

Drs. Broder and Goldman focus the spotlight on the "21st century relationship trends and norms in psychotherapy" in Chap. 9. They highlight that many couples who are committed and devoted to one another prefer to live together rather than marry. They are monogamous but feel no need to legalize the relationship. Their practices (usually separate) are located in Philadelphia, and they have an upper middle to upper-class clientele. I tend to think some of what they describe is more typical in urban and suburban communities of large, metropolitan areas and of "upper middle and upper class" couples rather than less wealthy, agricultural and religious communities and cannot be generalized. They provide a vivid, well-documented description of long-term committed relationships between unmarried couples that an increasing number of couples find preferable.

As I am writing this summation of Chap. 10, which focuses on Handling Couples Issues Pertaining to Relocation and Finances, I am cooped up in my apartment not knowing if Category 4 Hurricane Milton (October 2024) or some of the raging tornadoes will hit our area. It is when such unexpected external crises, like hurricanes, tornadoes, massive flooding, and/or explosions hit and destroy ones' homes that people are faced with having to relocate immediately (even if just for the immediate future). This is not something they were planning to do. These losses associated with the dramatic, unforeseen event are extensive, and can include credit cards, cash, check books, bank information, one's computer which stored all such critical information, as well and beloved possessions. There is often no way to access insurance purchased to cover emergencies quickly and relocation must take place immediately. Other relocations occur because of job transfers, the desire to live someplace else, sometimes to live nearer to other family members, or to move into a more upscale community, which they can now afford. Planned relocations based on choice are much easier than sudden ones emanating from unanticipated crises, which can be overwhelming and take months to finalize. Help should be sought from such agencies as FEMA, Family Service Associations, churches, and appropriate state and local municipal agencies. This tragedy is often overwhelming, and it takes a long time to resolve and for the individuals involved to recuperate.

In Chap. 11, Dr. Wilner describes the reasons for and processes of engaging in the adoption of a child from another country. She discusses the importance of working with a well-reputed adoption agency or law firm that provides this kind of service, visiting the adoption agency in the country from which he/she/they will adopt and meeting the child in the orphanage or other facility has designated to be theirs. If it seems like a good match, then they agree to take the assigned child. If not, they ask if another child is available and try to ascertain if this one is a better match. Before leaving home, they should explain to any children they already have as well as any grandparents who will be awaiting the new member of the family what they might expect and how to welcome the child. Over the years, Americans have adopted from different countries—most recently, China has been the major source, but early in 2024 some of their policies were altered. Adoption agencies should keep abreast of such legal changes. Whether the child in from China, another Asian country, or an African or Latin American country, it is essential that the adoptive parent(s) help them deal with looking and sounding "different." Many international adoptions bring much happiness to those involved, others do not. Hopefully the original (local) adoption agency or a family service agency has staff that can help them deal with the problems that have evolved.

In Chap. 12, I summarize the major themes and challenges described throughout the book on some of the contemporary issues and problems confronting individuals, couples, and families being brought into therapy in the 21st century. If the reader has any feedback, please send it to me or the specific chapter authors. I hope you have garnered some new ideas and information and found this book well worth reading.

Palm Beach Gardens, FL, USA Florence W. Kaslow

Acknowledgements

I would like to extend my appreciation to my daughter, Dr. Nadine Kaslow, who in addition to contributing a chapter on a little-written about subject, helped me organize the final version of the book for publication; my son, Howard, who kept my computer functioning so I could complete this volume; and my editor and good friend at Springer, Sharon Panulla. Without their assistance and encouragement, this volume would not have been successfully completed.

Florence W. Kaslow, PhD, ABPP
Editor

Contents

1 **Evolving Identities of Family and Self in Times of Turbulence** 1
Lilli Friedland

2 **The Use of Psychedelics in Couples Therapy** 29
Alan Groveman

3 **Four and Five Generation Families: A Relatively New Phenomenon** 41
Florence W. Kaslow

4 **Understanding Postpartum Disorders and Their Impact on the Family** 51
Michele Harway

5 **Contemporary Issues in Primary Care Medicine: A Multifactorial Analysis of How Primary Care Has Changed in the 21st Century and How It Affects Patients and Physicians** 63
Laurie Plitcha Rothman

6 **The Interface Between Relational Family Dynamics, Interventional Neurosurgery, and Neuropsychology** 81
Yolanda C. León and K. Brianalysse Nicolena Cedeño

7 **Partners in Time: Multigenerational Family Businesses in the Twenty-First Century** 109
Mark I. Sirkin

8 **Navigating Love Across the Political Spectrum** 129
Nadine J. Kaslow, Samantha C. Patton, and Kallio Hunnicutt-Ferguson

9 **Twenty-First Century Relationship Trends and Norms in Psychotherapy** 151
Michael S. Broder and Arlene Goldman

10 Handling Couples Issues Pertaining to Relocation and Finances . . . 165
Florence W. Kaslow

11 The Rewards and Challenges of International Adoption 177
Karyne B. Wilner

12 Summation and Epilogue 201
Florence W. Kaslow

Index 203

About the Editors and Contributors

About the Editor

Florence W. Kaslow, PhD, ABPP is in private practice as an individual, couples and family psychologist and Family Business Consultant in West Palm Beach, FL. She has been a Professor at a Medical School in Philadelphia and a former Dean of a Psychology graduate school in Florida. She has guest lectured in over 50 countries, is the author or editor of 32 books, and a contributor to over 100 other books.

Contributors

Florence W. Kaslow, PhD, ABPP Kaslow Associates, Palm Beach Gardens, FL, USA

G. Andrew H. Benjamin, PhD, JD, ABPP University of Washington, Seattle, WA, USA

Lilli Friedland, PhD, ABPP Executive Advisors, Inc., Beverly Hills, CA, USA

Alan Groveman, PhD, ABPP Northwestern University, Evanston, IL, USA

Michele Harway, PhD, ABPP Fielding Graduate University, Santa Barbara, CA, USA

Laurie Plitcha Rothman, MD, ABFM, ABOM Tampa General Hospital, Palm Beach Gardens, FL, USA

Yolanda C. León, PsyD, APBdN University of South Florida, Tampa, FL, USA

K. Brianalysse Nicolena Cedeño, BA University of South Florida, Tampa, FL, USA

Mark I. Sirkin, PhD Sirkin Advisors, White Plains, NY, USA

Nadine J. Kaslow, PhD, ABPP Emory University, Atlanta, GA, USA

Samantha C. Patton, PhD, ABPP Emory University, Atlanta, GA, USA

Kallio Hunnicutt-Ferguson, PhD, ABPP Emory University, Atlanta, GA, USA

Michael S. Broder, PhD Media Psychology Associates, Philadelphia, PA, USA

Arlene Goldman, PhD Media Psychology Associates, Philadelphia, PA, USA

Karyne B. Wilner, PsyD Core Energetics Academy, Newtown, CT, USA

Introduction

Family psychology continues to celebrate Florrie Kaslow, PhD, ABPP. Once again, she has amassed colleagues in our discipline to discuss emerging issues in family psychology and has added to our literature, too. As a result, readers will appreciate the comprehensive compendium of the 21st century subjects that can inform all mental health practitioners including the clinicians (psychologists, neuropsychologists, psychiatrists, social workers, counselors) and their teachers and researchers. It will also enlighten concierge physicians and family business consultants.

Truly the book is a stimulating complement to the existing literature as family psychology continues to address a myriad of new challenges and opportunities that families experience. The book also reminds us of time-tested knowledge, such as how familial homeostasis and resistance to change is a dynamic that still exists; it demands consideration no matter what contexts face the family (Bowen, 1978). The chapters are lucidly written and cover the topics with informed, enjoyable, and compelling approaches. The book magnifies clinical interventions and throughout the chapters, case studies flesh out the applications of the skills.

Readers will feel heartened as they appreciate the depth of family psychology reflected throughout the chapters in *Contemporary issues in individual, couple, and family lives and treatment*. They will greatly benefit from the far-reaching coverage of the chapters. I certainly did.

Bowen, M. (1978). *Family therapy in clinical practice*. Jason, Aronson, Inc.

G. Andrew H. Benjamin
Clinical Professor of Psychology
Affiliate Professor of Law
University of Washington
Seattle, WA, USA

Chapter 1
Evolving Identities of Family and Self in Times of Turbulence

Lilli Friedland

Redefining the Family

The family unit has long been recognized as the fundamental building block of human societies, serving as the primary source of nurturance, education, and socialization for individuals from birth through adulthood. Historically, the family was often defined as a social and economic unit connected by blood, marriage, cohabitation, or adoption. For children, the family's attachment bonds and connectedness offer necessary support and a secure base for exploring the world while providing a sense of stability and connection. Traditionally, the family has been the central structure in transmitting cultural and societal values and providing emotional and economic support to its members. The core of an individual's sense of "belonging" and social identity is shaped by the values, customs, languages, traditions, and culture passed down through their family (Schwartz et al., 2009). Intergenerational stories foster a sense of identity continuity and connection across generations. (Fivush ct al., 2011). When families and communities work together, a child's sense of belonging and emotional connection is stable and positive, enabling them to thrive.

L. Friedland (✉)
Executive Advisors, Inc, Beverly Hills, CA, USA
e-mail: lillif@executiveadvisors.org

F. W. Kaslow (ed.), *Contemporary Issues in Individual, Couple, and Family Lives and Treatment*, https://doi.org/10.1007/978-3-031-90006-8_1

Evolving Definitions and Compositions of Family

In recent decades, amidst a fundamental shift in how families are formed and maintained, the concept of family has undergone significant transformation challenging traditional definitions and expanding our understanding of what constitutes a family unit.

Many Americans are increasingly pessimistic about the institution of marriage and the family (Parker & Minkin, 2023). These views reflect the increasing number of single-parent households, same-sex couples with or without children, blended families resulting from divorce and remarriage, multigenerational households, "chosen families" of close friends or non-biologically related individuals, and co-parenting arrangements between non-romantic partners. *This broadening definition reflects a shift toward viewing families as socially constructed units rather than biologically or legally defined entities as they have been historically.*

The traditional structure and role of the family unit are undergoing significant changes. As families play a critical role in the health, reproduction, and well-being of current and future generations, understanding how these transformations are reshaping family dynamics is vital (Pesando et al., 2019).

Demographic Shifts and Evolving Family Structures

While the structure and dynamics of the family are evolving, its fundamental importance in shaping individual identities and providing a foundation for identity development, health and well-being, and resilience remains as crucial as ever.

In prior generations, authority structures, predictable rules, and stable, secure environments were established by parents in the home, at school, and by employers in the workplace. Broader society, the media, academic and religious institutions, and communities tended to espouse values and ethics like those fostered by the family (e.g., the importance of loyalty, hard work, and responsibility to and for the family). Shared values and ethics contribute to the formation and stability of individual, group, and family identities (Hogg et al., 2017). A person could choose not to abide by these cultural standards (e.g., have an affair), yet they knew that it was considered "wrong" by the prevailing societal and family norms. However, in the twenty-first century, values and ethics have become *fluid.* The psychosocial landscape has shifted from strong family ties to more individualistic and transient relationships, undermining the stability of children's primary environment during their formative years. Since the 1960s, people have been marrying and having children later in life, with 14% of babies now born to women aged 35 or older. Rising divorce rates have increased the prevalence of single-parent and blended families. The proportion of heterosexual couples with children dropped from 40% in 1970 to 20% in 2012. About 10% of children in the USA now live with a grandparent. Smaller family sizes are increasingly common, especially in high-income countries, driven by declining fertility rates. These evolving family dynamics highlight the need to adapt support systems to foster resilience and well-being in future generations.

The increase in cohabitation has contributed to a rise in non-marital unions and births outside of marriage (Smock & Schwartz, 2020). Longer life expectancies have led to more multigenerational households, altering caregiving roles and often reducing the stability of the family's support system (Seltzer, 2019). Notably, children are more likely to achieve success in adulthood if they grow up with both married parents, particularly if their parents remain married into their adulthood (Powell et al., 2016). The Global Family Change (GFC) study identified strong links between women's family-related behaviors—such as lower fertility rates, delayed milestones of adulthood, and increased autonomy—and higher Human Development Index (HDI) scores in low-to-middle-income countries (Pesando et al., 2019). These patterns indicate that shifts in family structures and dynamics are intertwined with broader societal progress, including enhanced gender equality in both domestic and professional spheres.

The Role of Family in Identity Development

Early Identity Development

From childhood, the family serves as the primary context for identity formation. The quality of familial interactions has direct consequences on children's developmental outcomes (Arias & Punyanunt-Carter, 2017). Attachment theory emphasizes the role of early relationships in shaping identity (Bowlby, 1988). Secure attachment relationships with caregivers provide a strong foundation for healthy physical and psychological development by offering emotional support and a safe, secure base to explore the world and providing a sense of "belonging," a fundamental human need (Allen et al., 2022). "Belonging" refers to a sense of psychological safety and security allowing a child to develop a strong sense of self in a positive environment for learning, exploration, and collaboration. Early experiences within the family lay the foundation for how individuals perceive themselves and their place in the world. Complementing this, the concept of "mirroring" emphasizes how family members' responses and feedback help children develop a sense of self (Winnicott, 1971). Positive childhood experiences occur when individuals have their needs met and experience and perceive a sense of safety, stability, and support. The following strategies can promote an emotionally healthy child-raising environment.

- Developing core parental knowledge, attitudes, and practices is associated with positive parent–child interactions and healthy early child development (National Academies of Sciences, Engineering, and Medicine, 2016).
- Educating families about emotional intelligence and critical thinking is valuable. This includes helping children recognize that they may have multiple, sometimes

conflicting feelings about experiences, that emotions can change over time, and that feelings provide valuable data about their reactions to the world. Similarly, it is important to help children realize they may have multiple thoughts or opinions of a given matter, upon which they can consider and reflect to facilitate wise decision-making.
- Guiding families to understand and navigate the tendency of dichotomous thinking involves encouraging families to view experiences, opinions, and emotions on a continuum rather than in all-or-none terms, which in turn can foster more nuanced, empathetic understanding within family units.

The family unit serves as the primary channel through which cultural, moral, and social values are passed down, shaping a child's self-concept and understanding of the values and rules of society (Grusec & Hastings, 2015). Children are imprinted by their family's dynamics, customs, rules, values, and culture. Kinship is spawned by these factors and the geographic proximity in which families live to one another. The family's customs of sharing rituals, values, and celebrations generate a feeling of community and "belonging." Family narratives, traditions, and shared experiences form the context for shaping an individual's family and community identities and learning social roles. Successful socialization occurs by internalizing or taking the parent's values, attitudes, and behaviors as one's own. As individuals develop, they choose which familial values they want to continue.

Emerging Adulthood and Identity Formation

As family structures diversify, the process of identity exploration and commitment characterizing the emerging adult years has become increasingly complex. In the past, reaching adulthood was defined by adopting adult roles, such as finishing one's education, obtaining full-time employment, getting married, becoming financially independent, or becoming a parent. Today, young adults view transitions to *adulthood as processes, rather than discrete events*, reflecting their newly dominant values of self-sufficiency and individualism.

The journey from adolescence to adulthood has become increasingly complex in contemporary society, with the period of emerging adulthood playing a crucial role in identity formation. This developmental phase, typically spanning ages 18–25, is characterized by significant psychological, social, and neurological changes that profoundly impact an individual's sense of self and relations with others. The emerging adulthood period is essential to the development of cognitive flexibility, inhibitory control, and emotional regulation.

Emerging adulthood is a time of transition, marked by the exploration of new environments, relationships, and ideas. As individuals leave the familiar environments of home, family, and childhood friends, they embark on a journey of self-discovery and identity consolidation. Arnett (2007) identifies *emerging adulthood* as a period having five features: (i) age of identity exploration: a time for trying out various life possibilities, particularly in love and work; (ii) age of instability: a period marked by frequent changes in relationships, work and living situations; (iii) age of self-focus: a time of heightened autonomy and self-reflection; (iv) age of feeling "in-between": neither adolescent nor fully adult, leading to a "sense of liminality"; and (v) age of possibilities: a time of optimism and belief in multiple available life paths. These features collectively create a unique psychological milieu in which emerging adults consistently grapple with two central questions: "Who am I?" (personal identity defining a sense of "I" and "me") and "How do other people see me?" (social identity defining self in terms of "we" and "us").

Social group affiliations and identities are increasingly solidified at this time, a period when the individual develops a sense of connection with group members, shared meaning, and support from others in groups with whom the individual wishes to identify (Hogg et al., 2017). The interplay between personal identity and social identity becomes paramount during the emerging adult period. Social group membership is internalized into the individual's sense of self, influencing the individual's thinking, feelings, and actions. When people experience a lack or loss of social identity, they experience social disconnection, loneliness, and lower well-being (Haslam et al., 2022). The desire to "belong" and to "be accepted" is particularly strong during emerging adulthood. In the past twenty years, there have been significant increases in loneliness, depression, and anxiety being reported across nearly every population, especially young adults. Many emerging adults report feelings of vulnerability, loneliness, and a sense of being "lost." Nearly 20% of the 203,070 adolescents interviewed from 2005–2017 reported prior-year treatment or counseling for mental health problems. The largest increase reported was with internalizing problems (e.g., anxiety, depression, suicidal thoughts, and somatization disorders), particularly in young women (Mojtabai & Olfson 2020). Social identity interventions can build and strengthen social group membership and are effective in improving mental health, well-being, and social connectedness (Haslam et al., 2016).

Feeling supported and connected with parents and family's social community is important because emerging adults who experience these positive connections are more likely to feel safe to explore their own identities and expand the possibilities for their future. This identity security leads to positive outcomes such as higher self-esteem and well-being, less internalizing and externalizing of problematic behaviors, and improved quality of familial relationships (Crocetti et al., 2016). Fostering a *strong family unit with healthy relationships is the most powerful tool* to embed capabilities of positive self-identity, connection, and mutual support. Family imbues the core features necessary for healthy relationships (Cacioppo et al., 2015): (a) intimate connectedness—having someone in your life who affirms who you are; (b) relational connectedness—having mutually rewarding, face-to-face contact with people; and (c) collective connectedness—feeling you are part of a group beyond individual existence.

Developing self-esteem, constructive social relationships, and thus positive well-being is central to identity consolidation, social connectedness, and resilience. The *key to healthy identity development lies in how families and communities support adolescents and emerging adult members through their identity development processes.*

The Rise of Self-Focus and Individualism

In recent years a significant shift toward self-focus and individualism has reshaped family relationships, identity formation, and the individual's resilience. Currently, self-interest and personal autonomy have increasingly taken precedence over family or communal concerns. The commitments and obligations that once characterized an individual's connection to their family, such as shared values and responsibilities, have dissipated. There is a growing emphasis on self-authorship, individual autonomy, self-fulfillment, and higher "quality" demands on adult relationships (Bianchi & Casper, 2004). This trend is particularly pronounced in Gen Z's, who expect to make their own choices, find jobs that align with their personal values, and focus on their unique feelings and desires (Botsman, 2024). This shift has led to a reevaluation of family roles, expectations, and legacies, with many young people viewing the traditional tenants of family life as less relevant or important than prior generations did or still do.

This increased focus on "self" is particularly evident in major life decisions made by young adults. They are increasingly likely to question traditional life trajectories, carefully weighing whether to commit to long-term careers or optimize for job flexibility, have children, enter long-term relationships, purchase homes, or integrate their lives with their families of origin. These decisions are often made with a focus on personal fulfillment and individual goals, rather than family or societal expectations. *Work is increasingly defining their life and identity* as compared to the past when tribes, including family, were more central to self-definition.

Ultimately, the very notion of what constitutes a fulfilling life has dramatically altered. A 2023 Pew Research study found that individuals increasingly define life fulfillment in terms of friendships and job satisfaction, placing less emphasis on traditional markers such as marriage or having children (Schaffer, 2023). This represents a significant departure from past generations, where family formation was often seen as central to the meaningfulness of life.

This shift toward individualism and self-focus has been accompanied by changes in how many young people conceptualize relationships. For example, some family members may perceive a lack of sustained emotional support from other members or feel reluctant to support to other members. Other individuals may not feel psychologically safe expressing diverse viewpoints within their family or may believe, rightly or wrongly, that they are not accepted by other family members. This can lead to a sense of being "related, yet not family"—a recognition that they cannot rely on other family members or do not want to be relied upon. Therefore, for many young adults their sense of "self" may be somewhat unstable and seemingly "always in formation," which often produces heightened anxiety and loneliness and a feeling of constantly being "in search of community." Some researchers describe this as the "family decline theory," pointing to the family's diminishing ability to fulfill its central societal roles (Laplant, 2016).

As self-interest increasingly supersedes communal or family concerns (e.g., the role of family members in providing support and guidance), the sense of familial connection and community has diminished, potentially impacting an individual's ability to cope and flourish, especially during times of turbulence and uncertainty.

Psychological interventions are recommended to address these weakened family support functions:

(a) Recognize the impact of family history on identity formation. More specifically, psychotherapists need to consider each individual's narrative of their family's history as it yields an understanding of their personal identification within the context of the family's past and current relationships.
(b) Supporting individuals and families through transitions, such as divorce or remarriage, requires understanding of how these changes may affect identity development. Having access to a diverse array of role models can be helpful, as it can offer people a broader perspective on their identity, enhance their adaptability and self-acceptance, and widen their view of interpersonal dynamics (Biblarz & Stacey, 2010).
(c) Incorporating cultural, ethnic, shared history, and religious diversity as well as demographic and societal changes may require careful navigation to ensure individuals feel secure and supported in their identity exploration.

The challenge for individuals, family, and society is to find ways to balance these individualistic tendencies with the human need for continuity, support, and belonging.

The Rise of "Chosen" Families and Non-Traditional Family Units

The rise of "chosen" families represents another significant shift in how family bonds are conceptualized. As societal acceptance of diverse lifestyles has grown, so too has the recognition of groups of individuals who deliberately choose to create family-like bonds without biological or legal ties. The "chosen family" refers to nonbiological kinship bonding formed to provide mutual support, often occurring when individuals do not feel accepted by their biological families, such as in the LGBTQ community (Pahl & Spencer, 2004).

The concept of "chosen families" challenges traditional notions of kinship and highlights the importance of emotional bonds and mutual support in defining family relationships. The rise in "chosen" families implies that some individuals do not experience the "safe haven" that those within traditional stable family structures historically did.

The Rise of Family Estrangement

One of the consequences of these demographic shifts is the rise in family estrangement. The frequency with which family members are excluded or sidelined, parent–child alienation, and parent–child estrangement within contemporary families is increasing (Scharp & Hall, 2017). Recent research highlights that estrangement is more common among fathers (26%) than among mothers (6%). Among the additional factors influencing family connectedness are race (e.g., black adult children are less likely to be estranged from their mothers than their fathers), gender (e.g., daughters are less likely to be estranged from their mothers than sons are), and sexual orientation (e.g., bisexual adult children are more likely to be estranged from their fathers than heterosexual children).

In the past, the family has functioned as a safety net or "assurance policy" that made it both harder to join and more difficult to leave (Ermisch et al., 2023). In times of trouble family would be there to help one another. Attitudes, expectations, and inclinations of individuals and families toward this "assurance policy" have been changing in recent years. The recent shifts have given rise to instability, a lack of psychological safety, anxiety, loneliness, and depression, all negatively affecting the individual's sense of stability, security, and continuity of traditional family systems. For many people, this has resulted in a reduced sense of feeling connected and supported, often accompanied by a loss of sense of meaning in their lives.

During periods of transition and instability, individuals and families become more vulnerable to societal pressures and group dynamics of acceptance, rejection, or exclusion. Managing oneself and attending to others becomes more challenging during these uncertain times. As families experience instability, familiar practices, continuing legacy, and a sense of community lose their grip, leading individuals to either try new approaches or remain "frozen" in past behaviors that may no longer be effective.

Case Study #1: The Jackson family

The Jackson family has two adult children. The family moved away from New York City about 40 years ago. The mother had worked as a principal of a school and the father as an accountant. The 45-year-old daughter is a lawyer, never married, and has no children. She stays connected to the family with weekly phone calls and monthly visits. The son, 40 years old, lives at home with his parents while he is trying to find his niche job. The daughter feels that the parents are "enabling" the son by not pushing him to support himself. She views the son as their parents' favorite child. The parents want their children to be happy. Describing the family as close when the children were raised, the parents admit they are heartbroken that their children aren't happily married with children, as their own experience was rewarding.

By asking the parents to identify and process their fears, and hopes, for their children, the parents can be more available to accept their adult children. It would be wise for the therapist to first meet individually with the adult children to learn their perspectives and desires, as well as to separately meet with the parents to identify and process their hopes and fears for their children. With the increasing questioning about the relevance of marriage in today's contemporary society, the therapist needs to ask, "Do the Jackson parents view marriage as necessary to live a happy, fulfilling life?"

After these steps, the therapist can ask family members what might constitute family connectedness, and how each would imagine their relationships to look, what they want in terms of family connectedness and community. Then the therapist would guide the strengthening of the family relationships where possible. By illuminating the changing family structures of the last couple of decades, the therapist may be able to promote greater mutual understanding and acceptance within the family. An increasing number of people in the USA feel marriage is old-fashioned or not relevant, including 71% of 18–20-year-olds and 77% of those over 65. The therapist should enquire as to how their children not marrying will impact the Jackson family's viability and mutual support, especially when the parents are older and therefore more physically and psychologically vulnerable.

Despite these challenges, there is hope for the future of family connectedness and continuity. If families wish to promote ongoing connection and relationships, they must engage in purposeful actions to facilitate the meaning, connection, familial pride, and the adoption of family values and traditions by future generations. While the environment of family life is changing, there are still opportunities to foster strong, meaningful family bonds. Psychological interventions need to promote respect for individual autonomy while strengthening the family's sense of community and continuity. This might involve helping families develop new traditions that align with changing values or facilitating open respectful dialogues about expectations and responsibilities within the family unit. Non-directive support, coupled with knowledge about the complexities of estrangement, helps individuals navigate difficult family dynamics.

The Significance of Psychological Safety and Stability in Families

The multiplicity of lifestyles, changing family structures, and evolving family dynamics contribute to instability and uncertainty. High rates of divorce, remarriage, and family reconfiguration can disrupt the stability children need to thrive (Furstenberg, 2019). Economic pressures, including financial instability and job insecurity, can create stress and tension within families, undermining psychological safety. The increased demands of balancing work–life can limit the time and energy parents have for fostering a psychologically safe home environment (Powell et al.,

2016). The pervasive use of digital devices and social media can interfere with face-to-face interactions and emotional attunement within families (Haidt, 2024). Changing societal norms and values can create intergenerational conflicts and uncertainty within families (Majeed & Kanwal, 2019). *As a consequence of this societal instability family bonds have become more fragile and the connectedness between members has decreased.*

The concept of psychological safety refers to a shared belief that the environment is safe for interpersonal risk-taking, is open to diverse ideas and actions, and promotes collaboration and learning (Edmondson & Lei, 2014). When applied to the family context, psychological safety can be understood as an environment where family members feel comfortable expressing themselves without fear of negative consequences, where mistakes are viewed as opportunities for learning rather than grounds for punishment, and where open communication ("active listening"), mutual respect, and emotional support exist.

"Relational health" refers to psychologically safe, stable, nurturing family relationships that promote emotional development in children (Willis & Eddy, 2022). Without a psychologically safe, stable, and supportive family environment, critical to the development of resilience and well-being, children are at risk for adverse childhood experiences ("ACEs"). ACEs are related to chronic health problems, mental illness, and substance abuse problems later in life (CDC, 2024).

Positive family environments can foster stronger family bonds and cohesion and increase individual resilience and coping skills. Open, respectful communication within families helps individuals navigate identity challenges. These positive family environments contribute to better academic and social outcomes for children (Arias & Punyanunt-Carter, 2017).

Despite the rapid changes in family structure and dynamics, strong family bonds are needed to continue to foster positive individual, family, and community identity formation and resilience.

Strategies for Psychological Safe Family Environments

Families that adapt to change and support individual growth promote resilience, which improves the individual's well-being over time (Walsh, 2016). Various strategies are offered for therapists to promote a psychologically safe environment:

- Psychologists and mental health professionals need to assess family dynamics and identify areas where psychological safety may be compromised. Develop tailored strategies to enhance communication dynamics, emotional regulation, and conflict resolution within families by employing strategies to promote psychological safety and stability.
- Establishing clear, open, and respectful dialogue is fundamental to creating a foundation of trust and understanding. This involves active listening and validating each other's experiences and emotions.

- Cultural competence is vital in this work, as different cultures may have varying approaches to direct/indirect communications whether they have an environment of psychological safety. Recognizing and respecting these differences while promoting overall family well-being is a delicate balance.
- At times, if fitting, adopting a trauma-informed approach is necessary, addressing the impact of past traumas on family functioning and helping families rebuild psychological safety.
- Promote the development of family resilience by fostering flexibility and adaptability. This process typically involves encouraging renegotiating roles and responsibilities as family circumstances change or finding new ways to connect during times of stress or separation (Moen & Wethington, 1992).
- Creating and maintaining family rituals and traditions are instrumental in providing a sense of continuity and belonging, especially when facing change (Fiese et al., 2002). These rituals can be as simple as regular family meals, weekend activities, or holiday celebrations. The key is consistency and shared meaning among the members. Adapting rituals to accommodate diverse family structures and cultural backgrounds can help maintain these benefits, even in evolving family contexts (Imber-Black & Roberts, 1998). Families that adjust to new circumstances while maintaining core values tend to be more resilient (Walsh, 2016).
- Balancing individual autonomy within the family community by promoting individual growth and independence while maintaining strong family connections, particularly as children mature.
- Learning to listen and appreciate differences, respect, and embrace and integrate diversity within the family unit can be a source of strength.

Case Study #2: O'Malley Family

Forty years ago, if you asked someone to tell you something about themselves, they might respond: "I am Tom O'Malley. I grew up in the Philadelphia suburbs. My grandparents immigrated to the U.S. about 70 years ago from Ireland. Proud of their heritage, my grandparents and their children actively participated in the Irish American community in their area. They had three children, though one died in a car accident in high school. Their son, my father, has four adult children. One son lives close to my grandparents, another son recently married a man, and their daughter and her family live across the country and established a life and close relationships with her husband's family in Idaho, who are not Irish. Our family, particularly my grandparents, continue to have difficulty accepting their gay grandson who married his partner about 10 years ago and now has a one-year-old child. The family has a tradition of gathering for a family vacation once a year, yet in the past few years my parents and I, the part of the family that live close to the grandparents, are the only ones who come regularly."

Tom indicated that his family needs help understanding gay and lesbian marriages if they are going to maintain the family's connection to one another. The treating psychologist or mental health professional should first ask each family member to describe their understanding of the family history. By listening to their personal narrative of the family's past, individuals can reconstruct their sense of cultural belonging and connection with their forebearers and where they see themselves fitting in.

The family needs help understanding that societies and cultural values have changed for many, permitting and accepting more gay and lesbian marriages. This diversification is accompanied by growing legal recognition and social acceptance of these family forms, reflecting broader shifts in societal values and norms. It is recommended that therapists speak to family members individually and together to explore concerns, biases, and goals as to whether they can positively adapt to and accept gay marriage. By focusing on the family's strengths and history of getting through stresses and difficult times by recounting the family's history, the therapist can provide a "safe" environment to discuss and accept the marriage of the gay son and his partner should the grandparents decide they want to continue their connection to one another to all family members. The next step would then be for the family to decide if want to continue as a family like they had before and explore how to integrate everyone into the expanded family definition. Are there respected members of the Irish American community that the family may consult (e.g., cultural leaders, clergy) who may support the inclusion of all? If not, are there other alternatives? Utilizing support systems beyond the immediate family can also bolster family acceptance and resilience. Engaging with extended family and community resources when needed can provide additional layers of support (Ungar, 2011).

The Role of Family in Developing Resilience

Resilience, the ability to adapt and thrive in the face of adversity, is necessary to successfully navigate life's challenges. The key components of resilience are positive adaptation (maintaining or regaining mental health and well-being despite adversity), protective factors (strengths and other resources that buffer against negative outcomes), and the ability to navigate risk factors (conditions or experiences that increase the likelihood of negative outcomes).

In the context of family psychology, resilience takes on a dual nature: it applies both to individual family members and to the family unit. Understanding how families foster resilience, and how different family structures contribute to this process, supports healthy family functioning. *Resilience is a dynamic interactive process that builds family and individual well-being with relational support and collaboration.*

Family resilience refers to the ability of the family unit to withstand and rebound from disruptive life challenges (Walsh, 2016). More specifically, family resilience is the capacity of the family, as a functional system, to withstand and rebound from internal conflicts or external stressors and emerge stronger and more resourceful.

Individual resilience is the capacity of the individual to positively adapt despite life's challenging circumstances (Masten, 2001).

Family and individual resilience are deeply intertwined, with individual resilience often drawing strength from family bonds, and family resilience emerging from the collective efforts of its members. Resilient families possess qualities and dynamics that enable them to manage adverse situations and maintain a sense of stability and harmony.

Therapy directed toward building family resilience entails the treating therapist and family members working through challenges collaboratively (Walsh, 2016). Psychotherapists can promote resilience when the family faces stressors and adversity:

(a) Elicit each family member's definition and description of their family, their own values and aspirations, and who the individual identifies as important in their family life. Fostering open, respectful communication is crucial, for creating safe spaces for family members to express concerns and emotions (Walsh, 2016).

    - Genograms can be used to focus on positive influences, relationship mapping, and questionnaires (Walsh, 2016).
    - Involving children in age-appropriate discussions about family challenges and decisions can help build their resilience and problem-solving skills (Fivush et al., 2011).
    - Keep in mind a systems approach to address the dynamic interplay of multiple factors impacting the family.

(b) Cultivating a positive family historical narrative supports family and individual continuity and resilience.

    - Recounting stories of family members who, over the generations, coped with challenges and succeeded in overcoming adversities fosters both individual self-efficacy and community resilience.
    - A strengths-based focus can help families identify and build upon their existing resources and coping strategies.

(c) Framing challenges as opportunities for growth and learning can help family members develop a resilient mindset (Walsh, 2016).
(d) Celebrating family strengths and successes, no matter how small, can build confidence and optimism in the face of difficult challenges (Fivush et al., 2011).

Resilience Strategies for the Modern Family

As family structures diversify, new family forms need to develop strengths that contribute to resilience building. Single-parent families, for instance, often develop strong parent–child bonds and increased self-reliance (McLanahan & Sandefur, 1994). Blended families can foster adaptability and skills in navigating complex relationships. Same-sex parent families frequently demonstrate high levels of commitment to parenting and openness to diversity (Patterson, 2017). In 2015 almost 30% of all children in the USA resided with a grandparent at some time during their childhood, with 25% living with their grandparent without a parent in the household, usually benefiting from intergenerational wisdom (Smock & Schwartz, 2020). Each of these diverse family structures offers unique pathways to building resilience, highlighting the adaptability of the family unit in fostering this crucial characteristic.

Case Studies: Resilience in Various Family Structures

To illustrate how resilience manifests in different family contexts, consider the following examples:

1. The Rodriguez family, a single-parent household, faced significant financial strain when Maria lost her job during an economic downturn. Despite these challenges, Maria maintained a positive outlook, openly communicated with her children about their situation, and involved them in problem-solving. The family's resilience was evident in their ability to adapt to new circumstances, support each other emotionally, and maintain hope for the future.
2. The Patel-Johnson family, a blended and multicultural unit, encountered challenges in merging their families and cultural traditions when Amir and Sarah married. By fostering open communication, celebrating diversity, and creating new family rituals that honored both cultures, they built a resilient family unit capable of navigating complex cultural and relational dynamics.
3. Lisa and Emily Thompson, a same-sex couple, adopted siblings with a history of trauma. They focused on creating a stable, nurturing environment, seeking professional support when needed, and advocating for their children in school and community settings. Their resilience as a family unit was demonstrated through their ability to adapt to each child's needs and overcome societal challenges.

The family unit remains a powerful source of cultivating and maintaining identity and resilience for individuals in contemporary society. These examples highlight how different family structures can foster resilience through open communication, adaptability, and a commitment to supporting each member's well-being. They also demonstrate the importance of drawing on both internal family resources and external support systems when facing adversity.

Strengths-based interventions, identifying and building upon existing family strengths and resources, can be particularly effective in promoting resilience. Systemic interventions that address family dynamics as a whole, rather than focusing solely on individual members, can enhance overall family resilience. Narrative therapy techniques can be valuable in helping families reframe their experiences and develop empowering narratives (White & Epston, 1990).

Families play a crucial role in nurturing the individual's identity and resilience through positive attachment bonds, which create a sense of safety, stability, and security, allowing individuals to explore their environment, learn from their mistakes, and develop emotional coping skills. Bandura's social learning theory (1977) describes how children learn from their parents and caregivers through observation, imitation, and modeling effective coping strategies to manage stress and adversity. Beyond the individual's genetic blueprint, the most significant factor in developing social and emotional resilience is good parenting.

By encouraging independence and problem-solving skills, families and caregivers build the child's confidence in their ability ("self-efficacy") to overcome adversity (Schunk & Pajares, 2009). Four key factors have been identified that help children develop resilience: (i) facilitating supportive adult–child relationships; (ii) building a sense of self-efficacy and perceived control; (iii) providing opportunities to strengthen adaptive skills and self-regulatory capacities; and (iv) mobilizing sources of faith, hope, and cultural traditions.

Serving as the primary context for developing identity and resilience in early life, through a safe learning environment, the family's transmission of values and beliefs provides meaning and purpose. The process of passing down family narratives can further inspire resilience in future generations, highlighting shared stories of overcoming adversity (Fivush et al., 2011). These narratives contribute to a sense of family continuity, identity, and historic legacy, offering a broader context of support and role models for the development of the individual's resilience in the face of life's challenges.

The Impact of Emerging Technologies on Family Dynamics

The rapid advancement of technology has profoundly influenced family life in the twenty-first century, reshaping communication patterns, redefining family boundaries, and altering the very nature of family interactions. This technological revolution presents both opportunities and challenges for family dynamics, requiring a nuanced understanding of its impacts to harness its benefits while mitigating potential risks.

The influence of new technologies is especially pronounced on children and young adults, though its effects ripple through all family members. One of the most significant consequences of this technological shift has been the loosening of traditional family ties. Today, family members, even when physically together, are often highly distracted or immersed in digital modalities and find their attention, focus, and the quality of their communication profoundly altered. The expectation of 24/7 availability through digital means has, paradoxically, often resulted in shallower connections, failing to replicate the depth of bonding possible through eye-to-eye, in-person interactions.

The very nature of information processing and communication has undergone a radical transformation. Whereas people once took time to read books and newspapers, discuss ideas, and attend lectures, today's information exchanges are predominantly online, quick, and often superficial. Many individuals, particularly adolescents and young adults, rely heavily on headlines and brief snippets of information, potentially compromising their ability to engage and communicate collaboratively. This shift has significant implications for how younger generations understand and interpret the world around them. According to a 2018 Pew Research study, 95% of 13–17-year-olds report they have access to a smartphone (Pew Research Center, 2018). The constant availability and ubiquity of personal media devices have fostered a culture of immediate gratification and "bottom line" thinking, often at the expense of deeper reflection, analysis, and thoughtful discourse. There has been a concerning reduction in critical thinking skills among college graduates, suggesting a growing disconnect from historical context, cultural understanding, and nuanced value systems (Flores et al., 2010). This trend is exemplified by the tendency of many adolescents and emerging adults to judge historical events and figures solely by contemporary standards, without consideration for the contexts of different eras (Archer & Matheson, 2024).

The phenomenon described as the "great rewiring of childhood" points to a paradoxical situation where parents have become overprotective of their children in the physical world while "underprotective" in the digital realm. By restricting children's freedom to explore and take risks in the "real world" (i.e., the physical world), parents may inadvertently hinder the development of crucial critical thinking and social skills (Haidt, 2024). Simultaneously, many children have unrestricted access to social media and online gaming, exposing them to a virtual world that can be even more challenging to navigate than the real world.

The consequences of this shift are becoming increasingly apparent. Gen Z and other younger adults, having grown up in this "wired," "always online" environment, often struggle with face-to-face interactions and are prone to making quick judgments based on limited information. The asynchronous nature of many digital interactions, available 24/7 through "glass" connections (e.g., smartphones, tablets), has contributed to a growing sense of disconnection from real-world engagement and communities.

For emerging adults, ages 18–29, online interactions and the constant distraction from real-life engagement have impacted their relationships and self-perceptions. Over the past two generations, society and new technologies have promulgated three "Great Untruths" to the young: (i) the Untruth of Fragility—we should be shielded against adversity because we are fragile ("what doesn't kill you makes you weaker"); (ii) the Untruth of Emotional Reasoning—that we should always trust our feelings; and (iii) the Untruth of Us. vs. Them—that we should judge others for their faults while avoiding self-evaluation (Haidt & Lukianoff, 2018). These beliefs, combined with the curated nature of online self-presentation, have contributed to a culture of heightened self-focus and decreased empathy. The implications of these changes for family dynamics and individual development are profound. There is a growing tendency toward dichotomous thinking, the "you're either with me or against me" mentality, which often strains familial relationships and hinders communication. The increased importance placed on self and self-satisfaction has led to what some describe as moral narcissism, in which individuals believe their personal views and morals are superior to others. This reduces tolerance for, or even willingness to listen to, differing perspectives within families, communities, and society at large.

Digital Communication and Family Relationships

Digital communication has transformed the way families *can* interact offering new avenues for connection, but also presenting unique challenges. The ability to share updates, photos, and experiences in real time can foster a sense of connection even when family members are physically apart (Coyne et al., 2014). Moreover, the rise of asynchronous communication allows for interaction among family members despite busy schedules or remote living, potentially increasing the frequency of family communication. Families spread across national borders due to migration and global careers must develop new strategies for maintaining family connections (Baldassar & Merla, 2014). These families often rely heavily on technology to bridge physical distances (Madianou & Miller, 2012).

However, this increased connectivity comes with its own set of risks and challenges. Overreliance on digital communication may decrease in-person engagement, potentially weakening the depth of family relationships (Turkle, 2015). The lack of non-verbal and non-visual cues in digital communication can lead to misunderstandings, potentially exacerbating family conflicts and misunderstandings (Hertlein & Blumer, 2014). Furthermore, the constant connectivity enabled by technology can blur work–life boundaries, encroaching on dedicated family time. To combat this, families can establish guidelines for healthy technology use to help members maintain strong bonds in the digital age.

Social Media's Influence on Family Identity and Interaction

The impact of social media on family dynamics is noteworthy. Platforms like Facebook, Instagram, and TikTok have become integral to many families' lives, influencing how they present themselves and interact with others. Individuals and families often present idealized versions of their lives on social media (Blum-Ross & Livingstone, 2017) because they feel pressured to maintain a façade of "perfection," potentially straining family relationships or produce anxiety or depression in individuals.

Social media also serves as a platform for creating and sharing family narratives. While this can strengthen family bonds by celebrating shared experiences, it also raises questions about privacy and consent, especially concerning children's presence online. Parents must navigate the delicate balance between sharing family moments and protecting their own and their children's digital footprint.

Balancing Technology Use and Face-to-Face Family Time

The pervasive nature of technology in family life necessitates strategies for maintaining a healthy balance between digital and face-to-face interactions. Establishing tech-free zones and times, such as during family meals, can create space for meaningful in-person communication (Turkle, 2015). Developing family "tech etiquette" rules about device use during shared activities can help prioritize face-to-face engagement (Hiniker et al., 2016). Parents play a crucial role in modeling appropriate technology use, as children often emulate their parents' digital habits (Sanders et al., 2016).

Fostering meaningful offline interactions is essential for maintaining strong family bonds. Scheduling regular family activities that promote face-to-face engagement can counterbalance the draw of digital devices (Coyne et al., 2014). Encouraging outdoor and physical activities provides shared experiences that do not involve screens yet strengthen family bonds (Larson et al., 2019).

Technology can also be leveraged to enhance family bonding. Collaborative digital projects, such as creating family blogs or digital scrapbooks, can be engaging shared activities. Video calls can connect distant family members, maintaining relationships across geographic divides. Educational technology, when used judiciously, can promote family learning and interaction.

Families who effectively navigate balancing digital and face-to-face communication can access resources, information, and support networks that enhance their resilience (Farnham & Churchill, 2011). Learning to manage technology use can help families strike a healthy balance between connectedness and individual space and autonomy, contributing to both overall family well-being and individual resilience (Carvalho et al., 2015).

Economic and Social Pressures on Modern Families

Contemporary families face a complex array of economic and social pressures ranging from work–life balance, struggles with economic stability, and evolving social expectations, which shape family dynamics in substantial ways. Understanding these pressures and their effects is crucial for developing strategies to support healthy families and individuals.

Work–Life Balance and Its Impact on Family Units

The struggle to balance work demands with family life has become a central issue for many contemporary families. Rising workplace demands often lead to reduced family time, a trend exacerbated by technological advancements that blur the boundaries between the workplace and home life. The expectation of constant availability, facilitated by smartphones and remote work capabilities, can significantly encroach on family time and emotional energy.

Dual-income households, while offering financial benefits, often face increased stress and time pressures. Coordinating childcare and household responsibilities becomes a complex juggling act, particularly when both parents have demanding careers. This balancing act can lead to work-related stress spilling over into family interactions, affecting relationship quality and overall family well-being (Perry-Jenkins & Gerstel, 2020).

Many families are experiencing reduced time for family rituals and bonding activities. These rituals, which traditionally served to strengthen family identity, connectedness, and continuity, are often sacrificed in the face of competing demands for the individual's time.

Economic Instability and Its Effects on the Family

Economic factors play a crucial role in shaping family structures and dynamics. Low SES (i.e., Socio-Economic Status) can lead to lower satisfaction and stability, increased stress, and negative parent–child interactions (Conger et al., 2010). The stress of financial instability frequently strains relationships altering family roles and impacting children's development. Long-term unemployment may result in role changes within the family, potentially challenging traditional family structures and expectations.

Despite the increase of women in the workforce, the division of work is not equally divided among parents. Women still take care of more household and childcare responsibilities even in households where they earn the same as their husbands or when women are the primary breadwinners (Fry et al., 2023). The increase in work and family responsibilities has strained contemporary families and contributed to family instability and fewer children. When income inequality occurs, it can affect family formation patterns and stability dynamics (McLanahan & Percheski, 2008).

Strategies that can foster the family's ability to manage economic challenges include:

(a) Developing flexible roles and responsibilities within the family can help adapt to changing circumstances (Moen & Wethington, 1992). Encouraging shared responsibility and teamwork within the family can distribute the burden of coping with stressors and strengthen family bonds.
(b) Cultivating relationships with extended family, friends, and community promotes needed support and resilience in the face of adversity (Ungar, 2011).
(c) Promoting financial literacy within the family can also be a powerful tool for building family and individual resilience. Teaching children about budgeting, saving, investing, and responsible financial management can prepare them for

future economic challenges. Developing family financial goals and strategies together can foster a sense of shared purpose and control over economic circumstances (Serido et al., 2010).

Social and Cultural Factors Influence on Family Dynamics

Shifting social norms and expectations significantly impact how the family functions and perceives themselves. Changing gender roles have led to varied expectations for men and women in the workplace and family environment. This trend has significant implications for work–family balance and family dynamics as it may lead to more egalitarian family structures that require careful negotiation of roles and responsibilities (Nomaguchi & Milkie, 2020). Currently, almost one in five stay-at-home parents in the USA are dads (Fry, 2023). While this shift has introduced new possibilities for family arrangements, it has also created new challenges as families navigate evolving roles and responsibilities.

Parenting pressures have intensified, particularly in the age of social media. Intensive parenting norms can create stress and guilt, particularly for working parents striving to meet heightened expectations of involvement and achievement (Hays, 2016). Social media amplifies these pressures, facilitating constant comparisons and perceived judgments about parenting choices (Blum-Ross & Livingstone, 2017).

Educational expectations have also shifted, with increasing pressure for academic achievement impacting family schedules and resources. This pressure can lead to overscheduled children and stressed parents, potentially undermining family unity and well-being. Moreover, disparities in access to educational opportunities can exacerbate social inequalities, further straining families already facing economic challenges.

Family composition affects children. Children in blended families sometimes struggle with loyalties and the integration of multiple family identities. Single-parent households impact gender role development and self-esteem in unique ways (McLanahan & Sandefur, 1994).

Cultural diversity adds another layer of complexity to the stresses and pressures within the family. Immigrant families often face challenges in balancing cultural traditions with new social norms (Suárez-Orozco & Suárez-Orozco, 2001), while intercultural families navigate blending different cultural expectations and practices (Crippen & Brew, 2007). These families often need to manage stressors related to acculturation and discrimination, while trying to maintain their historic cultural identity in a new environment.

Multicultural or multiethnic families, whether formed through intermarriage, cohabitation, adoption, or immigration, face unique opportunities and challenges. Language barriers within the family or with the broader community can complicate communication and cultural transmission. Conflicting cultural values and practices can lead to family tensions as members navigate between different cultural expectations (Rosenblatt, 2009). Family structures and concepts of identity vary significantly across cultures, reflecting deeply held values and traditions. When working with multicultural families, it is important to distinguish between collectivist and individualist cultures. Collectivist cultures often emphasize extended family networks and interdependence, while individualist cultures tend to focus more on nuclear families and personal autonomy (Triandis, 2001). This fundamental difference in perspective can significantly impact family dynamics and individual identity development.

For psychotherapists, cultural competence with the family's ethnicity or culture is essential when working with culturally diverse families:

- This involves psychotherapists developing awareness of their own cultural biases and assumptions (Sue et al., 2022), as well as knowledge about various cultural perspectives on family and mental health (Hays, 2016).
- Using culturally appropriate assessment tools and techniques and considering cultural factors in interpreting family dynamics and individual behaviors are crucial for effective practice (McGoldrick et al., 2005).
- Culturally adapted interventions may involve modifying therapeutic approaches to align with cultural values and practices and incorporating cultural strengths and resources into treatment plans (Bernal & Domenech Rodríguez, 2012).
- Facilitate families to identify and navigate cultural conflicts and identity issues and support individuals in developing bicultural competence (Rosenblatt, 2009) without losing their cultural identity or having to choose one culture over another.
- Foster open communication about cultural differences within the family, as well as encourage the exploration of multiple cultural identities in children and adolescents.
- Consider cultural transmission within families including maintaining language through bilingual education or heritage language classes and sharing family histories and cultural narratives (Fivush et al., 2011).
- Connecting with cultural communities and organizations can provide support and resources for cultural preservation.
- Celebrating the contributions of each family member and cultivating an inclusive family identity that accommodates various perspectives and experiences can enhance family community and adaptability.
- Observing cultural traditions and values can serve as sources of strength during adversity, providing a sense of continuity and meaning in the face of challenges (Ungar, 2008). When facing challenges, diverse cultural perspectives can offer multiple problem-solving and creative approaches, enhancing a family's ability to adapt. Different cultural communities interact with family and individual practices and can create conditions promoting children's capability of navigating multiple cultures and identities (Mistry & Wu, 2010), while exposure to diverse viewpoints can foster cognitive flexibility and resilience. Cultural diversity also provides connections to multiple communities that can provide diverse sources of support.

Family roles and hierarchies also demonstrate cultural variation (Bornstein, 2010). The concept of self and identity also varies across cultures. Some cultures view identity as primarily relational and context-dependent, with individuals defining themselves largely in terms of their relationships and social roles, whereas other cultures emphasize individual traits and personal achievements (Heine, 2001). These different perspectives on identity can lead to varying expectations and potential conflicts within families, especially in multicultural contexts.

Case Study #3: The Mas family

Sandi Mas had two children on her own (via sperm bank). She viewed herself as very close and devoted to them, yet when her son married, the family connection erupted. Sandi felt abandoned by her son's loyalty to his new wife and her family as he joined his newly expanded family for many holidays. She was depressed and felt unappreciated by her son and blamed his wife for turning her son against her. The treating psychologist would first need to emotionally support and work with Sandi through her depression and sense of loss of closeness with her son. The therapist should then prompt Sandi to label her fears and work with her to process them. After these steps, the therapist can ask Sandi whether she could envision a different "connectedness" with her son given his expanded family, how she might imagine this broader relationship would look, and then guide the strengthening of the relationships where possible. It would be prudent to provide Sandi with research demonstrating how in-laws bring their own personal and family values, history, traditions, and culture that may differ from the family of origin's connections. Facilitated by her therapist, Sandi can reflect on her expectations and understandings of an expanding family (i.e., with new members) and explore possible types and ways of restructuring or connecting as a newly expanded kinship unit if she chooses to do so.

Role of Culture

Intergenerational relationships frequently reflect significant variations of values. Many African and Asian cultures place a high value on filial piety and elder care, with expectations that adult children will care for their aging parents, whereas Western cultures often prioritize the independence of adult children, which can lead to different family structures and caregiving arrangements in later life (Pyke, 1999). Experiences of discrimination or social exclusion can also impact multicultural families, potentially affecting family cohesion and individual well-being (Killian, 2001). Family members may have to navigate multiple cultural identities, a process that can be enriching, but also complex and potentially stressful (Benet-Martínez & Haritatos, 2005).

Despite these challenges, diverse families offer unique opportunities for growth and resilience. Exposure to multiple cultures can enhance cultural competence and global perspective, valuable skills in our interconnected world. Navigating cultural differences can increase cognitive flexibility and problem-solving skills, potentially benefiting all family members (Leung et al., 2008). Multicultural families possess a rich cultural heritage and diverse family narratives, which can serve as sources of strength and identity (Fivush et al., 2011).

Concluding Comments

As families navigate the 21st-century society, it becomes clear that while the forms may vary, the *fundamental functions of family—providing nurturance, support, a sense of belonging and connection, and continuity—remain as necessary as ever in fostering positive individual identity development, family connectedness, resilience, and well-being.*

References

Allen, K. A., Kern, M. L., Rozek, C. S., McInerney, D. M., & Slavich, G. M. (2022). Belonging: A review of conceptual issues, an integrative framework, and directions for future research. *Australian Journal of Psychology, 73*(1), 87–102. https://doi.org/10.1080/00049530.2021.1883409

Archer, A., & Matheson, B. (2024). It was a different time: Judging historical figures by today's moral standards. *Journal of Applied Philosophy*. https://doi.org/10.1111/japp.12713

Arias, V. S., & Punyanunt-Carter. (2017). Family, culture, and communication. *Oxford Research Encyclopedia of Communication*. https://doi.org/10.1093/acrefore/9780190228613.013.504

Arnett, J. J. (2007). Emerging adulthood: What is it, and what is it good for? *Child Development Perspectives, 1*(2), 68–73. https://doi.org/10.1111/j.1750-8606.2007.00016.x

Baldassar, L., & Merla, L. (Eds.). (2014). *Transnational families, migration and the circulation of care: Understanding mobility and absence in family life*. Routledge.

Bandura, A. (1977). *Social learning theory*. Prentice Hall.

Benet-Martínez, V., & Haritatos, J. (2005). Bicultural identity integration (BII): Components and psychosocial antecedents. *Journal of Personality, 73*(4), 1015–1050. https://doi.org/10.1111/j.1467-6494.2005.00337.x

Bernal, G., & Domenech Rodríguez, M. M. (Eds.). (2012). *Cultural adaptations: Tools for evidence-based practice with diverse populations*. American Psychological Association. https://doi.org/10.1037/13752-000

Biblarz, T. J., & Stacey, J. (2010). How does the gender of parents matter? *Journal of Marriage and Family, 72*(1), 3–22. https://doi.org/10.1111/j.1741-3737.2009.00678.x

Blum-Ross, A., & Livingstone, S. (2017). "Sharenting," parent blogging, and the boundaries of the digital self. *Popular Communication, 15*(2), 110–125. https://doi.org/10.1080/15405702.2016.1223300

Bornstein, M. H. (Ed.). (2010). *Handbook of cultural developmental science*. Psychology Press.

Botsman, R. (2024). To Keep Gen Z, companies need to level up. *Wired*. https://www.wired.com/story/to-keep-gen-z-companies-need-to-level-up/

Bowlby, J. (1988). *A secure base: Parent-child attachment and healthy human development*. Basic Books.

Bianchi, S. M., & Casper, L.M. (2004). Explanations of Family Change. In Sourcebook for Family Theory and Research, Ed. Bengtson, V. L., Acock, A. C., Allen, K.R., Diworth-Anderson, P. & Klein, D.M. Sage Publications.

Cacioppo, J. T., Cacioppo, S., Capitanio, J. P., & Cole, S. W. (2015). The neuroendocrinology of social isolation. *Annual Review of Psychology, 66*, 733–767. https://doi.org/10.1146/annurev-psych-010814-015240

Carvalho, J., Francisco, R., & Relvas, A. P. (2015). Family functioning and information and communication technologies: How do they relate? A literature review. *Computers in Human Behavior, 45*, 99–108. https://doi.org/10.1016/j.chb.2014.11.037

Centers for Disease Control (CDC). (2024). *Adverse Childhood Experiences (ACE's)*. https://www.cdc.gov/aces/about/index.html https://www.cdc.gov/vitalsigns/aces/index.html

Conger, R. D., Conger, K. J., & Martin, M. J. (2010). Socioeconomic status, family processes, and individual development. *Journal of Marriage and Family, 72*(3), 685–704. https://www.jstor.org/stable/40732503

Coyne, S. M., Padilla-Walker, L. M., Fraser, A. M., Fellows, K., & Day, R. D. (2014). "Media time = family time": Positive media use in families with adolescents. *Journal of Adolescent Research, 29*(5), 663–688. https://doi.org/10.1177/0743558414538316

Crippen, C., & Brew, L. (2007). Intercultural parenting and the transcultural family: A literature Review. *The Family Journal, 15*(2), 107–115. https://doi.org/10.1177/1066480706297783

Crocetti, E., Branje, S., Rubini, M., Koot, H. M., & Meeus, W. (2016). Identity processes and parent-child and sibling relationships in adolescence: A five-wave multi-informant longitudinal study. *Child Development, 87*(1), 210–228. https://doi.org/10.1111/cdev.12547

Edmondson, A. C., & Lei, Z. (2014). Psychological safety: The history, renaissance, and future of an interpersonal construct. *Annual Review of Organizational Psychology and Organizational Behavior, 1*(1), 23–43. https://doi.org/10.1146/annurev-orgpsych-031413-091305

Ermisch, J., Gambetta, D., Iacono, S. L., & Sonmez, B. (2023). Trust and strength of Family ties: New experimental evidence. *Social Psychology Quarterly, 86*(2), 195–207. https://doi.org/10.1177/01902725231162074

Farnham, S. D., & Churchill, E. F. (2011). Faceted identity, faceted lives: Social and technical issues with being yourself online. In *Proceedings of the ACM 2011 conference on Computer supported cooperative work* (pp. 359–368). https://doi.org/10.1145/1958824.195888

Fiese, B. H., Tomcho, T. J., Douglas, M., Josephs, K., Poltrock, S., & Baker, T. (2002). A review of 50 years of research on naturally occurring family routines and rituals: Cause for celebration? *Journal of Family Psychology, 16*(4), 381–390. https://doi.org/10.1037/0893-3200.16.4.381

Fivush, R., Bohanek, J. G., & Zaman, W. (2011). Personal and intergenerational narratives in relation to adolescents' well-being. *New Directions for Child and Adolescent Development, 131*, 45–57. https://doi.org/10.1002/cd.288

Flores, K. L., Matkin, G. S., Burbach, M. E., Quinn, C. E., & Harding, H. (2010). Deficient critical thinking skills among college graduates: Implications for leadership. *Educational Philosophy and Theory, 44*(2), 212–230. https://doi.org/10.1111/j.1469-5812.2010.00672.x

Fry, R. (2023). *18% of stay-at-home parents in U.S. are dads*. Pew Research Center. https://www.pewresearch.org/short-reads/2023/08/03/almost-1-in-5-stay-at-home-parents-in-the-us-are-dads/

Fry, R., Aragao, C., Hurst, K., & Parker, K. (2023). *In a growing Share of U.S. marriages, husbands and wives earn about the same*. Pew Research Center. https://www.pewresearch.org/social-trends/2023/04/13/in-a-growing-share-of-u-s-marriages-husbands-and-wives-earn-about-the-same/

Furstenberg, F. F. (2019). Family change in global perspective: How and why family systems change. *Family Relations: An Interdisciplinary Journal of Applied Family Studies, 68*(3), 326–341. https://doi.org/10.1111/fare.12361

Grusec, J. E., & Hastings, P. D. (Eds.). (2015). Handbook of socialization: Theory and research (2nd ed.). The Guilford Press.
Haidt, J. (2024). *The anxious generation: How the great rewiring of childhood is causing an Epidemic of mental illness*. Penguin Random House.
Haidt, J., & Lukianoff, G. (2018). *The coddling of the American mind: How good intentions and bad ideas are setting up a generation for failure*. Penguin Press.
Hays, P. A. (2016). *Addressing cultural complexities in practice: Assessment, diagnosis, and therapy* (3rd ed.). American Psychological Association. https://doi.org/10.1037/14801-000
Heine, S. J. (2001). Self as cultural product: An examination of East Asian and North American selves. *Journal of Personality, 69*(6), 881–905. https://doi.org/10.1111/1467-6494.696168
Hiniker, A., Schoenebeck, S. Y., & Kientz, J. A. (2016). Not at the dinner table: Parents' and children's perspectives on family technology rules. In *Proceedings of the 19th ACM Conference on Computer-Supported Cooperative Work & Social Computing*.
Hogg, M. A., Abrams, D., & Brewer, M. B. (2017). Social identity: The role of self in group processes and intergroup relations. *Group Processes & Intergroup Relations, 20*(5), 570–581. https://doi.org/10.1177/1368430217690909
Haslam, C., Cruwys, T., Haslam, S. A., Dingle, G., Chang, M. X-L., (2016) Group 4 Health: Evidence that a Social Identity Intervention thatBuilds and Strengthens Social Group Membership Improves Mental Health. *Journal of Affective Disorders, 194* (188–195). https://doi.org/10.1016/j.jad.2016.01.010
Haslam, S. A., Haslam, C., Cruwys, T., Jetten, J., Bentley, S. V., Fong, P., & Steffens, N. K. (2022). Social Identity Makes Group-Based Social Connection Possible. *Current Opinion in Psychology, 43*, 161–165. https://doi.org/10.1016/j.copsyc.2021.07.013
Hertlein, K. M., & Blumer, M. L. C. (2014). The couple and family technology framework: Intimate relationships in a digital age. Routledge/Taylor& Francis Group.
Imber-Black, E., & Roberts, J. (1998). *Rituals for our times: Celebrating, healing, and Changing our lives and our relationships*. HarperCollins.
Killian, K. D. (2001). Crossing borders: Race, gender, and their intersections in interracial couples. *Journal of Feminist Family Therapy, 13*(1), 1–31. https://doi.org/10.1300/J086v13n01_01
Laplant, K. (2016). Family decline theory. *Encyclopedia of Family Studies,* Wiley OnLine Library. https://doi.org/10.1002/9781119085621.wbefs248
Larson, L. R., Szczytko, R., Bowers, E. P., Stephens, L. E., Stevenson, K. T., & Floyd, M. F. (2019). Outdoor time, screen time, and connection to nature: Troubling trends among rural youth? *Environment and Behavior, 51*(8), 966–991. https://doi.org/10.1177/0013916518806686
Leung, A. K.-Y., Maddux, W. W., Galinsky, A. D., & Chiu, C.-Y. (2008). Multicultural experience enhances creativity: The when and how. *American Psychologist, 63*(3), 169–181. https://doi.org/10.1037/0003-066X.63.3.169
Madianou, M., & Miller, D. (2012). *Migration and new media: Transnational families and polymedia. Routledge.* https://doi.org/10.4324/9780203154236
Majeed, M. T., & Kanwal, S. (2019). The global integration and transmission of social values: A case of family ties. *Social Indicators Research, 141*, 703–729. https://doi.org/10.1007/s11205-018-1847-x
Masten, A. S. (2001). Ordinary magic: Resilience processes in development. *American Psychologist, 56*(3), 227–238. https://doi.org/10.1037/0003-066X.56.3.227
McGoldrick, M., Giordano, J., & Garcia-Preto, N. (Eds.). (2005). *Ethnicity and family therapy* (3rd ed.). The Guilford Press.
McLanahan, S., & Percheski, C. (2008). Family structure and the reproduction of inequalities. *Annual Review of Sociology, 34*, 257–276. https://doi.org/10.1146/annurev.soc.34.040507.134549
McLanahan, S., & Sandefur, G. (1994). *Growing up with a single parent: What hurts, what helps.* Harvard University Press.
Mistry, J., & Wu, J. (2010). Navigating cultural worlds and negotiating identities: A conceptual model. *Human Development, 53*(1), 5–25. https://doi.org/10.1159/000268136

Moen, P., & Wethington, E. (1992). The concept of family adaptive strategies. *Annual Review of Sociology, 18*(1), 233–251. https://doi.org/10.1146/annurev.so.18.080192.001313
Mojtabai, R., & Olfson, M. (2020). *Survey data confirm increases in anxiety, depression and suicidal thinking among U.S. adolescents*. Johns Hopkins Bloomberg School of Public Health. https://publichealth.jhu.edu/2020/survey-data-confirm-increases-in-anxiety-depression-and-suicidal-thinking-among-u-s-adolescents
National Academies of Sciences, Engineering, and Medicine. (2016). Division of Behavioral and Social Sciences and Education; Board on Children, Youth, and Families; Committee on Supporting the Parents of Young Children. In H. Breiner, M. Ford, & V. L. Gadsden (Eds.), *Parenting matters: Supporting parents of children ages 0-8*. National Academies Press (US). https://www.ncbi.nlm.nih.gov/books/NBK402020/
Nomaguchi, K., & Milkie, M. A. (2020). Parenthood and well-being: A decade in review. *Journal of Marriage and Family, 82*(1), 198–223. https://doi.org/10.1111/jomf.12646
Pahl, R., & Spencer, L. (2004). Personal communities: Not simply families of 'fate' or 'choice'. *Current Sociology, 52*(2), 199–221. https://doi.org/10.1177/0011392104041 80
Parker, K. & Minkin, R. (2023). *Public has mixed views on the modern American family*. Pew Research Center. https://www.pewresearch.org/social-trends/2023/09/14/public-has-mixed-views-on-the-modern-american-family/
Patterson, C. J. (2017). Parents' sexual orientation and children's development. *Child Development Perspectives, 11*(1), 45–49. https://doi.org/10.1111/cdep.12207
Perry-Jenkins, M., & Gerstel, N. (2020). Work and family in the second decade of the 21st century. *Journal of Marriage and Family, 82*(1), 420–453. https://doi.org/10.1111/jomf.12636
Pesando, L. M., Castro, A. F., Andriano, L., Behrman, J. A., Billari, F. C., Monden, C., Furstenberg, F., & Kohler, H. P. (2019). Global family change: Persistent diversity with development. *Population and Development Review, 45*(1), 133–168. https://doi.org/10.1111/padr.12209
Pew Research Center. (2018). *Social media fact sheet*. Retrieved from https://www.pewresearch.org/internet/2018/05/31/teens-social-media-technology-2018/
Powell, B., Hamilton, L., Manago, B., & Cheng, S. (2016). Implications of changing family forms for children. *Annual Review of Sociology, 42*, 301–322. https://doi.org/10.1146/annurev-soc-081715-074444
Pyke, K. (1999). The micropolitics of care in relationships between aging parents and adult children: Individualism, collectivism, and power. *Journal of Marriage and the Family, 61*(3), 661–672. https://doi.org/10.2307/353568
Rosenblatt, P. C. (2009). *Shared obliviousness in family systems*. State University of New York Press.
Sanders, W., Parent, J., Forehand, R., Sullivan, A. D., & Jones, D. J. (2016). Parental perceptions of technology and technology-focused parenting: Associations with youth screen time. *Journal of Applied Developmental Psychology, 44*, 28–38. https://doi.org/10.1016/j.appdev.2016.02.005
Schaffer, K. (2023). *Striking findings from 2023*. Pew Research. https://www.pewresearch.org/short-reads/2023/12/08/striking-findings-from-2023/
Scharp, K. M., & Hall, E. D. (2017). Family marginalization, alienation, and estrangement: Questioning the nonvoluntary status of family relationships. *Annals of the International Communication Association, 41*(1), 28–45. https://doi.org/10.1080/23808985.2017.1285680
Schunk, D. H., & Pajares, F. (2009). Self-efficacy theory. In K. R. Wenzel & A. Wigfield (Eds.), *Handbook of motivation at school* (pp. 35–53). Routledge/Taylor & Francis Group.
Seltzer, J. A. (2019). Family change and changing families. *Demography, 6*(2), 405–426. https://doi.org/10.1007/s13524-019-00766-6
Serido, J., Shim, S., Mishra, A., & Tang, C. (2010). Financial parenting, financial coping behaviors, and well-being of emerging adults. *Family Relations, 59*(4), 453–464. https://doi.org/10.1111/j.1741-3729.2010.00615.x
Smock, P. J., & Schwartz, C. R. (2020). The demography of families: A review of patterns and change. *Journal of Marriage and Family, 82*(1), 9–34. https://doi.org/10.1111/jomf.12612
Suárez-Orozco, C., & Suárez-Orozco, M. M. (2001). *Children of immigration*. Harvard University Press.

Sue, D. W., Sue, D., Neville, H. A., & Smith, A. (2022). *Counseling the culturally diverse: Theory and practice* (9th ed.). Wiley.

Schwartz, S. J., Zamboanga, B. L., Weisskirch, R. S., & Wang, S. C. (2009). The Relationships of Personal and Cultural Identity to Adaptive and Maladaptive Psychosocial Functioning in Emerging Adults. *The Journal of Social Psychology, 150*(1), 1–33. https://doi.org/10.1080/00224540903366784. published online 2010

Triandis, H. C. (2001). Individualism-collectivism and personality. *Journal of Personality, 69*(6), 907–924. https://doi.org/10.1111/1467-6494.696169

Turkle, S. (2015). *Reclaiming conversation: The power of talk in a digital age*. Penguin Press.

Ungar, M. (2008). Resilience Across Cultures. *The British Journal of Social Work, 38*(2), 218–235. https://doi.org/10.1093/bjsw/bcl343 downloaded. https://www.researchgate.net/publication/30949809_Resilience_across_Cultures

Ungar, M. (2011). The social ecology of resilience: Addressing contextual and cultural ambiguity of a nascent construct. *American Journal of Orthopsychiatry, 81*(1), 1–17. https://doi.org/10.1111/j.1939-0025.2010.01067.x

Walsh, F. (2016). *Strengthening family resilience*. Guilford Press.

White, M., & Epston, D. (1990). *Narrative means to therapeutic ends*. Norton & Company.

Willis, D. W., & Eddy, J. M. (2022). Early relational health: Innovations in child health for promotion, screening, and research. *Infant Mental Health Journal, 43*(3), 361–372. https://doi.org/10.1002/imhj.21980

Winnicott, D. W. (1971). *Playing and reality*. Tavistock Publications.

Lilli Friedland PhD, ABPP, is board certified by the American Board of Professional Psychology in clinical psychology, with specialties in family and organizational systems. Dr. Friedland is a highly respected family psychologist, consultant, and executive coach to business leaders. She served on the American Psych. Association's Council of Representatives; and as president, Division 46 Society for Media Psychology & Technology; and on the California Psych. Association. Board; and as president of Division 3, Organizational & Consulting Psychology, and president of Division 6, Media Psychology; as governor-appointed member of the California Board of Psychology, the state licensing board; and, as President of the Los Angeles County Psychological Association. The Los Angeles Board of Supervisors has honored her for distinguished services on several occasions. Dr. Friedland has been cited in the Wall Street Journal, New York Times, Harvard Business Review, Los Angeles Times, Time Magazine, and other national publications. She has published articles, co-authored a book, and made over two hundred national and local TV and radio appearances.

Chapter 2
The Use of Psychedelics in Couples Therapy

Alan Groveman

The History of Psychedelics

Psychedelics have played a long and complex role in human history. The use of psychoactive substances in religious and healing practices dates back thousands of years. People in China used cannabis in 3000 BCE. In 2500 BCE people in Switzerland ate poppy seeds. Early Indigenous people in the Amazon brewed ayahuasca and in West Africa, they ate the Iboga shrub (George et al., 2022). Art historians have hypothesized that the 15th-century artist Hieronymus Bosch suffered from ergotism (caused by ingesting ergot by eating grains such as rye, an extremely toxic and hallucinogenic alkaloid found in the ergot fungus, such as lysergic acid -LSD), which accounted for his demonic paintings (Fuller, 1968). In the eighteenth and nineteenth centuries, poets such as Samuel Taylor Coleridge composed works while under the influence of Opium (Charpentier, 1970). In more recent times, LSD was synthesized in 1938 by Albert Hofmann (Osmond, 1957). By the 1950s, it was being explored for various therapeutic applications, especially as an adjunct to psychotherapy. Stanislav Grof, a prominent researcher during this period, performed many sessions (over 40,000) using LSD to treat a range of conditions (Grof, 2008). Unfortunately, growing public interest in LSD precipitated unsupervised and unregulated recreational use of the drug, and in 1970 the USA passed the Controlled Substance Act listing LSD and psilocybin as Schedule I drugs (Vattano, 1981). The Controlled Substance Act was signed into law by Richard Nixon. It organized federally regulated drugs into five schedules with varying restrictions and penalties (*Controlled Substance Schedules*, n.d.)

In 1971, the United Nations convened a conference to establish a protocol for psychotropic substances known as the Convention on Psychotropic Substances

A. Groveman (✉)
Northwestern University, Evanston, IL, USA

F. W. Kaslow (ed.), *Contemporary Issues in Individual, Couple, and Family Lives and Treatment*, https://doi.org/10.1007/978-3-031-90006-8_2

(*Convention on Psychotropic Substances*, 1971). Despite a backlash against psychedelics, the 1990s saw a resurgence of scientific research in psychedelic-assisted therapy (PAT), as evidenced by numerous studies listed in the NIH's National Library of Medicine database (*Drug Scheduling*, n.d.). Collaborative efforts among neurologists, psychiatrists, psychologists, and pharmacologists have shown that PAT is an effective treatment. Large-scale clinical trials have been conducted, showing positive results for a variety of mental health conditions. FDA granted "breakthrough therapy" designation to psilocybin for treatment-resistant depression and to MDMA for PTSD. (Carhart-Harris et al., 2018).

Below is a list of Schedule I-IV drugs. The list was created in 1970 by United States Drug Enforcement Agency (DEA) which maintains a list of controlled medications and illicit substances categorized from Schedule I to V (Gabay, 2013). The list is used to inform the medical community and the public about the accepted use and potential abuse of Drugs. Schedule I drugs include MDMA and Psilocybin. MDMA is currently illegal in the United States. Psilocybin is legal, in Oregon and Colorado with specific regulations governing its use.

- **Schedule I—**Drugs with no currently accepted medical use and a high potential for abuse.
- **Schedule II—**Drugs with a high potential for abuse, with use potentially leading to severe psychological or physical dependence. These drugs are also considered dangerous.
- **Schedule III**—Drugs with a moderate to low potential for physical and psychological dependence. Schedule III drugs abuse potential is less than Schedule I and Schedule II drugs but more than Schedule IV.
- **Schedule IV**—Drugs with a low potential for abuse and low risk of dependence.
- **Schedule V—**Drugs with lower potential for abuse than Schedule IV that consist of preparations containing limited quantities of certain narcotics (LSD, psilocybin, psilocin, mescaline, peyote, cannabis, MDMA (3,4-methylenedioxymetham phetamine), and DMT (N, N-Dimethyltryptamine)) were listed as Schedule I drugs.

Ketamine, originally used as an anesthetic, received FDA approval as an adjunctive medication for treatment-resistant depression (TRD) in adults (Anand et al., 2011). MDMA demonstrated efficacy in psychedelic-assisted psychotherapy for the treatment of PTSD (Jerome et al., 2020). Over the past thirty years hundreds of studies have been conducted in PAT demonstrating the efficacy of the treatment for a variety of neuropsychiatric conditions (Kelly et al., 2022).

In 1988 the Controlled Substance Act listed MDMA as a Schedule I drug. However, because of several successful controlled studies, in 2017 the FDA designated MDA as a breakthrough therapy for PTSD (Lewis, 2000). Consequently, several studies have used MDMA as an adjunct in treating couples when a partner has PTSD (Anand et al., 2011). Wagner (2021) has described a transtheoretical model using MDMA in couple therapy. The exploration of systemic factors, the reduction of disruptive dyadic interactions, and a focus on strengthening attachment bonds are often listed as the foundational goals of couple therapy (Johnson, 2019). "MDMA elevates serum oxytocin (Wolff et al., 2006; Dumont et al., 2009) and vasopressin (Bershad et al., 2016), as well as cortisol and prolactin (Harris et al., 2002). MDMA causes a decrease in cerebral blood flow to the amygdala and hippocampus, an increase in activity in the prefrontal cortex, action in the occipital cortex and insula, a decrease in functional connectivity between the hippocampus and prefrontal cortex, and an increase between the hippocampus and amygdala" (Wagner, 2021 p. 2). The neurochemical effect of MDMA, including oxytocin and vasopressin, appears to enhance a person's experience of loving emotions (Carhart-Harris et al., 2013). In an uncontrolled trial Monson and colleagues (Monson et al., 2020) tested the safety, tolerability, and efficacy of MDMA-facilitated CBCT. Six couples with varying levels of baseline relationship satisfaction in which one partner was diagnosed with PTSD participated. There were significant improvements in PTSD, depression, sleep, emotion regulation, trauma beliefs, and relationship satisfaction.

In a psilocybin-assisted group study Stauffer and colleagues (Stauffer et al., 2020) found that individuals who had preoccupied attachment styles experienced a reduction in their anxiety and increased feelings of unity probably because of the mystical-type of experiences that can accompany psilocybin. PAT for couples is an emerging approach that continues to be explored as a viable treatment to help a couple enhance their relationship. An overview of the key factors that inform PAT for couple therapy is presented below.

MDMA and the Brain

MDMA has been shown to decrease the reactivity of the amygdala and hippocampus resulting in a reduced fear response. Oxytocin, vasopressin, dopamine, and serotonin levels in the brain are elevated and feelings of attachment and a more positive mood are experienced (Wagner, 2021). Couples report feeling more secure in sharing feelings and issues that have impeded the relationship. They are more amenable to therapeutic interventions. MDMA appears to mimic the neurobiology of love and rekindle the positive memories of connectedness, including sexual arousal.

Legal and Ethical Issues

Denver was the first city to decriminalize psilocybin in 2019. Oakland and Sata Cruz, California, Washington, D.C., Somerville, Cambridge, and Northampton. Massachusetts, Seattle, Washington, and Detroit Michigan have all decriminalized psilocybin. Oregon was the first. Mount Sinai Icahn School of Medicine: Center for Psychedelic Psychotherapy and Trauma Research

- Massachusetts General Hospital: Center for the Neuroscience of Psychedelics

- University of Wisconsin: Transdisciplinary Center for Research in Psychoactive Substances.

In 2017 the FDA approved MDMA as a breakthrough treatment for PTSD (Mithoefer et al., 2019). Almond and Allan (2019) incorporated MDMA with an Emotionally Focused Therapy (EFT) protocol for couples experiencing the impact of PTSD. Greer and Tolbert (1998) concluded that under the right circumstances, "MDMA reduces or somehow eliminates the neurophysiological fear response to a perceived threat to one's emotional integrity, allowing clients to feel more comfortable being aware of, communicating about, and recalling thoughts and feelings that were usually accompanied by fear and anxiety" (p. 377). Using MDMA enhanced a couple's ability to communicate more openly and with a lower fear response. Attachment bonds were strengthened, and dyadic adjustment was improved.

The legal and ethical concerns about the misuse of MDMA parallel the concerns 50 years ago about LSD. Moving out of the lab and into unsupervised and unregulated public use risks dangerous repercussions to the public. Quality assurance, accurate dosage calibration, and a clear understanding of potential risk are required to reduce harm (Pilecki et al., 2021). Popular media has reported on the research support for MDMA-assisted couple therapy and has cautioned its use without professional guidance, particularly with individuals who have experienced significant trauma, or psychotic episodes in their lives (Ducharme, 2023). Pilecki and colleagues have recommended a harm reduction approach that presents clients with the risk/benefit ratio prior to using psychedelics and forming clear expectations and intentions (Pilecki et al., 2021). Clearly, there is a need for psychotherapy support in psychedelic-assisted therapy.

Training and Competencies

Clinicians need to be trained in the appropriate therapeutic techniques when working with psychedelic-assisted treatment. Couples seeking MDMA adjunctive treatment should be encouraged to consult a professional who follows a three-step protocol: (1) Screening prior to an MDMA session, (2) Guidance and support during the MDMA session, and (3) Follow-up and ongoing therapy, if required, post the MDMA session.

Therapists working in the PAT field require empathic listening skills, attunement, an ability to work with catharsis, and a knowledge of psychedelic/brain interaction. It is critical for the therapist engaged in PAT to have a clear understanding of set (expectations and intentions of the client) and setting (the environment where PAT is conducted, and the psychedelic is administered). Twelve domains for training therapists in PAT have been suggested by Phelps (2017, pp. 474–475). Those domains are: (1) The history of clinical research and current legal status of psychedelic-assisted therapy; (2) Neurobiology, neuropharmacology, drug disposition, and drug interactions; (3) Best practices in sets and settings: preparation, psychedelic session, and integration; (4) Psychedelics and therapeutic relationships: transference, boundaries, ethics, and self- care; (5) Supervised observation of psychedelic session videos; (6) Variations in therapeutic models: client-centered and psycholytic psychedelic therapy; (7) Complementary therapeutic techniques in psychedelic-assisted therapy; (8) Co-therapy methods and interprofessional skills for working on multidisciplinary teams; (9) Current models of consciousness, spiritual intelligence, and mystical experiences; (10) Ceremonial use of psychedelics in religious and community settings; (11) Individual and group clinical supervision during an internship as a psychedelic therapist in FDA-approved clinical trials or expanded access to clinical research programs; and (12) Personal experience of being guided as a research participant in an FDA-approved study.

Many authors highlight the importance of the therapist in successful MDMA-assisted therapy and a focus on the inner experience catalyzed by MDMA (Metzner & Adamson, 2001; Mithoefer, 2015). Mithoefer (2015) emphasizes empathic listening skills including: (1) Minimal encouragement, verbal and non-verbal; (2) Invitation rather than direction; (3) Paraphrasing; (4) Reflecting; (5) Emotional labeling; (6) Validating; (7) Reassurance and waiting; (8) Allowing participants to come to conclusions themselves. Non-directive communication also uses invitation rather than direction. For example: (1) "We encourage you to …"; (2) "This might be a good time to …"; (3) Use the gerund of a word: instead of "breathe" say "breathing" because it is suggestive rather that directive; and (4) Reflecting back to the participant what they are saying in order to continue conversation without being directive.

MDMA Abuse

The use of MDMA under research conditions is generally safe (Pollan, 2019). However, the recreational use of MDMA as a "party drug" can be dangerous (*MDMA (Ecstasy) Abuse*, n.d.). Often, MDMA obtained illegally is adulterated with methamphetamine, caffeine, the over-the-counter cough suppressant dextromethorphan, the diet drug ephedrine, and cocaine. Reported undesirable effects of street obtained MDMA include: (*MDMA (Ecstasy) Abuse*, n.d.) anxiety, restlessness, irritability, sadness, impulsiveness, aggression, sleep disturbances, lack of appetite, thirst, and reduced interest in and pleasure from sex. In addition to undesirable effects, MDMA obtained illegally can also cause serious adverse health conditions including involuntary jaw clenching and teeth grinding, muscle cramping, blurred vision, marked rise in body temperature (hyperthermia), dehydration, high blood pressure, heart failure, kidney failure, and arrhythmia.

Unfortunately, reports of successful treatment with psychedelics precipitate misuse by the public. Popular media outlets such as Time (Ducharme, 2023) and the New York Times (Caron, 2022) may tempt couples to obtain MDMA illegally and experiment without proper medical and psychological oversight. Unknown dose level, adulteration, lack of medical and therapist screening and guidance perpetuate the myth of the dangers of MDMA. Charpentier (1970) quoting the Swiss-German scientist Paracelsus, in the 1500s said "What is there that is not poison? All things are poison, and nothing is without poison. Solely the dose determines that a thing is not a poison."

At the time this chapter is being written MDMA is illegal, except for clinical trials for individuals who have been diagnosed with PTSD. Providers cannot prescribe MDMA but can serve as guides for those couples that want to experience MDMA and self-administer the drug. Of course, this does not resolve the issues of dose level and possible adulteration. Several authors have described protocols that are used for MDMA-assisted treatment (Greer & Tolbert, 1998; Monson et al., 2020) and the necessity for MDMA to be used in conjunction with psychotherapy. Below is a sample protocol for working with MDMA-assisted couple therapy modeled after the Multidiscipline Association for Psychedelic Studies recommendations (Mithoefer, 2015).

Sample MDMA-Assisted Couple Therapy Protocol

Initial Steps

Couples that are interested in participating in MDMA-assisted therapy should be encouraged to review written information about possible benefits and risks. Questions about treatment should be discussed with potential participants in full. Issues of confidentiality, including that the couple is considered the "patient" and holds the privilege of releasing information, therapist training, and the purpose and setting of each session need to be specified. In addition, expectations related to treatment need to be explored and clarified. MDMA is not a magic bullet that results in full-blown dyadic harmony. Both partners sign a consent to treat form.

MDMA-assisted couple therapy requires a team approach. A medical provider (preferably a psychiatrist, or psychiatric nurse practitioner familiar with Psychedelic-Assisted Therapy—PAT) needs to meet with each partner and review each one's medical and psychiatric history. This can be accomplished by using the Structured Clinical Interview for Axis I Diagnosis (SCID) and the SCID II for personality disorder as well as obtaining a medical history, physical examination, serum chemistry profile, complete blood count, thyroid-stimulation hormone (TSH), free thyroxine, HIV serology, urinalysis, and electrocardiogram (ECG). Mithoefer (Mithoefer et al., 2010) has listed psychiatric and medical exclusion criteria that need to be considered prior to MDMA-assisted therapy. Psychiatric exclusion criteria include any Axis I disorder with the following exceptions: anxiety disorders, affective disorders other than bipolar disorder type 1, substance abuse or dependence in remission for 60 days, and an eating disorder without active purging. In addition, a diagnosis of borderline personality disorder is an exclusion criterion. There should be urine drug testing for cocaine, marijuana, amphetamines, MDMA, opiates, and benzodiazepines at the initial screening and immediately before each experimental session.

The extensive screening prior to MDMA-assisted therapy is part of the protocol for a randomized controlled pilot study (Mithoefer et al., 2010) and is, therefore, extensive. Non- clinical trial use will probably not require as many tests. However, psychiatric exclusion criteria for any MDMA-related treatment need to be considered for psychotic processes, bipolar I and borderline personality disorders, when working with couples.

Setting, Structure, and Safety

Following the initial screening the couple meets with a couple therapist for one to two sessions. Current relationship status, history of dyadic interactions, including distress, strengths, abuse, points of disagreement, and agreed to goals are reviewed. The couple agree to participate in both the MDMA experience and couple counseling. The number of psychedelic and therapy sessions is discussed, and concerns and expectations are considered. The setting for the therapy and MDMA sessions needs to be seen by the couple, and any concerns, such as setting arrangements and therapist location, need to be addressed. If music is used during the MDMA session, the couple, in consultation with the therapist, decided on the play-list. Lighting, room temperature, and size of the room are reviewed so that the couple and therapist feel comfortable.

The use of MDMA necessitates careful participants preparation and assessment because it can have significant emotional and physical impacts. During the preparation sessions, the participant and therapists discuss the parameters of each session and establish agreements to support a collaborative therapeutic partnership and promote a therapeutic attitude.

The potential of providing the participant with nurturing touch or targeted bodywork through physical contact is discussed by the therapists and the participant. Throughout the experimental sessions, the participant and the therapists should work out a comfortable physical distance between them. The therapists should also be aware of any potential shifts in the participant's comfort level about their proximity.

The duties of the therapists are defined and enhanced by agreements for appropriate behavior before, during, and after therapy sessions. Therapists and participants are expressly prohibited from having any kind of sexual interaction. In addition to ensuring that the patient's enhanced vulnerability won't be exploited, this contract establishes a safe environment for the patient to get physical comfort during treatment. Throughout the whole MDMA-assisted session, two therapists are present. For the duration of the MDMA-assisted sessions, both therapists agree to stay in the room with the participant, except for brief intervals during which one therapist at a time may leave the room. This is done to assess the participant's level of self-reported distress (SUD), which must be equal to or less than baseline, by looking at physiological signs, and by using clinical judgment regarding stability.

Both the therapists and the couple must concur that they are in a stable and safe state for the therapy session to end successfully. In addition, the couple must consent to accepting transportation home from the integrative follow-up session after the MDMA-assisted session, whether it is provided by the therapists or by a friend. The participant and the therapist consent to continue daily phone communication for a maximum of one week following each MDMA-assisted session.

Two MDMA dosing sessions for each participant are implemented. A dosing session is defined as *individuals administered a specific dose of a psychedelic substance*, without psychotherapy taking place. The first is individually conducted with each participant, with two therapists present. At least one of the therapists is always present in the room throughout the entire MDMA-assisted session. The participant is reminded that the therapists are there for support, if needed. The participant can either share what they are experiencing or remain silent. Following the first MDMA dosing session two or three 90-minute integration sessions are conducted. During these sessions the participant can explore feelings, and reactions to the dosing session with the therapist(s). The therapist(s) do not engage in interpretation of the material presented by the participant, but rather the goal is to encourage and be attuned to what the participant is describing so that the participant can integrate the experience. The therapists need to be both empathetically present and maintain boundaries. By doing this, the therapists support the client in remaining aware of her or his own inner experience and establish a secure space that encourages openness to investigate novel and surprising insights that might surface throughout the healing process.

The second MDMA dosing session is conducted with both partners in the same room. Instructions provided for the first dosing are repeated and partners are informed that they can choose to interact with each other during the session, or with the therapists in the room. The second session is more interactive, and partners are encouraged to share feelings. Two to three integration sessions are held after the second dosing. The emphasis in these sessions is to help the couple better understand their interactional patterns and how their communication can be more effective. It is recommended that one aspect of therapy with the couple focuses on attachment theory and the effects early attachment has on adult relationships (Mikulincer & Shaver, 2016). Psychedelics may facilitate deep emotional processing, allowing partners to revisit early attachment experiences and reframe early attachment trauma. Therapists may assist couples in exploring their attachment styles and how they manifest in their relationship dynamics within the framework of psychedelic-assisted couple therapy. By learning more about how their respective attachment patterns interact, couples can develop a deeper level of empathy and understanding.

Good interaction patterns are essential to a happy relationship. Improving couples' interactional patterns and self-expression is the main goal of communication theory in the context of couple therapy. Psychedelics can improve communication by encouraging candid and open discussion. People may feel more connected, sympathetic, and capable of expressing their thoughts and feelings when under the influence of psychedelics. Couples can use this improved communication to address underlying issues, communicate unmet needs, and create post-session communication strategies, with the assistance of their therapist.

A third component facilitated by MDMA is transpersonal psychology, which examines the relationship between psychology and spirituality. Transpersonal psychology can assist couples in exploring their spiritual and existential aspects together in psychedelic-assisted marital therapy. Couples using psychedelics may have deep spiritual and mystical experiences that increase their feeling of purpose and interconnectedness in their relationship. To foster both personal and interpersonal development, therapists can assist couples in incorporating these experiences into their everyday life and relationships.

If the couple agrees, and the therapist feels it is useful, family members can be invited to join the couple in their session. Having the couple explain the changes in the relationship because of treatment to family members can serve to alter negative expectations about the couple that the family may harbor (Lafrance et al., 2020).

Conclusion

Couples receiving MDMA therapy can reach greater depths of self-awareness, emotional recovery, and personal development by incorporating these frameworks into their sessions. The use of psychedelics as a catalyst for therapeutic exploration can amplify the effectiveness of traditional couples therapy approaches and provide a unique opportunity for couples to reconnect, heal, and strengthen their bonds.

References

Almond, K., & Allan, R. (2019). Incorporating MDMA as an adjunct in emotionally focused couples therapy with clients impacted by trauma or PTSD. *The Family Journal, 27*(3), 293–299. https://doi.org/10.1177/1066480719852360

Anand, A., Mathew, S. J., & Janicak, P. G. (2011). Ketamine treatment for major depression. *Psychopharmacology Review, 46*(12), 89–96. https://doi.org/10.1097/01.psyphr.0000410133.47951.30

Bershad, A. K., Weafer, J. J., Kirkpatrick, M. G., Wardle, M. C., Miller, M. A., de Wit, H. (2016). Oxytocin receptor gene variation predicts subjective responses to MDMA. *Social Neuroscience, 11*(6), 592–599. https://doi.org/10.1080/17470919.2016.1143026

Carhart-Harris, R. L., Bolstridge, M., Day, C. M., Rucker, J., Watts, R., Erritzoe, D. E., & Taylor, D. (2018). Psilocybin with psychological support for treatment-resistant depression: Six-month follow-up. *Psychopharmacology, 235*(2), 399–408. https://doi.org/10.1007/s00213-017-4771-x

Carhart-Harris, R. L., Wall, M. B., Erritzoe, D., Kaelen, M., Ferguson, B., De Meer, I., Tanner, M., Bloomfield, M., Williams, T. M., Bolstridge, M., Stewart, L., Morgan, C. J., Newbould, R., Feilding, A., Curran, H. V., & Nutt, D. J. (2013). The effect of acutely administered MDMA on subjective and bold-*f*MRI responses to favourite and worst autobiographical memories. *The International Journal of Neuropsychopharmacology, 17*(04), 527–540. https://doi.org/10.1017/S1461145713001405

Caron, C. (2022, January 8). Can MDMA save a marriage? *NY Times*. Retrieved January 5, 2024.

Charpentier, J. (1970). *The sublime somnambulist*. Haskel House.

Controlled substance schedules. (n.d.). Retrieved December. 2023

Convention on psychotropic substances. (1971). United Nations. https://www.unodc.org/unodc/en/treaties/psychotropics.html

Drug scheduling. (n.d.). Drug Enforcement Agency. Retrieved December 22, 2023, from https://www.dea.gov/drug-information/drug-scheduling

Ducharme, J. (2023, March 14). Psychedelics could revolutionize couples therapy. *TIME*. https://time.com/6262291/psychedelics-mdma-couples-therapy/

Dumont, G. J. H., Sweep, F. C. G. J., van der Steen, R., Hermsen, R., Donders, A. R. T., Touw, D. J., van Gerven, J. M. A., Buitelaar, J. K., & Verkes, R. J. (2009). Increased oxytocin concentrations and prosocial feelings in humans after ecstasy (34-methylenedioxymethamphetamine) administration. *Social Neuroscience, 4*(4), 359–366. https://doi.org/10.1080/17470910802649470

Fuller, J. G. (1968). *The day of St. Anthony's fire*. MacMillan and Co.

Gabay, M. (2013). The federal controlled substances act: schedules and pharmacy registration. *Hospital Pharmacy, 48*(6), 473–474.

George, D., Hanson, R., & Wilkinson, D. (2022). Ancient roots of today's emerging renaissance in psychedelic medicine. *Culture, Medicine, and Psychiatry, 46*(4), 890–903. https://doi.org/10.1007/s11013-021-09749-y

Greer, G. R., & Tolbert, R. (1998). A method of conducting therapeutic sessions with MDMA. *Journal of Psychoactive Drugs, 30*(4), 371–379. https://doi.org/10.1080/02791072.1998.10399713

Grof, S. (2008). *LSD psychotherapy* (4th ed.). MAPS.

Harris, D. S., Baggott, M., Mendelson, J. H., Mendelson, J. E., & Jones, R. T. (2002). Subjective and hormonal effects of 34-methylenedioxymethamphetamine (MDMA) in humans. *Psychopharmacology, 162*(4), 396–405. https://doi.org/10.1007/s00213-002-1131-1

Jerome, L., Feduccia, A. A., Wang, J. B., Hamilton, S., Yazar-Klosinski, B., Emerson, A., Mithoefer, M. C., & Doblin, R. (2020). Long- term follow-up outcomes of MDMA-assisted psychotherapy for treatment of PTSD: A longitudinal pooled analysis of six phase 2 trials. *Psychopharmacology, 237*(8), 2485–2497. https://doi.org/10.1007/s00213-020-05548-2

Johnson, S. M. (2019). The basics of eft interventions: Emotions and the macro-intervention, the EFT tango. In *The practice of emotionally focused couple therapy* (pp. 51–84). Routledge.

Kelly, D. F., Heinzerling, K., Sharma, A., Gowrinathan, S., Sergi, K., & Mallari, R. (2022). Psychedelic-assisted therapy and psychedelic science: A review and perspective on opportunities in neurosurgery and neuro-oncology. *Neurosurgery, 92*(4), 680–694. https://doi.org/10.1227/neu.0000000000002275

Lafrance, A., Henderson, K. A., & Mayman, S. (2020). *Emotion-focused family therapy: A transdiagnostic model for caregiver-focused interventions*. American Psychological Association. https://doi.org/10.1037/0000166-000

Lewis, D. D. (2000). *Therapeutic MDMA (ecstasy) & the federal government: a cloudy past & a hopeful future*. Harvard Library. https://dash.harvard.edu/handle/1/8889454

MDMA (ecstasy) abuse. (n.d.). National Institute on Drug Abuse. Retrieved January 3, 2024, from https://nida.nih.gov/sites/default/files/rrmdma_0.pdf

Metzner, R., & Adamson, S. (2001). Using MDMA in healing, psychotherapy and spiritual practice. In J. Holland (Ed.), *Ecstasy, A complete guide: A comprehensive look at the risks and benefits of MDMA* (pp. 192–207). Inner Traditions.

Mikulincer, M., & Shaver, P. (2016). *Attachment in adulthood* (2nd ed.). Guilford Publications, Inc.

Mithoefer, M. (2015). *A manual for MDMA assisted psychotherapy in the treatment of PTSD* (Manual V.7). Multidiscipline Association for Psychedelic Studies. https://maps.org/research-archive/mdma/MDMA-Assisted-Psychotherapy-Treatment-Manual-Version7-19Aug15-FINAL.pdf

Mithoefer, M., Mithoefer, A., Feduccia, A., Jerome, I., Wagner, M., Hoilland, J., Hamilton, S., Yazar-Klosinski, B., Emerson, A., & Doblin, R. (2019). S.08.06 MDMA-assisted psychotherapy for PTSD: A promising novel experimental treatment moving into phase 3 trials with FDA breakthrough therapy designation. *European Neuropsychopharmacology, 29*, S11–S12. https://doi.org/10.1016/j.euroneuro.2018.11.930

Mithoefer, M. C., Wagner, M. T., Mithoefer, A. T., Jerome, L., & Doblin, R. (2010). The safety and efficacy of ±3,4-methylenedioxymethamphetamine-assisted psychotherapy in subjects with chronic, treatment-resistant posttraumatic stress disorder: The first randomized controlled pilot study. *Journal of Psychopharmacology, 25*(4), 439–452. https://doi.org/10.1177/0269881110378371

Monson, C. M., Wagner, A. C., Mithoefer, A. T., Liebman, R., Feduccia, A. A., Jerome, L., Yazar-Klosinski, B., Emerson, A., Doblin, R., & Mithoefer, M. C. (2020). MDMA-facilitated cognitive-behavioural conjoint therapy for posttraumatic stress disorder: An uncontrolled trial. *European Journal of Psychotraumatology, 11*(1). https://doi.org/10.1080/20008198.2020.1840123

Osmond, H. (1957). A review of the clinical effects of psychotomimetic agents. *Annals of the New York Academy of Sciences, 66*(3), 418–434. https://doi.org/10.1111/j.1749-6632.1957.tb40738.x

Phelps, J. (2017). Developing guidelines and competencies for the training of psychedelic therapists. *Journal of Humanistic Psychology, 57*(5), 450–487. https://doi.org/10.1177/0022167817711304

Pilecki, B., Luoma, J. B., Bathje, G. J., Rhea, J., & Narloch, V. (2021). Ethical and legal issues in psychedelic harm reduction and integration therapy. *Harm Reduction Journal, 18*(1). https://doi.org/10.1186/s12954-021-00489-1

Pollan, M. (2019). *How to change your mind*. Perfection Learning Corporation.

Stauffer, C. S., Anderson, B. T., Ortigo, K. M., & Woolley, J. (2020). Psilocybin-assisted group therapy and attachment: Observed reduction in attachment anxiety and influences of attachment insecurity on the psilocybin experience. *ACS Pharmacology & Translational Science, 4*(2), 526–532. https://doi.org/10.1021/acsptsci.0c00169

Vattano, A. J. (1981). Psychedelic drugs reconsidered. *Children & Schools, 4*(1), 71–72. https://doi.org/10.1093/cs/4.1.71

Wagner, A. C. (2021). Couple therapy with MDMA—proposed pathways of action. *Frontiers in Psychology, 12*. https://doi.org/10.3389/fpsyg.2021.733456

Wolff, K., Tsapakis, E. M., Winstock, A. R., Hartley, D., Holt, D., Forsling, M. L., & Aitchison, K. J. (2006). Vasopressin and oxytocin secretion in response to the consumption of ecstasy in a clubbing population. *Journal of Psychopharmacology, 20*(3), 400–410. https://doi.org/10.1177/0269881106061514

Alan Groveman PhD, ABPP, has been a licensed New Jersey Psychologist since 1980. In 1997, he served as the President of the New Jersey Psychological Association and is the immediate past-chair of the New Jersey State Board of Psychological Examiners. Dr. Groveman is a Board-Certified Couple and Family Psychologist by the American Board of Professional Psychology and currently serves as the president of the American Academy of Couple and Family Psychology. He is part of the affiliate faculty at the Family Institute of Northwestern University.

Chapter 3
Four and Five Generation Families: A Relatively New Phenomenon

Florence W. Kaslow

Four and Five Generation Families

Case #1: Green Family

Jerry Green was turning 90 years old (Generation 1) and had just retired as CEO of a chain of kitchen appliance stores which he had started 50 years earlier. He had been and still was well liked and respected by his employees and executives from the firms he bought equipment and supplies from, as well as by customers who had gotten to know him. He was referred to me by a former client of mine and requested an appointment to deal with the enormous changes being wrought by his retirement, and what to do in the next and final stage of his life.

Mr. Green's wife had died five years earlier and he still missed her enormously. He continued to live in the lovely apartment they had shared in Jupiter, Florida. His son, Gary, now 65 years of age (Gen 2), managed their store in South Carolina and did not want to relocate his family and his company responsibilities to live closer to his still competent, but very distressed, discontent father. Gary's grown children (Gen 3) were settled in the same city as their parents, along with their adult children, ages 35 and 40, and grandchildren, ages 15 and 20 (Gen 4).

Janine, Jerry's 55-year-old daughter (Gen 2) resided in North Carolina and was the CEO of the family enterprise branch there. Like her brother, she liked her position and her lifestyle and saw no reason to uproot to be near her dad. It was difficult for her to envision him being lonely and despondent. He had always been so self-sufficient and positive. Both children had agreed they would alternate traveling to visit their father every other month for a weekend. It was unclear if it would be just

F. W. Kaslow (✉)
Kaslow Associates, Palm Beach Gardens, FL, USA

F. W. Kaslow (ed.), *Contemporary Issues in Individual, Couple, and Family Lives and Treatment*, https://doi.org/10.1007/978-3-031-90006-8_3

his son and daughter visiting or also their spouses and children, with whom he wanted more contact.

Jerry still played golf on the weekend and bridge once or twice a week. But he missed running the business, being involved with employees, customers, and suppliers, having a place to go six days a week and feeling useful and important. He felt hurt, dejected, and rejected when he realized that seeing him was not a priority for his children and their families. He had considered them a "close" family until he "needed and wanted" them to visit him more frequently and also to come to visit him for a long stay-over weekend every few months. As he began to feel comfortable in therapy with me, he talked about how shocked and hurt he was by his children not wanting to be more involved with his life. He felt they were ungrateful for his continuous generosity and investment in them and indifferent to his loneliness (Office of the U.S. Surgeon General, 2023). He was unaccustomed to talking to them about his feelings and his needs; it took about seven sessions before he was ready to articulate this to his son and daughter and their partners.

When he was ready to deal with his needs and wants, I recommended we hold an extended family therapy session (Framo, 1992) to which he would invite his son and daughter and their partners. Eventually, he asked them to arrange coverage at their stores so they could come to town for the same three days and have two extended family therapy sessions with me—with one day in-between to process and reflect on what was transpiring and get better (re)acquainted with their lonely, retired dad (Boszormenyi-Nagy & Spark, 1973). Fortunately, they did care for him and were pleased he had gone into therapy and had then invited them to join him and get to know him better in this stage of his life. I recommended we hold a session for the entire family (except children under 10) during a visit when both his son's and daughter's family could attend such an intergenerational family of origin session. Such sessions should be led by a knowledgeable and skilled therapist and provide a time and comfortable place for everyone to describe what they saw as the issues and contribute their thoughts toward resolution of the dilemmas (Speck & Attneave, 1974). This is what was done, with my serving as therapist/leader. (Sometimes a co-leader is invited to co-conduct the session.) Several long-term grudges emerged, including that they felt he was often too autocratic. Fortunately, there was much cross discussion with the intent of resolution. Much healing and forgiveness resulted (Hargrave, 1994; Hargrave & Pfitzer, 2011).

They all decided they would call him more frequently, do a family Facetime or Zoom call weekly, and that for as long as he could still drive, he would also visit them during the month they didn't come to see him. That way he would get to know his grandchildren and great-grandchildren better and perhaps be able to accompany them to some of their activities and have an occasional breakfast, lunch, or dinner with them all and celebrate some holidays together. When it became necessary, he could hire a driver.

Jerry was very gratified with the outcome and learned he had to be more open with his children and grandchildren about himself. He continued in therapy once a month for six more months and left saying he would call when he needed "some guidance" (which he did periodically) and that he delighted having his grandchildren and great-grandchildren in his life more and that he was no longer so lonely.

Unlike Jerry's situation, many people in the first and second generations of their four and five generation families, who are in their 80s, 90s, or even 100s, do not have the financial resources and intact cognitive capacity that Jerry did. If for any number of reasons, they cannot live alone, what are the other possible choices which can be considered?

Other Options to be Considered

Moving In with an Adult Child or Grandchild

Can the senior grandparent(s) or parent(s) move in with any of their adult children? Is there a guest house on the premises or a vacant guest bedroom in the house or apartment? If so, do they all get along well enough to live together over time? Would it be necessary for one of the adult children to stay home and take care of their parent(s) or grandparent(s)? Are they willing to do so? What would the financial arrangement be? Can they afford to pay for an aide part- or full-time, if one is needed, or can any of the children?

Over several decades of doing therapy with families and friends dealing with these mammoth issues I have heard responses ranging from "no way," "it just wouldn't work," "I can't quit my job," "I'd feel like a prisoner," and "nothing I would do would be enough." No doubt their assessment of their personal situation was accurate for them. The situation is even more complex if there have been divorces and remarriages and there are stepchildren whose ideas and wishes need to be taken into consideration.

Nonetheless, I've also had both men and women respond, "My parents have been wonderful to me and now it is my (our) turn to reciprocate. We will find a way to make it work, without giving up our privacy and independence. I (we) will treat them as I hope my (our) children will do in the future, should the need arise." And making such an arrangement ultimately gives them much satisfaction.

Moving Into an Apartment or Home in a Retirement Community

The Generation 1 senior great-grandparent(s) or grandparents (2) might consider moving into an apartment or a home in a retirement community, if they are still mobile and functioning well intellectually, i.e., no dementia, Alzheimer's, or severe physical impairment. They, hopefully with some or all their adult children, can discuss and explore this option to see if it is financially feasible. Are any of their children or grandchildren able to "chip in" on a regular basis to help defray expenses?

Are they nearby and able to help with errands? Do they want to remain in the same geographic area where they have been residing and may still have some friends and activities which they can continue to be involved in? Should they move into an apartment building? It is not only important to consider location, but access to transportation and if the building has activities they would like to participate in. Can they afford a full- or part-time aide, caretaker, or driver? If not, this is not a suitable choice.

A Retirement Residence

If after exploring these options to determine if they are viable, it is decided that they are not, the next possibility to be considered is a retirement residence where they either buy in (usually quite expensive) or rent at a substantial monthly fee. They should first explore what type of residents the facility appeals to, what kind of and how many meals per day are included, the quality of the meals and service, the availability of transportation on and off the premises to doctors' offices or outside activities, the visible and not-so-visible expenses, and whether and how policies are discriminatory. Are there maintenance services available evenings and weekends if something goes awry in the apartment? Often they are not. Is the facility independent and free-standing or one of a regional or national conglomerate with facilities in several or many states. If the latter, how much authority and discretion is there in the policies to allow for variations in different locales? Are there interesting activities, besides bingo, bridge, and canasta, they would like to become involved in? Does the facility have inexpensive guest suites on the premises so that when family members visit it is convenient for them to stay near their relatives? If not, does the facility have a special arrangement with a nearby hotel/motel for such accommodation?

Many seniors suffer from severe loneliness. Questions to ask before placing a relative or oneself in a retirement home/community include: What does the facility provide to counter the loneliness and sense of isolation experienced? Are the staff competent in dealing with dementia? Will the person be taken to their doctors and receive vaccinations, when necessary? Can they help subsidize the cost of caregiving assistance?

Putting Together a Group of Friends to Buy or Rent a Home Together

A very different alternative is when three or four women or men, a mixed-gender group, or several couples buy or rent a house together with sufficient bedrooms, and a large enough kitchen, living room and dining area to accommodate all (Koedem, 2023). It is comparable to creating a small sorority or fraternity house. Those involved usually contemplate hiring a housekeeper who may or may not also serve as a cook/chef and laundress. I've seen this work out well on a few occasions, but only if all involved agree in advance as to how they will share expenses, who supervises the housekeeper, what happens if someone decides to move out, etc. They also need to agree about such matters as paying bills on time, integrity, and mutual consideration. Knowing beforehand that they are compatible and have similar ethical standards can make this a good alternative. Each person or couple will need to relinquish some of the control they are accustomed to as they make group decisions. Issues that may be addressed related to whether a couple have an open marriage and sometimes have a different person sleep over are only "straight occupants" to be included or could some members identify as LGBTQ, what is the certainty that all will pay their share of the expenses on time, and how will the rules and regulations they agreed upon be enforced. They may want to vacation together first before they venture into this type of arrangement to ascertain their level of compatibility. Such an arrangement offers more independence and choices than retirement facilities (Koedem, 2023).

Assisted Living Facilities

A lengthy article in the New York Times (Rau, 11/9/23) stated that the cost of residing in an assisted living center is "so crushingly high that most Americans can't afford them." According to Rau, these facilities often also charge $5000 per month (many such facilities in states like Florida charge considerably more) and continually layer on extra fees for items like "blood pressure checks, insulin injections, medications ordered from outside pharmacies and daily help with using an inhaler" and for assisting residents to get into the shower, go to the dining room or delivering their meals.

Rau reported that there are now 31,000 assisted living facilities in the U.S. Prices often escalate when a "resident develops dementia or another serious illness." Many people's assets quickly diminish, and they do not qualify for Medicaid (Rau, 2023). In response to Rau's article, David Schless, President and CEO, American Seniors Housing Association, in a Letter to the Editor of the New York Times (12/16/2023) wrote, "Many Americans do have sufficient savings and home equity to pay for long-term care at home or in assisted living. But many have underestimated the consequences of longer life spans and have either been unable to adequately save or have not prepared for the costs associated with the myriad physical and cognitive care needs that are common at advanced ages. Our society does not have an adequate answer in place to help those whose savings are insufficient or who do not qualify for Medicaid-assisted living (which is limited). Your reporting goes a long way in calling attention to the difficulty of finding solutions to address the cost of long-term care for our aging population. These challenges can be met with (by city, state, and national governing bodies and agencies dealing with seniors). (Line added by FK) to create more options for them. Policymakers need to think broadly about ways to incentivize retirement savings, reactivate the market for long-term care insurance, expand Medicare benefits and much more."

Our country has not come to grips with what has become a disastrous situation for many. As people age and do not have sufficient financial resources or family support to manage, they face a frightening future.

When an extended three, four, or five generation family must make decisions about the needs of a senior relative who is no longer capable of living alone, an assisted living facility may need to be considered. These, like retirement facilities, should be fully explored and many questions asked before a decision is made. Important information to be ascertained includes: is there a physician on the premises around the clock, or on call? What is the ratio of nurses to patients on each of the three shifts and are they RNs, LPNs, or Nurse Assistants? What is the quality of the food served? Do the residents eat alone in their room, or if they are capable of going to a dining room and being with others, is it conveniently located on the premises? Are any rehabilitation or physical therapy services provided? What is the overall atmosphere that you see and sense when you visit the facility to determine if it is suitable? Can the potential patient handle the cost, and for how long?

Move the Person Into a Low-Income/Low-Cost Senior Apartment

In some, but not all communities, there are extant facilities for seniors who qualify financially for low-income housing. These facilities rely on some federal, state, or local governmental funding assistance. Questions to be asked when considering this option for someone include: What will the facility do if the patient(s) can no longer afford to pay the fees (rent?) nor can the family? Will they need to be sent to another lower-income or lower or no-cost (Medicaid) facility? Is it in good condition; is it well staffed or is it rundown and seedy? Is this something the family will be comfortable with? Families need to inquire about the qualifying requirements and waitlists for low-income or low-cost senior housing.

Conclusions

Four and five generation families can be a joy. Reunions and other family events can be anticipated and lead to wonderful occasions. Every member of the family can relish such gatherings. However, the opposite is also true. Many members of the extended family might have no desire to see each other and may refuse to attend such events.

Many children and grandchildren disdain the idea of taking on any and certainly not much responsibility for senior family members. Unlike many families in Japan, where it had long been customary for someone in the family to take their aging relatives to live with them (and this was usually the oldest son's responsibility), it is no longer the frequent resolution in Japan. They too are resorting to having their senior relatives live in retirement facilities. In the United States the majority of families do not have such a tradition except perhaps in Latino, Italian, and Jewish families. In this country and much of western Europe, greater mobility in the last one-half to three-quarters of a century has dispersed families and the emphasis for children growing up has been more on "being independent," "being your own person," "doing what you want and moving where it suits you." This runs counter to pitching in and being available to Generation 1 and Generation 2 members of the family, when they are in need.

On MEDPAGE TODAY (2/23/24) under the subject of "America Doesn't Care About Us Elders," Randall Fisher said "ageism is the last acceptable bias." Unfortunately, "it's ok to lump all of us 'old people' together and dislike them all." How sad!

The extant age care literature has not documented the "support seeking" that occurs within family support contexts (Marshall et al., 2023) apparently because "there have been no validated support-seeking strategy scales to study a large sample of aging parents, all of whom were receiving support from an adult child." They developed such an instrument, "The Support-Seeking Strategies Scale," a twelve-item self-report scale for surveying and assessing "parents' perceptions of support received from adult children." Their findings included the following: 1) direct support seeking was associated with more positive perceptions of received support from an adult child (supporting what was discussed earlier in this chapter in the case of Jerry Green), whereas hyperactivated (harping on their problems and pleading for help) and deactivated (minimizing or hiding difficulties) support seeking were associated with many more negative perceptions of received support. The results of their study indicated that "direct seeking of support" is the most adaptive strategy. They carefully separated what they labeled "persistent and intense seeking of support and deactivated support seeking" or suppressing the need for support as "maladaptive strategies" (p. 841).

In their factor analysis model diagrams on hyperactive/deactivated, direct and indirect factors for seeking help (pp. 844–845) they list expressions used for these purposes. These strategies are summarized below from their sentences: (Marshall et.al., 2023). Direct/Indirect: (1) I hint I need help or ask in a roundabout way. (2) I ask him/her directly. (3) I cry or get upset in front of him/her. (4) I tell him/her exactly what I need. Hyperactivated/Deactivated: (1) I exaggerate or downplay my needs. (2) I keep my needs to myself. (3) I ignore or downplay my need for help.

Their study sheds light on the thinking behind how seniors who need help are likely or not to articulate what may be pressing needs. In a letter to the Editor of the New York Time, The President and CEO of the American Seniors Housing Association wrote, "Many Americans do have sufficient savings and home equity to pay for long-term care at home or in assisted living. But many have underestimated the consequences of longer life spans and have either been unable to adequately save or have not prepared for the costs associated with the myriad physical and cognitive care needs that are common at advanced ages. Our society does not have an adequate answer in place to help those whose savings are insufficient or who do not qualify for Medicaid funds toward assisted living. Your reporting goes a long way in calling attention to the difficulty of finding solutions to address the cost of long-term care for our aging population. These challenges can be met with some hard work in Congress, the states, and federal and state agencies to create more options for our seniors. Policymakers need to think broadly for ways to incentivize saving for retirement, reactivate the market for long-term care insurance, expand Medicare benefits and much more" (Schless, 12/16/2023).

Concluding Comments

Hopefully this chapter clarifies some of the salient issues to be addressed by family members making decisions with and/or about senior generation family members and their living arrangements. All too many Gen 4 and Gen 5 members that I've spoken to recently have told me "to be unwanted is to feel unloved," which is tragic for them—during what has often been mislabeled "The Golden Years." Loneliness is a frequent, overwhelming feeling that individuals attribute to their being "unloved" and "unwanted" when we are dealing with them in treatment. Yet, there is little mention of this pervasive feeling in the literature reviewed. Social connection and proximity to others is necessary for (almost) all people. Many 4th and 5th Generation seniors indicate unhappily that they feel unloved, unwanted, abandoned, unappreciated, discarded—with no one present to say good morning or good night to or to get a hug from in person. They have what I call "The Disease of Loneliness" which is not treatable with medication. Some mention experiencing suicidal ideation. It is hoped that the readers, be they therapists, professors, legislators, or family members confronted with this pressing serious problem, will come up with viable solutions and publicize them. Some thought and action need to be taken about subsidizing caregiver assistance. Hopefully it will serve as a call to action for some families and for communities, government officials, and experts in the sociology of the family to be aware of the needs of many of our senior citizens who are living in isolation and to engage in developing alternative kinds of viable, more humane solutions. Fortunately, there are some excellent retirement facilities, and they can be looked to as role models that focus on promoting healthier longevity.

References

Boszormenyi-Nagy, I., & Spark, G. M. (1973). *Invisible loyalties*. Brunner/Mazel.
Framo, J. L. (1992). *Family-of-origin therapy: An intergenerational approach*. Routledge.
Hargrave, J. B. (1994). *Families and forgiveness: Healing wounds in the intergenerational family*. Brunner/Mazel, Inc.

Hargrave, J. B., & Pfitzer, F. (2011). *Restoration therapy: Understanding and guiding healing in marriage and family therapy*. Routledge.

Koedem, W. (2023, September 15). *Personal consultation on "several individuals or couples chosing to live together"*.

Marshall, E. M., Karantzas, G. C., Romano, D., Lee, J., Feeney, J. A., Mullins, E. R., McCabe, M. P., & Simpson, J. A. (2023). Older adults' support seeking from their adult children: The Support-Seeking Strategy Scale. *Journal of Family Psychology, 37*(6), 841–852. https://doi.org/10.1037/fam0001063

Office of the U.S. Surgeon General. (2023). *Our epidemic of loneliness and isolation: The U.S. Surgeon General's advisory on the healing effects of social connection and community*. U.S Department of Health and Human Services. https://www.hhs.gov/sites/default/files/surgeon-general-social-connection-advisory.pdf.

Rau, J. (2023, November 23). Extra fees help drive up assisted-living centers' profit. *New York Times*. https://www.nytimes.com/2023/11/19/health/long-term-care-assisted-living.html

Schless, (2023, December 16). Letter to the Editor Re "Assisted-Living Fees Pile Up, as Do the Profits" (front page, Nov. 23). *New York Times*. https://www.nytimes.com/2023/12/16/opinion/elderly-long-term-care.html

Speck, R. V., & Attneave, C. L. (1974). *Familiy networks: A new approach to family problems*. Vintage Books.

Florence W. Kaslow PhD, ABPP, is in private practice as an individual, couples, and family psychologist and a Family Business Consultant in West Palm Beach, FL. She has been a Professor at a Medical School in Philadelphia and a former Dean of a Psychology graduate school in Florida. She has guest lectured in over 50 countries, is the author or editor of 32 books, and a contributor to over 100 other books.

Chapter 4
Understanding Postpartum Disorders and Their Impact on the Family

Michele Harway

Postpartum Disorders

Postpartum disorders have been described as affecting women who have recently given birth. Yet, postpartum disorders do not **only** affect women who are recent new mothers but also impact other members of the family. Because mental health issues with this population have not been studied very much until recently, little has been written about how to identify and treat this set of disorders and symptoms of emotional or psychological disorders often are missed.

The focus of this chapter, therefore, will be an exploration of postpartum disorders and their impact on the family. Let us begin with what is currently the norm for understanding postpartum disorders and focus first on the women who suffer from these disorders.

Prevalence estimates about postpartum issues vary widely because of the general lack of attention or understanding about postpartum disorders and their impact on pregnancy and the postpartum period. Some estimates are that as many as three quarters of women experience depression during pregnancy and that 20% or more maintain more severe symptoms that may last for several months after the birth. Vanderkruik et al. (2017) explored the literature of maternal morbidity which indicated that 10% of pregnant women and 13% of postpartum women experience some type of mental disorder (usually depression or anxiety). They also suggest that the consequences of perinatal morbidity are substantial because these disorders lead to maternal complications and increased likelihood of adverse outcomes for the child. Fisher et al. (2012) indicated that there are even higher prevalence rates of postpartum disorders in low- and middle-income countries, namely 16% after birth and 20% during the postpartum period. Sadly, while there are good results from the treatments available for mental health disorders in the perinatal period, few women

M. Harway (✉)
Fielding Graduate University, Santa Barbara, CA, USA

F. W. Kaslow (ed.), *Contemporary Issues in Individual, Couple, and Family Lives and Treatment*, https://doi.org/10.1007/978-3-031-90006-8_4

receive such treatment, especially in developing countries. While data from those countries are scarce; in the United States (U.S.), Marcus et al. (2003), studying ten obstetric clinics, reported that less than 15% of women patients who scored above a cut-off score for depression received any formal treatment. Also, in the U.S, even more unlikely to receive treatment are postpartum women suffering from rare or more serious mental disorders. For example, while most cases of psychosis diagnosed in the mother typically develop shortly after the baby's birth, in some cases psychosis present later in the postpartum period and patients suffering from these psychoses may not be treated properly nor within an appropriate time frame. More problematic is that the development of the disorder might be ignored entirely. Since postpartum psychosis can be a key marker for a future affective disorder, the lack of its timely identification can be a missed opportunity for providing the needed treatment at the right time. There is also some evidence that in the U.S., at least, women of color have more adverse or fatal outcomes during the perinatal period. Women of color are also said to have double the rate of postpartum depression than other women do (38% vs. 13–19%) and 60% of these women are said not to receive any mental health services (Keefe et al., 2016). These women are reported as having more frequent and/or more severe symptoms and a more negative outcome, but it is unclear whether this is due to lack of early medical intervention or other factors. Moreover, women of color are said (anecdotally) to receive less treatment for postpartum depression. While medical and psychological professionals are beginning to diagnose and treat postpartum disorders more frequently, there is still much to learn about the postpartum period and the impact that different medical treatments have on new mothers.

How the postpartum period affects the rest of the family is even less often studied. Therefore, an important issue for mental health professionals as well as medical personnel is to better understand this experience and develop effective intervention programs for those who suffer and their families after experiencing the birth of a child. This topic will be further elaborated in another section of this chapter. But first, it is important to understand what postpartum disorders are and how often they occur.

Prevalence estimates for postpartum disorders vary widely because of the general lack of attention to or understanding about these disorders and how they impact pregnancy and the postpartum period. Postpartum disorders are those that occur during the immediate period after the birth of a baby and are the most frequent complications of pregnancy and the postpartum period.

Biological, Psychological, and Familial Contributors

Although it is not always clear which woman will experience a postpartum disorder (and which one they will have), some common histories include:

(1) prior diagnosis of depression or anxiety,

(2) prior experiencing of any of the symptoms described for bipolar disorder,
(3) schizophrenia or schizoaffective disorder,
(4) a prior pregnancy with postpartum psychosis or a family history of any of the above-cited disorders.

Caropreso et al. (2020) completed a meta-analysis of new mothers who had experienced pre-eclampsia during pregnancy and gathered data on their functioning during the postpartum period. There was a significant relation between the diagnosis of pre-eclampsia and the later diagnosis of depressive symptoms and postpartum symptoms either as part of postpartum depression or postpartum psychosis. Caropreso et al. (2020) also suggest that the development of pre-eclampsia is not only a risk factor for development of depression in the postpartum period, with a risk of depression being severe.

In the next section, common postpartum disorders and their presentation are considered. A later section focuses, in particular, on how the family system is impacted by the mother's battle with depression and other symptoms developed during the postpartum period.

What Comprises Postpartum Disorders

Postpartum disorders do not always present in the same way. The typical presentations are usually onc of three common ones as listed below and as yet unnamed and unknown numbers of atypical presentations. These common presentations are described by many mental health organizations including: the MGH Center for Women's Mental Health: Reproductive Psychiatry & Information Center, the National Institutes of Health, and SAMHSA. While there are minor variations in the descriptions of those presentations, the most common schema involves:

1. Mild Depression (also referred to as postpartum blues)
2. Postpartum Depression
3. Postpartum Psychosis

Postpartum Blues

Estimates are that 50 to 85% of women experience postpartum blues either shortly before and/or after delivery. Symptoms are relatively mild, with sufferers possibly experiencing rapid changes in mood resulting in tearfulness, anxiety, and irritability. These symptoms may be experienced for either a relatively short period of time or may last longer.

Postpartum Depression

Symptoms typically last a longer period of time (at least two or three weeks and often much longer) and interfere with a woman's usual functioning after the delivery, including care and bonding with her baby, and her usual ways of interacting with other family members. In some cases, hospitalization may be necessary.

Symptoms for a woman experiencing this disorder may include: a sad mood over a prolonged period, feelings of inadequacy, guilt, anxiety, depression, sleep issues, concentration problems, or changes in appetite. She may also show a lack of interest in her family members including the newborn, her other children, and her partner. Suicidal ideation is also often expressed.

Postpartum Psychosis

The most severe manifestation of postparum disorders includes postpartum psychosis often in the form of a bipolar-manic episode, which typically may include rapidly changing mood states, erratic or unusual behaviors, hallucinations, delusional beliefs often about causing possible harm to the baby, violent thoughts, suicidality, and other severe symptoms. In these cases, it is critical that the woman receive medical care as soon as possible, from a physician and/or Ph.D. psychologist or psychiatrist.

Although it is not always clear which woman will experience one of the postpartum disorders, some common histories include prior diagnosis of depression or anxiety, prior experiencing of any of the symptoms described for bipolar disorders, schizophrenia or schizoaffective disorder, a prior disorder manifesting with postpartum psychosis, or a family history of any of the above-cited disorders. Some common history includes prior diagnosis of anxiety or depression.

An immediate crisis manifests with the inception of this type of postpartum disorder and concern for the well-being of the mother as well as the child rapidly increases, especially if the mother is unable to relate to or care for her child. Part of the crisis is the lack of information circulating in society as a whole about how to identify and then treat this type of postpartum issue. Often pediatric and other medical personnel (and midwives) are overall unprepared to make the diagnosis and then provide appropriate interventions, unless they are part of a specially trained postpartum team. The U.S. seems to be somewhat behind some European countries (especially Scandinavia) where special residential programs and interventions for postpartum disorders keep the mother and the newborn together so that mother–child bonding is not disrupted.

Meanwhile, due to postpartum difficulties, the father, who is apt to be very worried and involved, is likely to have even less support at a time when he often must undertake full care of the child (and care of older children, if there are any) while the mother may be hospitalized in a mental health unit until she regains her pre-delivery level of functioning.

If they are a lucky couple, they will have extended family nearby, who may be willing and able to provide some relief to the parents. But many couples do not have this kind of support system in the vicinity.

Impact of a Postpartum Disorder on the Couple and the Family at Large

Given the paucity of published material on and clear diagnosis of postpartum disorders, it is not surprising that there is also little understanding of the impact of these disorders on the couple and the family at large. In order to better understand why they have such a devastating impact on the entire family, it is important to consider what factors contribute to the development of postpartum disorders, how these disorders present, and then how they may persist often over an extended period of time. While not much data is available specifically on the impact of postpartum disorders on the family system, we will focus on how the entire family system is likely to be impacted by the mother's battle with depression and other symptoms developed during the postpartum period. In addition, the father's limited time (if employed) and possible inability to cope with a new baby while also managing his partner's partial incapacitation may contribute to the family's difficulties. Other factors such as lack of paternity leave may also limit his availability to help with the needs of his wife and baby (and perhaps other children).

Some couples may have the resources to hire a competent baby nurse in locales which include agencies to provide suitable candidates. The lack of these resources and the ensuing exhaustion and frustration many young couples may experience can rapidly lead to anger, guilt, or a sense of helplessness. The couple might also be concerned about their ability to keep their baby healthy and safe.

Case History #1: Sabrina (Twenty-Nine-Year-Old First Time Mother) and Her Family

Sabrina and Patrick had eagerly been anticipating the birth of their first child: however, the pregnancy experience had been difficult. After miscarrying her first pregnancy, Sabrina rapidly became pregnant again. This pregnancy was fraught with difficulty from the very beginning as she had had an early diagnosis of gestational diabetes. Diabetes oral medications were contraindicated because of the pregnancy, so daily injections of insulin were necessary. Sabrina nonetheless remained healthy, and the pregnancy proceeded well. Shortly before her due date, Sabrina was scheduled for a routine pre-delivery appointment with her obstetrician, who immediately diagnosed her with pre-eclampsia (a dangerous complication with an abnormally high increase in blood pressure, which can endanger both the mother and the child's life). At that point, Sabrina was scheduled for an emergency Caesarian section. While the surgery went well and a healthy baby boy was born, Sabrina was confined to the hospital for several days for treatment of the exceedingly high blood pressure, which is characteristic of pre-eclampsia. Patrick remained very involved in Sabrina's recovery and stayed with her and the baby until they were released from the hospital. Finally, when Sabrina and the baby were released, they were excited to be taking their baby home and continuing their life as a new family. All went well for a few days, until Patrick noticed that Sabrina seemed uninvolved with their baby, and she behaved erratically at times.

The baby continued to thrive, but unfortunately, something seemed wrong with Sabrina. After a few days of grave concern about the new mother, a tentative diagnosis of postpartum disorder was given by Sabrina's obstetrician. He recommended that a consultation with a mental health professional to help her with a faster recovery be considered.

Impact of Postpartum Disorders on the Family Members

The Mother

While awareness of postpartum issues and their possible effect on the mother and the family has increased somewhat in the recent past, that information has not yet reached a large proportion of medical and mental health professionals. Consequently, medical coverage of these issues is spotty in many regions of the U.S. A serious consequence is that treatment of the new mother's postpartum disorder may be delayed or absent, leaving her with emotional sequela. These in turn may also interfere with the baby's development.

The incidence of postpartum disorders is high. Nonacs and Cohen (1998) provide statistics ranging from 30 to 75% for women reporting mild depression, and from 10 to 15% for those reporting more severe postpartum depression. For the rarer, but more serious presentation of postpartum psychosis, the figures are lower (0.1% to 0.2% of new mothers). With some exceptions, it can be difficult to predict which women might develop any of the three most common forms of postpartum disorders. However, some biological and psychological background factors are related to the development of postpartum psychosis.

It is important to emphasize that without an early diagnosis, treatment is delayed or impeded with consequent more serious outcomes for the sufferer and the family. Thus, early diagnosis is crucial but difficult in an era where medical professionals are not well schooled in these diagnoses or the requisite treatments and their lack of knowledge may lead to serious consequences for the family as a whole and its individual members.

Case History #1: Sabrina, Continued

Sabrina had had a difficult pregnancy with several serious complications which threatened her health and that of the baby. Fortunately, Dr. Kermain, Sabrina's obstetrician/gynecologist, caught each health issue as it appeared and only released Sabrina and the baby from the hospital when they were healthy enough to go home. Many of the complications, however, appeared after Sabrina and the baby's release from the hospital and some developed two or three weeks after release from the hospitals. These complications included both Sabrina's behavior as a general issue and as related to her lack of involvement with her baby. Dr. Kermain, knowledgeable about the various postpartum diagnoses, immediately considered postpartum psychosis as her condition deteriorated and more symptoms of psychosis appeared. In consultation with Sabrina's extended family, her husband and a clinical psychologist who had previously treated Sabrina and her husband, Dr. Kermain recommended hospitalization in a special hospital unit. This unit housed both postpartum mothers and their newborns, making it possible for Sabrina to get the help she needed while not interfering too much with the maternal/child bonding. Luckily for this family, they lived in an area which has his type of facility, still relatively rare in most of the U.S. (It is more often available in some European countries).

As for Patrick, while he spent some time without his wife and baby, he was able to visit more often as Sabrina's recovery proceeded.

The Father

Patrick and his family were lucky to have an experienced obstetrician well-versed in postpartum issues involved in treating his family leading to more favorable outcomes. However, Patrick still needed to rise to the occasion to be available to his wife and baby during this difficult time. As national attention has begun to consider the impact of the postpartum period on fathers as well, it is clear that he experiences many challenges. The research data indicates that as many as 10% of fathers suffer from clinical symptoms of depression or anxiety following the birth of the baby (Paulson & Bazemore, 2010). Since the father may also be the first to notice significant changes in the mother's functioning during the postpartum period, the additional stress of monitoring the mother's postpartum behavior may contribute to a change in the father's functioning. Thus, it is especially important to monitor the father during this time because his role will also encompass seeking appropriate care for the mother, if her functioning declines during the postpartum period. Some early work on the development of partner-inclusive treatment interventions is underway but this deficit has not yet been rectified. Fortunately, public health advocates are now focused on the development of programs to support fathers.

The Extended Family: How the Mother and Father with Postpartum Issues Cope

The next section will focus on what we know occurs to the family and its members during a difficult postpartum period and what interventions are available. In general, studies of depression and other unfavorable postpartum conditions have focused primarily on mothers. Some studies suggest that postpartum depression and stress also affect fathers. In Sweden, Johansson et al. (2017) reported that both parents may experience depression up to 25 months after the birth of their child with 11.3% of mothers and 4.9% of fathers reporting being depressed.

It is not a rarity for fathers to develop postpartum depression. Paulson and Bazemore (2010) report a significant number of fathers who develop postpartum depression with 10% reporting depression both before the baby's birth and afterwards with a higher rate of depression at 3 to 6 months postpartum. Like new mothers, new fathers appear to have similar (but milder) mood changes early in parenthood. In the case of the father, no post-birth hormones are involved. And, for both parents, their mental health is clearly related to the child's ability to thrive and to the mental health of the entire family.

Johansson et al.'s (2020) qualitative study of lived experiences of postpartum depression by the mother indicates that sometimes the depression is unrelated to the postpartum experience. Nonetheless, depression may be related to feelings of inadequacy in parenting because of both internally imposed expectations and the expectation of others, or because of problems in pregnancy or traumatic delivery, experiences with child health care support, spouse relationship problems, and vulnerability resulting from previous trauma. In Johansson et al.'s (2020) study, both parents described their experiences of parental stress and their underlying feelings of inadequacy. However, fathers were likely to refer to work, the economy, and the stresses of being off from work to care for a sick child, as well as childcare restrictions, all accounting for their everyday stress. Fathers were also concerned about how important it was to them to participate in their child's life and to be engaged in daily care for the child. By contrast, mothers focused on the stress they experienced with how to care for their children, be attentive to their spouse and her relationship with her husband. Most concerning was that many of the mothers said that their well-being was going into a downward spiral due to the overwhelming and very consuming responsibilities of caring for the children and her family.

Parental stress reported by the mothers included significant depression with most mothers saying that they experienced this almost immediately after birth.

Several of these mothers reported complications during pregnancy and traumatic deliveries, with most indicating that they had not processed those feelings. They felt the need to talk about their feelings and how these impacted them. Despite their need, few women reported having a viable support system. Of particular concern were those mothers who expressed difficulty connecting emotionally with the baby. Most of the mothers also stated that there were few opportunities to process feelings with other mothers, family members, or female friends. Some also reported anxiety, panic attacks and social phobia but kept those feelings to themselves. Mothers who were depressed also said they felt shame or guilt at their reaction. Some mothers reported that their depression progressed to sadness, irritation, and aggression. The appearance of the latter feeling encouraged them to seek help. This typically occurred late in the postpartum period.

Finally, both parents indicated that they felt some level of inadequacy but how they described that inadequacy differed: while the mothers described their inadequacy as depression, the fathers described their inadequacy as stress. Fathers focused more on the external stressors in their working lives and external demands while the mothers focused on the internal requirements related to parenthood and the internal demands accompanying these.

In another study, Meghan et al. (1999) interviewed new fathers whose wife had developed a postpartum disorder. Most of these men indicated that they felt fear, confusion and the concern that they would not be able to help their wives overcome the postpartum disorder. They also indicated that they had made many sacrifices to keep their family functioning. While the postpartum disorders improved in most cases, these fathers indicated that they were concerned about the possible changes to their spouse's functioning as she now seemed different from the woman he had known prior to the birth.

Treating the Postpartum Family and Postpartum Functioning

Postpartum symptoms are real, whether physical or mental. Consequently, both physical symptoms and emotional or mental symptoms must be treated. At a minimum, the couple should have an obstetrician/gynecologist following the mother for some time after the delivery as she may have ongoing physical issues that need to be treated. The couple should also see a psychologist or psychiatrist who can focus on helping them deal with the emotional or psychological issues due to changes in the family structure and the individual responsibilities that new parents must undertake. They must also attend to underlying psychiatric disorders that developed after delivery. Mental health professionals with prescription privilege should be part of the team from the beginning as medication will be necessary, especially in cases of postpartum psychosis. It is particularly important to recognize that many of the emotional symptoms which surface are likely to have hereditary or biological causes. Familial issues with mental illness may also be important. And, changes in the family structure occasioned by the birth may also require professional mental health intervention. Postpartum psychiatric symptoms (especially those described earlier in the section on postpartum disorders) should never be ignored and a licensed mental health professional with experience with those disorders should be identified as early as possible.

Although a rarity, some geographical areas may sponsor residential treatment programs for mothers and baby or nonresidential programs for the entire family.

Concluding Thoughts

This chapter has presented information on the physical and the emotional impact of pregnancy and childbirth on the infant's biological mother and the impact of this birth on other family members. One conclusion that emerges from this review is there is much that remains to be accomplished to ensure that the entire family system thrives after birth. Our country's medical system has not done very well in providing post-birth programs, facilities, and interventions to allow the family to heal from the physical and psychological aspects of the birth. Few interventions have been developed to help impacted families learn how to develop a healthy system for their family to function well in, to include the extended family (as well as older children if any) and to return to an earlier time when one's family was a great source of support. Our families need to be stronger, and we need to have specialists trained to provide the support that these families need to flourish. Scandinavia and other European countries seem to be ahead of us here in the U.S. in providing medical facilities and social interventions and programs to enhance the experience of mothers, newborns, fathers, and the rest of the extended family during the birth process and its sequelae. This is especially an issue when a postpartum medical issue must be dealt with or when postpartum challenges present themselves. Our medical system and the obstetricians, gynecologists, and mental health professionals that participate in that system have to help redesign it for families of the future. What follows are some suggestions for interventions that may help improve the postpartum experience.

Additional Needed Interventions

Support Groups for Postpartum Illness

Support groups can "help (the women) normalize their experiences and minimize feelings of isolation. Information networks were not found to be sufficient to meet that need." This recommendation is based on Doucet, Letourneau, and Blackmore's (2012) work looking at the support needs of women with postpartum psychosis and their partners. These needs were identified based on input from their study members' suggestions. All participants in that study expressed the need for more information on postpartum psychosis. Anger and frustration with the health care system and inadequate access to information about their illness was a common refrain.

Interventions to Support Men Whose Spouses Develop a Postpartum Disorder

Mental health and medical professionals need to develop interventions for men whose wives suffer from postpartum disorders. This is particularly important, especially since men are less likely to seek out such help on their own. In the field of psychology, there is a Division on the Psychology of Men (part of the American Psychological Association) which is a good resource for professionals working with clients with this issue. Interventions in this category include men's groups to explore the men's feelings about their family's situation, to help them develop strategies to deal with the postpartum issues and their own feelings and functioning during this period. It is important to help men develop strategies to counter the impact of postpartum issues on the newborn, his wife and his extended family and to help protect the men themselves against developing their own post-birth disorders.

Routine Screening of Fathers Whose Partners Develop Postpartum Disorders

There is general awareness that women commonly suffer postpartum disorders after giving birth. However, there is much less awareness that many men may also suffer mental health challenges after the baby's birth (as described in an earlier section of this chapter). Increasing men's own awareness that they are also more vulnerable to mental health challenges during this period is very important. At the same time, it is also critical to train physicians and mental health professionals in the screening of new fathers for possible postpartum issues of their own. The development of new strategies for the recovery of these fathers is an important goal as well.

Resource Development

In collaboration with professionals from the mental health, medical, and allied communities (for example, religious leaders), it is important to **develop a list of resources to support the family during this time. It may help to think of this type of intervention as helping the family to build a village to support them** until the postpartum issues have largely been resolved.

References

Caropreso, L., Cardoso, T., Eltayebani, M., & Frey, B. N. (2020). Preeclampsia as a risk factor for postpartum depression and psychosis: A systematic review and meta-analysis. *Archives of Women's Mental Health, 23*, 493–505. https://doi.org/10.1007/s00737-019-01010-1

Doucet, S., Letourneau, N., & Blackmore, E. R. (2012). Support needs of mothers who experience postpartum psychosis and their partners. *Journal of Obstetric Gynecology and Neonatal Nursing, 41*(2), 236–245. https://doi.org/10.1111/j.1552-6909.2011.01329.x

Fisher, J., Cabral de Mello, M., Patel, V., Rahman, A., Tran, T., Holton, S., & Holmes, W. (2012). Prevalence and determinants of common perinatal mental disorders in women in low- and lower-middle-income countries: A systematic review. *Bulletin of the World Health Organization, 90*(20), 139G–149G. https://doi.org/10.2471/BLT.11.091850

Johansson, M., Benderix, Y., & Svensson. (2020). Mothers; and fathers' lived experiences of postpartum depression and parental stress after childbirth: A qualitative study. *International Journal of Qualitative Studies on Health and Well-being, 15*(1). https://doi.org/10.1080/17482631.2020.1722564

Johansson, M., Svensson, I., Stenstrom, U., & Massoudi, P. (2017). Parental depression and child outcomes: Is marital conflict the missing link? *Child: Care Health and Development, 38*(4), 520–529. https://doi.org/10.1111/j.1365-2214.2011.01270.x

Keefe, R. H., Brownstein-Evans, C., & Rouland Polmanteer, R. S. (2016). Addressing access barriers to services for mothers at risk for perinatal mood disorders: A social work perspective. *Social Work Health Care, 55*(1), 1–11. https://doi.org/10.1080/00981389.2015.1101045

Marcus, S. M., Flynn, H. A., Blow, F. C., & Barry, K. L. (2003). Depressive symptom among pregnant women screened in obstetrics setting. *Journal of Women's Health, 12*(*4*), 373–380. https://doi.org/10.1089/154099903765448880

Meghan, M., Davis, M. W., Thomas, S., & Droppleman, P. (1999). Living with postpartum depression: The father's experience. *Journal of Maternal Child Nursing, 24*(4), 202–208.

Paulson, J. F., & Bazemore, S. (2010). Prenatal and postpartum depression in fathers and its association with maternal depression: A meta-analysis. *JAMA, 303*(19), 1961–1969. https://doi.org/10.1001/jama.2010.605

VanderKruik, R., Barreix, M., Chou, D., Allen, T., Say, L., Cohen, L. S., & Maternal Morbidity Working Group. (2017). The global prevalence of postpartum psychosis: A systematic review. *BMC Psychiatry, 17*, 272. https://doi.org/10.1186/s12888-017-1427-7

Michele Harway PhD, ABPP, is a Licensed Psychologist who is Board Certified in Couple and Family Psychology. She is also Emerita Faculty, at Fielding Graduate University, where she was Research Faculty for 32 years. She is author or editor of 10 books with topics as follows: Battering, Violence and Abuse, Couples Therapy, Changing Families, Multiple Identities, Sex Discrimination, and Longitudinal Research.

Chapter 5
Contemporary Issues in Primary Care Medicine: A Multifactorial Analysis of How Primary Care Has Changed in the 21st Century and How It Affects Patients and Physicians

Laurie Plitcha Rothman

Primary Care

According to the American Academy of Family Practice, "primary care is the provision of integrated, accessible health care services by physicians and their health care teams who are accountable for addressing a large majority of personal health care needs, developing a sustained partnership with patients, and practicing in the context of family and community. The care is person-centered, team-based, community-aligned, and designed to achieve better health, better care, and lower costs" (https://www.aafp.org/about/policies/all/primary-care.html). A primary care physician is "a specialist in family medicine, general internal medicine or general pediatrics who provides definitive care to the patient at the point of first contact and takes continuing responsibility for providing the patient's comprehensive care. This care may include chronic, preventive, and acute care in both inpatient and outpatient settings" (https://www.aafp.org/about/policies/all/primary-care.html). Primary care is an essential aspect of an effective health care system. Patients who have a relationship with a primary care physician are more likely to receive recommended preventive screenings, have fewer preventable hospital admissions, and have lower mortality rates (Basu et al., 2019). Primary care providers can also be advanced practice providers (APPs) such as nurse practitioners or physician assistants, ideally working in collaboration with a supervising physician.

L. P. Rothman (✉)
Tampa General Hospital, Palm Beach Gardens, FL, USA

F. W. Kaslow (ed.), *Contemporary Issues in Individual, Couple, and Family Lives and Treatment*, https://doi.org/10.1007/978-3-031-90006-8_5

Primary Care Physicians as Mental Health Clinicians

> In examining disease, we gain wisdom about anatomy and physiology and biology. In examining the person with disease, we gain wisdom about life.—Oliver Sachs, MD, The Man Who Mistook His Wife for a Hat, 1985

One might question why there is a chapter on primary care medicine in a book about "Contemporary Issues in Individual, Couple, and Family Treatment?" As a family physician, the reason for inclusion of this chapter is crystal clear to me, however, it may not be to the readers of this book. It is not well known that primary care physicians provide a significant amount of the psychiatric and psychological care in the United States. In 2021, 57.8 million adults in the United States were diagnosed with some form of mental illness. This number represents about one in five adults. The conditions are mainly in the form of anxiety and depressive disorders, but also include obsessive compulsive disorder, post-traumatic stress disorder, bipolar disorder, and other psychiatric diagnoses (Substance Abuse and Mental Health Services Administration, 2022). Many people do not realize that it is primary care physicians who provide much of the care for depression, anxiety, and other mild to moderate mental illnesses. As a profession, we provide 50% of the prescriptions for people with these mental illnesses, and almost a third of the care for severe persistent mental illness (Jetty et al., 2021). Even colleagues in related fields, including those in psychiatry and psychology, are often unaware of the role of primary care in mental health.

When I chose the field of family medicine, I did not realize that treating mental health conditions would be such a significant part of my practice. In retrospect, however, it makes sense. It is impossible to separate the mind and body, and when treating patients, we treat the whole person. On any given day half of my patients may have a mental health diagnosis in addition to their primary reason for their appointment. Even when I am not the primary provider of mental health services, understanding these additional diagnoses plays a vital role in their care. Furthermore, some of my routine appointments are solely for the treatment of anxiety, depression, attention deficit disorder, or situational stress. These conditions often affect the patient's physical health in significant ways. For example, depression can cause fatigue, weight changes, sleep disruption, back pain, headaches, and appetite changes. Anxiety can elevate one's blood pressure and heart rate as well as cause palpitations, nausea, and vomiting. Chronic conditions such as irritable bowel syndrome, migraines, or asthma may worsen with anxiety and depression.

Case #1: Angela

Angela is an affable 48-year-old female patient who first came to see me with concerns over her elevated blood pressure and worsening headaches. She had a long-standing fear of doctors and the health care system in general and stated that her blood pressure was always higher in a doctor's office (white coat hypertension). In fact, her blood pressure was extremely high, and she needed immediate treatment to prevent a serious cardiovascular complication from hypertension. However, Angela was also suffering from extreme lifelong anxiety, worsened by situational stress with marital problems and her live-in mother-in-law. We worked together to create a treatment plan that over a period of months, included dietary changes, increased physical activity, counseling for stress management, and pharmacologic therapy. I prescribed a Serotonin Specific Reuptake Inhibitor (SSRI) for anxiety and an anti-hypertensive medication. For her hypertension, I chose to start with a beta-blocker because this class of anti-hypertensive can help with blood pressure as well decrease anxiety. Within a month of beginning treatment, Angela's anxiety decreased significantly, and her blood pressure normalized. In retrospect, she noted that she had been anxious her entire life, and this was the first time she felt calm. Over time, she was able to decrease the dose of the blood pressure medication, maintain a normal blood pressure, feel better, and function more effectively in her daily life with significantly less anxiety.

According to the Mental and Behavioral Health Care Services by Family Physicians Position Paper, "The fragmented nature of medical and mental health care in the United States has created a number of challenges to providing high-quality mental health care services" (American Academy of Family Physicians, 2023). Mental health services are not distributed evenly nationwide, and many communities lack complete access to these services. Roughly two-thirds of primary care physicians are unable to connect their patients to outpatient mental health services (American Academy of Family Physicians, 2023). This may be due to being in a rural or medically underserved area or having a lack of mental health providers who accept insurance. As a result, primary care physicians must assume a leading role in the management of mental illness. According to the World Health Organization, "integrating mental health services into primary care is the most viable way of closing the treatment gap and ensuring that people get the mental health care they need" (Ivbijaro & Funk, 2008, pp. 127–128.). Services at the primary care level tend to be the most accessible and affordable. When mental health is addressed as a part of primary care, patients are more likely to get diagnosed and treated. I have seen this manifested in my practice over and over throughout the years. For example, when I have had patients with a sleep disorder who need specialized cognitive behavioral therapy for insomnia rather than pharmacology, I have found very few local providers available. This makes it difficult to follow clinical guidelines for optimal care, and patients end up treated with medications rather than appropriate behavioral therapy for disordered sleep. Early in my career, I was surprised by the high number of patients who I was treating for anxiety, depression, and situational stress. It is not unusual for me to have days where I finish my clinic hours and realize I saw more patients with mental health concerns than with other diagnoses. As previously stated, it is impossible to separate the mental from the physical, as mental health and physical health impact each other enormously. Primary care doctors are doing a significant amount of caring for these patients, either alone or in tandem with our psychology and psychiatry colleagues.

I am grateful for my family medicine residency training which prepared me to take on these challenges. Family medicine endorses a biopsychosocial approach to medicine and is "the medical specialty which provides continuing, comprehensive health care for the individual and family. It is a specialty in breadth that integrates the biologic, clinical, and behavioral sciences. The scope of Family Medicine encompasses all ages, genders, each organ system, and every disease entity" (American Academy of Family Physicians, 1984). Some of the medical school classes that were part of my preparation for this aspect of my career were human physiology, human development, biochemistry, and pharmacology. There was also a clinical rotation in psychiatry that consisted of a lecture series and direct participation in the care of patients. When I was an intern and resident, my family medicine preceptors had had tremendous experience with mental health care and were able to teach about prescribing psychiatric medications and train me in brief counseling intervention techniques. We were also fortunate to have had an experienced behavioral medicine specialist on our faculty who gave seminars and was available in the clinic for patient consultations. I have taken continuing medical education classes to augment my knowledge and skills in this area. As physicians, we must be lifelong learners and continuously increase our knowledge base and clinical skills.

Case #2: Allison

"Allison," a 40-year-old mother with young children at home, came to see me when her father was diagnosed with stage 4 prostate cancer. They had a very close relationship, and this news was devastating to her. Allison was not sleeping, she was crying all the time, she had headaches, neck pain, and had lost her appetite. She was losing weight. It was becoming difficult for her to be present with her children and focus on her work. She met the Diagnostic and Statistical Manual of Mental Disorders, Fifth Edition Text Revision (DSM-5-TR) diagnostic criteria for a major depressive episode. I treated her with an SSRI and gave her a referral to get supportive psychological counseling. Allison's symptoms improve quickly, and she was able to manage her life and cope with her father's illness and eventual death. After his death, I referred her to a local grief support group. She stayed on the SSRI for about a year and then, when her life was calmer, we were able to taper her off successfully.

I have treated numerous patients with similar circumstances to Allison over the years. Her case is a prime example of where situational stressors can lead to a mental health condition and cause physical symptoms. This is something PCPs frequently encounter in the primary care setting. This type of medical treatment is part of family medicine training. For patients with straightforward psychiatric symptoms, I usually do not refer them to a psychiatrist, unless that is the patient's preference. I typically provide a referral for counseling with a psychologist or a well-qualified licensed clinical social worker (MSW). Oftentimes, patients do not want to meet with a therapist or there are financial or insurance barriers to doing so.

For patients with more severe symptoms, or for those who are non-responsive to my initial treatment, I always refer to a psychiatric specialist. I personally do not treat bipolar disorders, schizophrenia, or depression with psychotic features.

Primary Care Demographics

Primary care physicians (PCPs) represent about one-third of all physicians in the United States. According to the Council on Graduate Medical Education, optimal health outcomes occur when primary care represents 40% of the physician workforce. Primary care providers are professionals who typically start their careers in their late twenties or early thirties due to the requisite number of years of education and training, and then work for about forty years. In 2019, 25% of all PCPs were in their sixties. Women represent an increasing proportion of primary care providers, with 46% of all PCPs currently female. Primary care physicians may own their practices, work as an employee of another physician, be employed in a non-physician owned practice, work for a hospital or academic center, or work as an independent contractor. Most primary care offices are owned by an individual physician or by a physician group. Half of all primary care physicians are full or partial owners of their practices, which is a decline from the past. The other half are part of a growing number of employed physicians. Of the 48% of primary care doctors who are employed by others, two-thirds work in non-physician owned practices while one-third work in physician owned practices (Willis et al., 2020).

As a primary care physician who graduated from medical school in 1999 and finished residency training in family medicine in 2002, I have experienced many changes in the field over the past 25 years that have affected me as a physician, my patients, and how we relate to one another. These changes have been both positive and negative, and in both instances impact the physician–patient relationship, which is extremely important in all specialties, but especially in primary care. The quality of that relationship and the trust associated with it affects health outcomes and both patient and physician satisfaction (Sharkiya, 2023). Some of these changes are major technological innovations, the adoption of the electronic medical record, the influence of corporations and insurance companies on our practice, the increased presence of APPs, the increased use of dedicated hospitalists (physicians who specialize in the care of hospitalized patients and work exclusively in an inpatient hospital setting), and a multitude of impacts from the Covid-19 pandemic that began in March of 2020 and continue periodically in different locales. High amounts of physician burnout have accompanied many of these changes, leading many doctors to retire early or leave medicine for other fields. In addition, there are currently physician shortages in many geographic regions, or the looming threat of such shortages in the near future. According to the Association of American Colleges, it is estimated that the United States will face a physician shortage of 86,000 by 2036 (GlobalData Plc., 2024). These projections, combined with an aging population, create other potential concerns for the availability of health care over the next decade or so. The COVID-19 pandemic increased stress for all health care workers and brought another major change to the field, telehealth. Telehealth was being used prior to March of 2020; however, it became significantly more common during the pandemic and is here to stay.

Telehealth

As stated above, a major change that has occurred in health care in the past decade, and specifically skyrocketed in the last four years, is the increasing use and normalization of telemedicine. Telemedicine (or telehealth) can be defined as "a health-related service with the help of telecommunicating and electronic information technologies. It refers to the whole collection of deliverables designed to enable patients and their physicians or health care providers" (Haleem et al., 2021). Telehealth allows for a wide range of services available to patients which includes online consultations, remote health monitoring, telehealth nursing, and remote physical therapy. This technology also increases access to specialists, who might otherwise be difficult for patients to connect with due to geographical distance. For convenience, patients can access health care providers via their computer, tablet, or phone. The telemedicine visit can take place at the patient's home, workplace, or even their car; basically, anywhere they can have an internet or phone connection. Patients can save time and money, and health outcomes are improved (Butzner & Cuffee, 2021). Medical care via telehealth can be a valuable tool for both patients and clinicians. It allows the expansion of health care to medically underserved regions, gives patients increased access to their physicians, allows patients with transportation difficulties to have continuity of care, saves them time and money not needing to travel to and from appointments, and can help promote better health outcomes by improving follow up on the management of chronic diseases between in-person health visits. Telemedicine can be extremely convenient for both physician and patient; however, this change in communication can impact the patient–physician relationship.

There are several barriers to telemedicine that are worth noting. Access to technology is a major one. For a patient to have a successful virtual appointment, they must have a computer, tablet, or smartphone available to them that can support the telemedicine platform or app that is being used for the visit. If remote health monitoring is being done, patients must have the equipment needed to monitor blood pressure, heart rate, weight, and oxygen levels and be proficient at using it. Patients also must have reliable internet service. In addition, they need to be comfortable with the use of this technology. Some types of appointments are not conducive to a video visit. For example, there are times when the physical exam component of the visit is imperative for a proper clinical evaluation. Being able to listen to lungs, look in an ear, or examine the patient's abdomen are all good examples of this. Technology does exist so that some of the physical exam can be done remotely, where the patient has tools on hand to accentuate the video visit; however, these are not widely available at this time. For example, the patient can have in their possession a stethoscope, otoscope, pulse oximeter, blood pressure monitor, and other equipment that allow the physician to conduct an exam remotely. There is also the intangible benefit of in-person human interaction, which is absent when an appointment is conducted over video rather than in person.

Prior to March of 2020, telehealth visits were infrequent and inconsistently used. Out of necessity, the use of virtual visits increased dramatically during the COVID-19 pandemic, when many doctor's offices stopped seeing patients in person, and there were quarantines imposed on sick or symptomatic patients (Monaghesh & Hajizadeh, 2020). A national study of thirty-six million working-age individuals with private insurance claims data showed that telemedicine encounters increased 766% in the first 3 months of the pandemic, from 0.3% of all interactions in March to June 2019, to an astounding 23.6% of all interactions in that same period in 2020 (Weiner et al., 2021). During this time, telemedicine became a way for patients to receive care while remaining isolated and protect health care providers from being exposed to the virus. At the beginning of the pandemic, Congress made significant changes to Medicare restrictions as to where telemedicine must originate, what fees would be reimbursed, and what platforms could be used. This prompted similar relaxations on interstate practice and privacy regulations, leading to an increase in the reimbursements for telemedicine, with both government and private insurers (VanderWerf et al., 2022). These changes enabled physicians to add telemedicine visits to their schedules and continue to be compensated for their time. It is not clear whether this relaxation of regulations will remain in place.

During the peak of the pandemic, I was working at an employee health center that provided primary care to first responders and their dependents. While we were still seeing our sick patients in the office, using precautions with personal protective equipment, we also used telehealth visits to follow up on patients who had been diagnosed with COVID-19. This enabled my colleagues and me to check in with our sickest patients every few days and re-evaluate their recovery and health status. Before COVID-19 vaccinations were available, and as treatment protocols were emerging, these video visits allowed us to provide ongoing care for patients with COVID-19 infections, while protecting ourselves and our staff from getting sick. Patients were pleased with this type of care, as often they did not feel well enough to go out. If, during a telehealth encounter, I identified a patient who I felt needed to come into the office, I could still have them come in person for a more thorough evaluation. This was my first experience with using telemedicine consistently. In doing so, I gained comfort with the technology, and more importantly, with the concept that this could improve the way I provide care to my patients. Since that time, I have been able to integrate telehealth visits into my practice in a meaningful way that enhances the overall care of my patients. I use this option to review labs, follow up on depression and anxiety, monitor medications, follow up on other chronic diseases, assess compliance to plans of care, and to evaluate mild illnesses. I do not believe that telemedicine should replace traditional office practice; however, it can absolutely enhance it.

Advanced Practice Providers

APPs, such as nurse practitioners (NPs) and physician assistants (PAs), have changed the landscape of medicine in significant ways. These professionals play a key role in health care today. The World Health Organization defined mid-level health providers (an older way of referring to APPs) as "a health provider who is trained, authorized, and regulated to work autonomously, receives pre-service training at a higher education institution for at least 2–3 years and whose scope of practice includes (but is not restricted to) being able to diagnose, manage, and treat illness, disease, and impairments, prescribe medicines, as well as engage in preventive and promotive care" (Moola et al., 2021). With physician shortages in many areas, these professionals allow a greater number of people to have access to health care, especially in rural or underserved areas. APPs can manage both acute and chronic illness as well as provide preventive care services. Their presence in a busy medical practice can allow physicians to focus on the more complex patients, who may have a multitude of problems. In addition, they can make a primary care or specialty practice or an emergency room more efficient and cost-effective.

There are some concerns regarding the increased use of APPs in practice. States vary in what NPs and PAs are allowed to do in terms of their scope of practice and prescribing. In Florida, for example, NPs can practice within their specialty independently. However, in other states they may not be able to do so. They are required to have a nursing degree and advanced training at a master's or doctoral level to achieve this status. However, the quality of their training may vary depending on where their training took place, and the type of hands-on clinical experience obtained. They have fewer requisite training hours required as compared to physicians and may not have the experience to diagnose and manage complex conditions. Patients often do not realize that NPs can get their advanced degree in as little as eighteen months after becoming an RN, and there is no residency training requirement. PA programs usually run about two years long and have no residency requirement. In contrast, physicians must complete four years in person at a medical school (there is no online option) and three to seven years of residency training. Physicians have 12,000–16,000 hours of patient experience during their training, whereas NPs and PAs have around 500–2000 hours (Smith, November 2023). These differences in training do not mean that they are not valuable members of a patient care team. It does suggest though that they should work in collaboration with or under the supervision of a physician, and that patients should know who they are being treated by. I have had the privilege of working with many talented NPs and PAs throughout my career, and I have found the best ones to be self-aware of their knowledge base and competency. I always appreciate it when I am approached for consultation or collaboration. Like any other professional, their competency improves with their years of experience. It is especially important that physicians and APPs work in tandem and have ongoing communication regarding patient care. There is also the element of patient preference and perception. I have patients who are content to be treated by an NP or PA, and others who insist on only seeing a physician. It should be their choice.

Current Practice Models

Solo or Group Practice

Doctors have a variety of options to choose from when deciding what type of practice to work in. One traditional option is to be a solo practitioner who is self-employed and runs a small practice. This involves being a businessperson as well as a medical professional. The benefit of this type of practice is that the physician has a great deal of autonomy in how the practice is run and how they practice medicine. The disadvantages include increased financial risk, increased potential liability, additional personal responsibility, decreased on-site professional support, and often needing to spend time on administrative rather than clinical tasks. It also may be challenging to schedule time off as getting coverage can be difficult. It is getting much harder to afford to run a solo practice. Doctors can also choose to be part of a partnership or group. This may be a group that is limited to one's specialty or be a multispecialty practice. In this environment, there are more resources available to the physician and the financial risk is shared. In addition, there are colleagues with whom to share patient care responsibilities. It is also beneficial to have other professionals to exchange ideas with and to informally consult on challenging cases. Physicians can be employed by another doctor, a group, a hospital system, or an insurance company. The benefits of being an employed physician are less personal financial risk, a guaranteed income, a decrease in administrative burdens, and greater access to the resources of a larger organization. The downside to being employed is a loss of autonomy, potential productivity quotas, and possibly being subject to corporate or hospi**tal oversite.**

Direct Primary Care

Direct primary care (DPC) is a growing alternative practice model that benefits both patients and physicians. According to the Direct Primary Care Alliance, "Direct Primary Care is an innovative health care model where physicians partner with their patients to provide primary care services under a flat, periodic membership fee. By moving outside of the administrative burdens of the traditional insurance-based billing system, DPC practices can provide a wide spectrum of care in a transparent, affordable manner" (https://dpcalliance.org/about/what-is-direct-primary-care-dpc/). The basic DPC philosophy is to keep the insurance company out of the patient–physician relationship. Most DPC practices are smaller than traditional practices, with the average patient membership being around four hundred patients. "Members" can get same-day appointments and typically will see the same physician at each visit. They can also communicate with their physician by text, email, phone, or patient portal. Physicians who choose this model say they are doing so to provide better care, and they are significantly less likely to experience burnout. For non-primary care services, DPC patients should have some type of insurance, usually a high deductible plan. Uninsured patients who need costly procedures such as a colonoscopy or magnetic resonance imaging (MRI) often benefit from their DPC physician's ability to negotiate lower fee-for-service prices for their patients (Eskew & Klink, 2015). DPC is different than concierge care: it typically offers low monthly fees, does not participate in any payer programs, and applies the patient's membership fees to a broader range of services (Eskew & Klink, 2015). There are currently around 2300 DPC practices serving 300,000 patients in the United States (Nelson, 2023).

Concierge Medicine

According to Harvard Medical School, concierge medicine, also known as boutique medicine or retainer medicine, emerged in the 1990s as an alternative to traditional medical practice (Konstantinovsky, 2021). In the concierge model of primary care, patients pay an annual fee that can range anywhere from $1800 to over $40,000, with the average cost being $2000–$5000/year. The practice may still bill the patient's private medical insurance or Medicare for office visits, or they may be fee-for-service only. The benefits of concierge medicine are 24/7 access to their physician/health care team, same-day or next-day office visits, extended visits with their doctor, personalized care, and the ability to email or text with the doctor. Typically, lab testing is in the office, making it more convenient for the patient. Sometimes, concierge physicians will also offer home visits. There may be additional perks that are specific to each practice. The overall concept is that patients will have greater access to their health care team when they need it and build a more personal relationship with one physician. According to the Harvard report, more than one in five wealthy people will pay an extra fee for access to their doctor (Konstantinovsky, 2021).

To provide this level of service, the physician will limit the number of patients they accept into their practice. Typically, this number will be anywhere from 300–600 patients, which is significantly less than the typical 2000–4000 patients in a traditional practice. Doctors are choosing this model of care for many reasons. One of the most significant reasons is the administrative burden associated with a traditional primary care practice that can cause physician burnout. According to a *Medical Economics* Physician Report, prior authorizations consumed, on average, more than 4.6 percent of physician's time each week. Electronic health record and other administrative requirements are linked to the alarming increase in physician burnout rates, especially among primary care doctors (Gardner et al., 2019). In a concierge practice, there are fewer patients, and subsequently, much less paperwork. Staff have more time to assist with authorizations and administrative tasks.

Another important reason for choosing to practice concierge medicine is being able to spend more time with patients, and not having to rush through office visits. Currently, the typical office visit in primary care lasts just 18.0 minutes and these are scheduled to be anywhere from 10–20 min (Neprash et al., 2021). For complex medical conditions, this is not sufficient time for a doctor to take a history of the problem, examine the patient, review test results or consults from other physicians, and create a plan of care for the patient. Both the patient and doctor feel rushed, and that type of time pressure is not conducive to comprehensive, quality care. In a concierge practice, there is the ability to schedule visits that are 30–60 min or longer if needed. Personally, I appreciate having the extra time to spend with my patients and get to know them well. I believe I can provide better care when these relationships are strong, and I have much greater job satisfaction.

Case #3: Jane

"Jane" was a patient of mine from a previous practice where I had taken care of her for years. After not treating her for a long time, she came back to my care when I opened my concierge practice. She had been feeling poorly for the previous few months and had an extensive list of symptoms to address. The doctor who she had been seeing at the time, who Jane liked and respected, told her that she did not have time for her, and she should "go find a concierge doctor." That is when Jane came back to me. At the time, she was a middle-aged woman with extreme fatigue, sweats, unexplained weight loss, nausea, body aches, elevated blood pressure, and severe anxiety. She also had osteoporosis which was not being addressed. There were fourteen problems to address at the end of my initial consultation, which lasted about 90 min. This initial consultation resulted in ordering diagnostic tests including labs and imaging. In less than 2 weeks, I was able to get all the tests completed which resulted in being able to formulate a working diagnosis for her. I referred her to the appropriate specialists for co-management of her issues and she was able to be treated surgically for one of the problems. As her doctor, it was very satisfying to be able to have the time and focus to be able to assess her condition fully, formulate her multiple diagnoses, and create a treatment plan that addressed each diagnosis. Jane was relieved to know what was going on with her and be able to get treated and feel better. It would have been impossible to address all of her concerns in a typical standard 18-minute visit.

Since changing to a concierge medicine practice one and a half years ago, I have had other patients who, like Jane, presented to me with a complex set of symptoms and concerns whom I have been able to provide a higher level of care for because I have adequate time to spend with them, time to carefully consider their specific concerns, research their problems when needed, and the ability to coordinate care for them with respect to diagnostic testing and specialty consults. This leads to quicker diagnoses, overall improved medical management, and increased satisfaction for both the patient and for me as the physician. In general, I get to know my patients better and our relationships are strong. Other patients have changed to my practice even though they like their current doctor. They were finding themselves increasingly frustrated due to not being able to get an appointment with their doctor when needed, or only being able to see the Nurse Practitioner or Physician Assistant in the practice. Multiple patients have told me that their doctor had stopped seeing sick patients during the pandemic and they were referred to urgent care for a cough or fever. These patients joined my practice because they understand that when they are ill, they will be evaluated and treated by a physician who knows them well, and it will occur in a timely fashion.

Beckers Hospital Review reported that the most popular specialties in concierge medicine are primary care, family medicine, cardiology, and pediatrics. The average age of a concierge medicine physician is 40–59 years old, the number of patients seen per day is 6–8. The states with the highest number of concierge physicians are Florida, California, Pennsylvania, and Virgina (Becker's Hospital Review, 2013). It is estimated that there are about 12,000 concierge physicians in the United States currently and that number is growing (Konstantinovsky, 2021). Although concierge medicine is good for those who can afford it, the expansion of this type of practice will contribute to the growing shortage of primary care physicians. According to the Association of American Medical Colleges (AAMC), the U.S. could see an estimated shortage of between 21,400 and 55,200 primary care physicians by 2033 (https://archive.thepcc.org/2020/07/10/new-report-confirms-growing-shortage-primary-care-physicians).

Physician Burnout

Earlier in this chapter, physician burnout was referenced but not fully explained. As burnout rates continue to rise, it is important to understand what it means to our health care system. The recognition of physician burnout is not new. In the 1970s Christina Maslach described burnout as "an erosion of the soul caused by a deterioration in one's values, dignity, spirit, and will" (Maslach & Leiter, 2000; p. 17). The American Medical Association considers physician burnout to be **"a long-term stress reaction"** and breaks it down into the tangible elements of emotional exhaustion, depersonalization (i.e. lack of empathy for or negative attitudes toward patients), and a feeling of diminished personal achievement. Burnout effects health care workers in all specialties and all practice settings (American Medical Association, 2023). According to the American Academy of Family Physicians, physician burnout is a "systemic health care issue," as the consequences of burnout affect physician well-being and health outcomes for patients. A 2015 analysis links physician burnout to a multitude of negative consequences. These include decreased patient satisfaction, poorer quality of care, increased medical errors, higher rates of physician substance abuse, and increased rates of physician suicide (Drummond, 2015).

A 2021 survey of over 13,000 physicians in twenty-nine medical specialties answered the question of why physicians are experiencing burnout. They identified contributing factors as having too many administrative tasks (including time spent charting and doing paperwork), a lack of respect from colleagues and staff, excessive work hours, computerization of health records, government regulations, and stressors related to the COVID-19 pandemic. Almost 50% of physicians reported they felt burned out. The numbers were higher for women than for men, likely because women tend to assume more childcare and household responsibilities and must contend with more stressors at work than do men (Kane, 2022).

Although it is not a lack of resilience on the part of the physician that causes burnout, there are important things they can do to help prevent it. Strategies to combat burnout address things the health care provider can do individually as well as organizational changes. Addressing burnout amongst health care workers requires a systemic approach. The underlying workplace issues that lead to burnout must be addressed. Organizations can implement strategies to reduce clinician administrative tasks which will allow them to have more time to focus their attention on patients (Gerteis et al., 2023). Physicians and other health care professionals can help themselves by engaging in routine self-care including regular exercise, healthy eating, good sleep hygiene, and the use of stress management techniques such as meditation or yoga. They should also get professional counseling or therapy if needed. Organizations can provide support to physicians by reducing administrative burdens, avoiding overscheduling them, and providing an environment that is supportive to clinicians and staff. One example of supporting physicians is the use of medical scribes to reduce time spent charting and reviewing the electronic health record. A 2018 study in *JAMA Internal Medicine* concluded that the use of medical scribes was associated with a reduction in documentation time and marked improvements in both productivity and job satisfaction (Mishra et al., 2018). Another newer development is the use of Artificial Intelligence (AI) in medicine.

Patient–Physician Communication

> The doctor's duty is to cure sometimes, relieve often, and comfort always. —Hippocrates

Excellent communication between patients and their physician is imperative for patients to receive quality health care. Open communication will lead to stronger relationships and trust. This will enable patients to be more receptive to physician advice and more adherent to treatment plans. When patients are truthful and forthcoming and physicians are actively listening, the chances of reaching a correct diagnosis are increased and medical errors are less likely to occur. In these cases, both patient and physician are more satisfied with the relationship. This leads to happier, healthier patients and physicians who struggle less with burnout. When office visits are limited to 15–20 min, there is inadequate time for this communication to occur.

It is especially important for physicians to take the time to make eye contact, listen uninterrupted, show that they care, communicate in ways that are consistent with each patient's level of health literacy, and provide thoughtful feedback. I personally experience a great deal of satisfaction when my patients express to me that they feel heard and that they know I am listening to them. I remind them that our conversations are confidential. Often I summarize my recommendations in writing and give them to my patients at the end of the visit. It is a wonderful feeling when they tell me during future visits that they have kept those instructions and referred to them between our appointments. I have even been told they have hung my notes on their refrigerator to be reminded of my advice. In these instances, I know we are communicating well. Moreover, effective communication requires physicians to understand and take into account their patient's cultural background.

There are several ways in which the patient can contribute to ensuring optimal communication. For the patient to gain the most from their visits with their doctors, they must be honest and clear. I recommend making a list of concerns and highlighting the most important ones that they want addressed. It is incredibly helpful when the patient is knowledgeable about their own medical history, medications, and family history. It is a bonus if the patient brings in their past relevant medical records. At the beginning of appointments with new patients, I will ask them what their goals are for the visit. This allows us to set a focus for the appointment about what is important to them and let them know their concerns will be addressed.

Conclusions: Finding the Joy in Medicine

> May I always act so as to preserve the finest traditions of my calling and may I long experience the joy of healing those who seek my help—Hippocrates.

For me, the joy of being a physician is all about the relationships I create with my patients. I have patients who I have been a physician for over 20 years, and I know a great deal about their lives. They know about mine as well and will often ask how my three sons are doing or inquire about some other aspect of my life that they are privy to. There is great satisfaction in these long-term relationships. There is also great satisfaction in getting to a challenging diagnosis, seeing improvements in their health and well-being, or being able to assist a patient through a difficult time. The pleasure of my job gets lost when my days are mired down in administrative tasks, when I am overscheduled and rushed through appointments, and when I experience barriers to providing the best possible care. When electronic medical records became popular, the physicians' attention turned from the patient to the computer screen. Over the years, I have employed technology to bring my eye contact back to the person in front of me, first, by using google glasses to connect to an off-site medical scribe, and more recently by using artificial intelligence technology to create highly accurate documentation in the patient chart. By embracing the newest technology, I can go back to being a more old-fashioned type of physician.

For physicians who are experiencing symptoms of burnout, I would recommend trying to figure out what the root cause is and determining how it can be addressed. The American Medical Association and the American Academy of Family Physicians offer many resources to help their members combat burnout and reignite the love of medicine. Changing to the concierge model has allowed me to take excellent care of patients, continue to develop those relationships I cherish, practice solid evidence-based medicine, and have time for my family and personal interests. In 2018, I knew I was going to need some type of change to want to continue to work as a family physician. I was exhausted from long days at work, administrative overload, poor communication in the office, and needing to bring work home every night to finish my documentation in my charts. Initially, my three years in employee health gave me back some of what I was looking for in terms of work–life balance and less pressure to see as many patients as possible each day. Now, as a concierge medicine physician, I can continue a similar path in a health system that supports its physician's well-being. When physicians have a healthy work environment, professional satisfaction, a reasonable work–life balance, and engage in self-care, they are most likely to find joy in their work and provide the best possible care for whatever type of patients' ailments they are treating.

References

American Academy of Family Physicians. (1984). Definition of family medicine. Published 1984. Accessed October 5, 2022. https://www.aafp.org/about/policies/all/family-medicine-definition.html

American Academy of Family Physicians. (2023). *Mental and behavioral health care services by family physicians (Position paper).* https://www.aafp.org/about/policies/all/mental-health-services.html

American Medical Association. (February 16, 2023). *What is physician burnout?* https://www.ama-assn.org/practice-management/physician-health/what-physician-burnout#

Basu, S., Berkowitz, S. A., Phillips, R. L., Bitton, A., Landon, B. E., & Phillips, R. S. (2019). Association of Primary Care physician supply with population mortality in the United States, 2005–2015. *JAMA Internal Medicine, 179*(4), 506. https://doi.org/10.1001/jamainternmed.2018.7624

Becker's Hospital Reviewer. (2013, June 6). *Concierge medicine in the US: 10 statistics*. https://www.beckershospitalreview.com/compensation-issues/concierge-medicine-in-the-us-10-statistics.html

Butzner, M., & Cuffee, Y. (2021). Telehealth interventions and outcomes across rural communities in the United States: Narrative review. *Journal of Medical Internet Research, 23*(8), e29575. https://doi.org/10.2196/29575

Drummond, D. (2015). Physician burnout: Its origin, symptoms, and five main causes. *Family Practice Management, 22*(5), 42–47. https://pubmed.ncbi.nlm.nih.gov/26554564/

Eskew, P. M., & Klink, K. (2015). Direct primary care: Practice distribution and cost across the nation. *Journal of the American Board of Family Medicine, 28*(6), 793–801. https://doi.org/10.3122/jabfm.2015.06.140337

Gardner, R. L., Cooper, E., Haskell, J., Harris, D. A., Poplau, S., Kroth, P. J., & Linzer, M. (2019). Physician stress and burnout: the impact of health information technology. *Journal of the American Medical Informatics Association, 26*(2), 106–114. https://doi.org/10.1093/jamia/ocy145

Gerteis, J. S., Booker, C., Brach, C., & De La Mere, J. (2023). *Burnout in primary care: Assessing and addressing it in your practice*. Agency for Healthcare Research and Quality; February 2023. AHRQ Publication No. 23-0025. https://www.ahrq.gov/sites/default/files/wysiwyg/evidencenow/tools-and-materials/burnout-in-primary-care.pdf

GlobalData Plc. (2024). *The complexities of physician supply and demand: Projections from 2021 to 2036*. AAMC. https://www.aamc.org/media/75236/download?attachment

Haleem, A., Javaid, M., Singh, R. P., & Suman, R. (2021). Telemedicine for healthcare: Capabilities, features, barriers, and applications. *Sensor International, 2*, 100117. https://doi.org/10.1016/j.sintl.2021.100117

Ivbijaro, G., & Funk, M. (2008). No mental health without primary care. *Mental Health in Family Medicine, 5*(3), 127–128.

Jetty, A., Petterson, S., Westfall, J. M., & Jabbarpour, Y. (2021). Assessing primary care contributions to behavioral health: A cross-sectional study using Medical Expenditure Panel Survey. *Journal of Primary Care & Community Health, 12*. https://doi.org/10.1177/21501327211023871

Kane, L. (2022, January 21). Physician Burnout & Depression Report 2022: Stress, Anxiety, and Anger. *Medscape*. https://www.medscape.com/slideshow/2022-lifestyle-burnout-6014664?faf=1

Konstantinovsky, M. (2021). Many doctors are switching to concierge medicine, exacerbating physician shortages. *Scientific American*. https://www.hsph.harvard.edu/horp/wp-content/uploads/sites/94/2021/10/scientificamerican.com-Many-Doctors-are-Switching-to-Concierge-Medicine-Exacerbating-Physician-Shortages.pdf

Maslach, C., & Leiter, M. P. (2000). *The truth about burnout: How organizations cause personal stress and what to do about it*. Jossey-Bass.

Mishra, P., Kiang, J. C., & Grant, R. W. (2018). Association of Medical Scribes in primary care with physician workflow and patient experience. *JAMA Internal Medicine, 178*(1), 1467–1472. https://doi.org/10.1001/jamainternmed.2018.3956

Monaghesh, E., & Hajizadeh, A. (2020). The role of telehealth during COVID-19 outbreak: A systematic review based on current evidence. *BMC Public Health, 20*(1), 1193. https://doi.org/10.1186/s12889-020-09301-4

Moola, S., Bhaumik, S., & Nambiar, D. (2021, May 10). Mid-level health providers for primary healthcare: A rapid evidence synthesis. *F1000Research*. https://doi.org/10.12688/f1000research.24279.2

Nelson, J. (2023, November 1). The evolution of direct care and concierge medicine. *Medscape*. https://www.medscape.com/viewarticle/997969?form=fpf

Neprash, H. T., Everhart, A., McAlpine, D., Smith, L. B., Sheridan, B., & Cross, D. A. (2021). Measuring primary care exam length using electronic health record data. *Medical Care, 59*(1), 62–66. https://doi.org/10.1097/MLR.0000000000001450

Sharkiya, S. H. (2023). Quality communication can improve patient-centered health outcomes among older patients: A rapid review. *BMC Health Services Research, 23*, 886. https://doi.org/10.1186/s12913-023-09869-8

Smith, T. M. (2023, November 22). *What's the difference between physicians and nurse practitioners?* American Medical Association. https://www.ama-assn.org/practice-management/scope-practice/whats-difference-between-physicians-and-nurse-practitioners

Substance Abuse and Mental Health Services. (2022). 2022 National Survey on Drug Use and Health (NSDUH). Retrieved from https://www.nimh.nih.gov/health/statistics/mental-illness

VanderWerf, M., Bernard, J., Barta, D. T., Berg, J., Collins, T., Dowdy, M., Feiler, K., Moore, D. L., Sifri, C., Spargo, G., Taylor, C. W., Towle, C. B., & Wibberly, K. H. (2022). Pandemic action plan policy and regulatory summary telehealth policy and regulatory considerations during a pandemic. *Telemedicine and e-Health, 28*(4), 457–466. https://doi.org/10.1089/tmj.2021.0216

Weiner, J. P., Bandeian, S., Hatef, E., Lans, D., Liu, A., & Lemke, K. W. (2021). In-person and telehealth ambulatory contacts and costs in a large US insured cohort before and during the COVID-19 pandemic. *JAMA Network Open, 4*(3), e212618. https://doi.org/10.1001/jamanetworkopen.2021.2618

Willis, J., Antono, B., Bazemore, A., Jetty, A., Petterson, S., George, J., Rosario, B. L., Scheufele, E., Rajmane, A., Dankwa-Mullan, I., & Rhee, K. (2020, October). *The state of primary care in the United States: A chartbook of facts and statistics.* https://www.graham-center.org/content/dam/rgc/documents/publications-reports/reports/PrimaryCareChartbook2021.pdf

Laurie Plitcha Rothman MD, ABFM, ABOM, graduated from The Technion Israel Institute of Technology with a Doctor of Medicine in 1999. She is a Board-Certified Family Physician (2003) who is also Board Certified in Obesity Medicine (2011). Her practice experience covers women's primary care, obesity medicine, general family medicine, and health care for law enforcement personnel. She currently practices primary care and concierge medicine with Tampa General Hospital Concierge Health in Palm Beach Gardens, Florida.

Chapter 6
The Interface Between Relational Family Dynamics, Interventional Neurosurgery, and Neuropsychology

Yolanda C. León and K. Brianalysse Nicolena Cedeño

The Interface Between Relational Family Dynamics, Interventional Neurosurgery, and Neuropsychology

Neuropsychology: Evaluation, Testing, & Psychometric Application

Neuropsychology is a subspecialty in the field of psychology that examines how disorders of the nervous system shape the relationship between the mind, brain, and human behavior. It is a branch of science dedicated to studying neuro-typical and atypical brain behavior relationships in terms of the physiological and cognitive processes associated with certain neuropathologies. Coupled with a clinical interview and psychometric testing, evaluations provide unique information about a patient's cognitive and behavioral functioning, that which is quantified and medically necessary, and can be essential for diagnosis, describing neurological status, treatment planning or program placement, monitoring treatment effects, and identifying underlying processes for cognition (Schoenberg & Scott, 2011).

Neuropsychological Testing & Psychometric Application

In clinical neuropsychology, neuropsychological testing, also known as psychometric testing, constitutes a significant portion of neuropsychological evaluations and is fundamental in terms of assessing cognitive dysfunction that arises due to a

Y. C. León (✉) · K. Brianalysse Nicolena Cedeño
University of South Florida, Tampa, FL, USA
e-mail: ycleon@usf.edu; kcedeno@usftgp.org

F. W. Kaslow (ed.), *Contemporary Issues in Individual, Couple, and Family Lives and Treatment*, https://doi.org/10.1007/978-3-031-90006-8_6

neurological disorder or disease. Psychometrically based assessment allows clinicians to evaluate cognitive performance from a quantitative standpoint and to assess the magnitude of neuropsychological deficits more deeply than what is done in a routine mental status or neurological exam. Another important component of testing establishes a baseline for the patient's performance to which serial performance can be monitored over time utilizing nomothetic and statistical measurements. "Thus, the neuropsychologist can interpret whether deficits or strengths exist in relation to normative comparison standards (i.e., how the patient performs compared to others), as well as to individual comparison standards (i.e., how the patient's current performance compares to his/her own premorbid level of baseline functioning)" (Schoenberg et al., 2019).

Use of Psychometrists

Psychometrists, highly trained professionals who specialize in the administration and scoring of both psychological and neuropsychological testing, demonstrate aptitude in the statistical aspects of neurocognitive assessment. Recognized by the American Psychological Association (APA), these adept professionals demonstrate the knowledge, experience, and ongoing education to administer and score psychometric measures, thereby setting the gold standard on which clinicians rely (National Association of Psychometrists, 2016).

Psychometrists in clinical contexts have administered neurocognitive assessments since the 1930s. In conducting lengthy testing batteries ranging from 2–4 h within an 8-hour workday, the cognitive load and time constraint for many clinicians [e.g., clinical psychologists, neuropsychologists, neurologists (in some cases)] has been significantly reduced, leading to the addition more of psychometrists in neuropsychology divisions over the last few decades. By using non-doctoral technicians to administer assessments, neuropsychologists have more time for report writing, clinical interviewing, test selection, and interpretation of data (National Association of Psychometrists, 2016). Further, psychometrists' competency in test assessment, preparedness in prompting and repeated instruction, skillful task switching between a multitude of testing materials, manuals, and stimuli, and adaptability to the demands of a capricious testing environment continue to support their utility across clinical, research, and forensic settings.

The Interface Between Neuropsychology and Family Psychology

Across multiple contexts, including the literature and clinical practice, formal application of family systems theory and frameworks in neuropsychology are absent and reflect a stark deficit in efficacious neuropsychological consultation. Yet, key to effective neuropsychological consultation is considering family systems factors as critical to the neuropsychologist's task of answering the referral question. Although the referral questions that prompted the consultation to neuropsychology may seem linear, it becomes more complex when family dynamics are considered while attempting to ascertain differential diagnosis, identify etiology, and engage in treatment planning. Ideal case conceptualization within a neuropsychology setting requires consideration of interacting family systems dynamics that collectively impact differential diagnosis and case conceptualization of the patient's presenting neuropsychological dysfunction, although without the expectation that neuropsychologists act as family psychologists.

Paucity of Research

The assessment and understanding of family systems dynamics in this process is not widely addressed in the literature. One early model to introduce family systems into medical treatment was Kazak and colleagues (2002) consultation treatment framework based on family systems and developmental theories for pediatric cancer patients. Koay and colleagues proposed collaboration between neuropsychology and neurosurgery and note the utilization and process of neuropsychological services within a neurosurgery setting is evolving (Koay et al., 2023; Koay et al., 2023; McLean et al., 2023). Cedeño and colleagues explored these frameworks across Latino and ethnocultural contexts and concluded by advocating the consideration of these dynamics during the consultative and treatment planning stages in which the reason for referral may falsely appear linear (Cedeño et al., 2024).

Clinical Practice

Neuropsychological assessment and consultation do not necessarily require identifying and addressing family systems dynamics but knowledge of them is essential. Sometimes when obtaining a comprehensive overview of the patient's medical, psychiatric, psychosocial, and family history to answer the referral question, family dynamics may become clearer. This may involve a disruption in family dynamics, a dysfunctional family dynamic, or a family member with severe problems other than the neurosurgical patient. This may or may not involve actual clinical psychopathology of the patient's family member or simply a dysfunctional dynamic that needs to be identified and understood to the extent that it impacts the referral question and decision-making for the patient as well as treatment planning by the treatment team.

Consultation frequently reveals a larger framework of family issues, implying that at least something has gone awry in the family system. To adequately serve the needs of the patient, especially if one is a minor or is not legally recognized as independent in their medical care, addressing dysfunctional family dynamics becomes paramount. This task becomes part of the process of answering the referral question and is as important as obtaining medical, developmental, and psychiatric history from other clinicians on the patient's treatment team.

Relational family dynamics are far from static in that they shift, taking on unique forms that are dependent upon the disruption in familial homeostasis, that is, the tendency of families to resist change in order to maintain a steady state (Bowen, 1978). This breakdown in equilibrium in family relations may occur randomly with equal probability of emerging at any point in answering the referral question, either before, during, or after the comprehensive review of medical, psychiatric, psychosocial, and family history. These dynamics reveal themselves during different stages of clinical evaluation, at different intensities and may not all emerge at once due to their complexity and intricate circuitry. Thus, recognizing and qualifying them early plays an indispensable role in meeting the needs of the patient and in directing continuity of care to other clinicians on the patient's care team.

The Multidimensional Role of the Neuropsychologist

The role of the neuropsychologist continues to evolve as it becomes more extensive, complex, and diverse. Initially, the neuropsychologists' role was that of a more medically and neuroanatomically oriented one. Neuropsychologists traditionally contributed to localization and lateralization of pathologic brain areas, identification of eloquent cortex (surface areas of the brain that directly control function), and evaluation of both preoperative and postoperative neuropsychological functioning to determine if there is cognitive dysfunction. Koay and colleagues point out that patient-specific demographic, linguistic, and educational considerations present challenges for neuropsychologists that must be addressed to effectively qualify as cognitive dysfunction (Koay et al., 2023). Particularly, they conceive that said challenges emanate from "patient specific level as neuropsychologists strive to serve the needs of a diverse, multilingual, multiethnic patient base" (Koay et al., 2023).

The Role of Neuropsychological Practice in a Neurosurgical Service

In a neurosurgery service, neuropsychological evaluations are often required to determine a patient's decision-making ability (e.g., medical, legal, financial), assess functional capacities, and assist with determination of candidacy for medical and surgical procedure (s), as a function of their overall cognition. Surgical candidacy is the extent to which the patient is a suitable candidate for a surgical procedure. Assessing variables that may impede their probability of a positive outcome is one of the main areas of focus, given that the role of the neuropsychologist is to answer the referral question that's *specific* to the neurosurgical team question, and ultimately articulate whether patients have met the eligibility preoperative requirements from a *neuropsychological* perspective. Psychiatric comorbidities, cognitive deficits, expectations (realistic or unrealistic), and the patient's decision to undergo the surgery to please another person (usually the spouse) are all variables to take into consideration when assessing surgical candidacy.

An essential task of the neuropsychologist conducting a presurgical assessment is to determine whether the patient can appreciate and make decisions regarding the risks/benefits of having or declining the procedure. The neuropsychologist will discuss the risk of cognitive decline, what it entails, and whether it is attributed to the procedure itself or to the natural disease course. For example, if deep brain stimulation is being considered, the neuropsychologist will discuss with the patient the possible risk for decline in verbal fluency, mood changes, and recurrence of a previous impulse control disorder. An evaluation also provides a baseline with which to compare later neurocognitive performance, as the procedures may contribute to an increased risk for decline in neurocognitive functioning, mood changes, and recurrence of a previous impulse control disorder. Koay et al. (2023) have described the evolving role of neuropsychology and collaborative care in a setting that integrates neuropsychological services into neurosurgical care.

In the context of neurosurgery, the role of the neuropsychologist is not to gate keep, but rather to serve as a type of "broker" between the patient, the family, and the neurosurgery team. They are an allied service provider giving a clinical opinion about a patient's neuropsychological status and probable outcomes of undergoing a proposed surgical procedure. Generally speaking, patients are "cleared" if they are considered good candidates (from a neuropsychological perspective) and at minimal risk of decline or doing harm to themselves. Conversely, if the patient's clinical presentation suggests cause for concern, they are not "cleared" nor exactly "blocked" from proceeding. Rather, in a multidisciplinary consensus conference, the neuropsychologist advises the surgery team of the limitations, caveats, dynamics, or disorders (e.g., obsessive, compulsive, or impulsive behaviors; dementia; mood disorders) that present increased risk of psychological, emotional, or behavioral sequelae.

As neuropsychology in neurosurgery continues to grow as a subspecialty, we propose that a greater knowledge of family systems dynamics be required to help expand the ability of the neuropsychologist to conceptualize cases, describe the patient's neurocognitive status, and predict outcome to better assist and inform the neurosurgery team. The present authors are hereby proposing our model for identifying family systems dynamics and incorporating them into the assessment process.

Neurosurgical Intervention Techniques

Functional neurosurgery is a medical discipline that utilizes structural and functional neuroimaging techniques to perform specific surgical interventions on specific afflicted areas of the nervous system (both central and peripheral). Interventions include neurostimulation, neuromodulation, and ablation. Functional neurosurgery "has the risk of modifying essential features of a patient's personhood, including mood, personality, and cognitive abilities" (Synofzik, 2013).

Patients are often considered possible surgical candidates for advanced neuromedical procedures (both surgical and treatment-based) that can help to alleviate unfavorable disease-specific symptoms (e.g., tremors, seizures, degenerative disc disease) that patients or their families often find significantly disconcerting. Neurosurgical interventions are defined as any procedure on the nervous system with a therapeutic purpose, either invasive (that which involves purposeful/deliberate access to the body via an incision) or minimally invasive (that which involves less and smaller incisions). Neuromodulation is a branch of functional neurosurgery that treats chronic neurological disorders by targeting deep brain nuclei and pathways involved in the mediation of the symptoms in order to stimulate, inhibit, or otherwise modify pathological activity (Amadio, 2015). Current neurosurgical interventions include deep brain stimulation (DBS), focused ultrasound (FUS), vagus nerve stimulator (VNS), responsive neurostimulation (RNS), resection and ablation.

DBS is a neuromodulation procedure involving implantation of a neurostimulator (electrodes) within areas of the brain. The electrodes produce electrical impulses that affect brain activity to treat various medical conditions and symptoms. A battery powered implantable pulse generator is inserted under the skin below the clavicle via a small wire that connects the device to the small electrodes within the brain. Stimulation parameters including frequency, pulse width, and voltage are adjusted to achieve maximum efficacy (See Fig. 6.1).

FUS thalamotomy is an ablative procedure used to treat refractory essential tremor divided into two classes: low intensity FUS and high intensity FUS [also referred to as MRI-guided FUS (MRIgFUS)]. The thalamus is ablated using high frequency sound waves that create heat and lesion target areas of the thalamus, preventing the circuits responsible for tremors from firing and reducing tremors. Possible adverse effects include temporary speech and swallowing difficulty, sensory (mild to moderate numbing or tingling in fingertips, face or lips), motor, gait/balance problems, and dysmetria (ability to coordinate and control movement) (see Fig. 6.1).

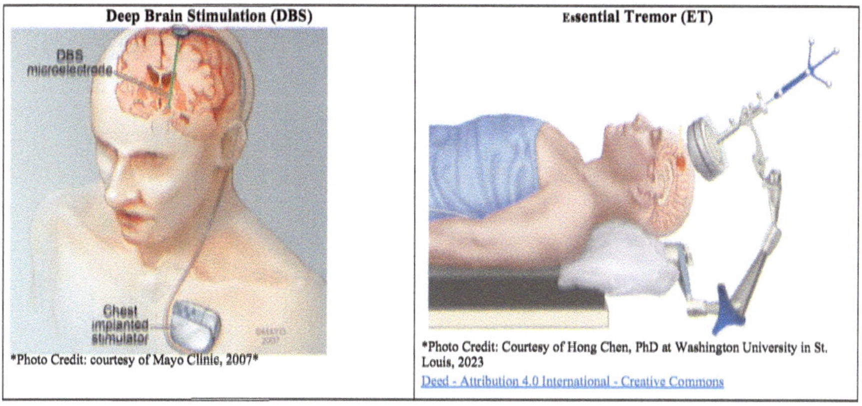

Fig. 6.1 Courtesy of Mayo Clinic, 2007 and Washington University, 2024 (left) and Hong Chen, PhD at Washington University in St. Louis (right)

VNS is a procedure that uses electrical impulses to send mild pulses of electrical energy through the left vagus nerve in the neck to the brain, interrupting irregular brain activity that leads to seizures, to prevent or shorten a seizure. The VNS device can be an implantable device. Possible adverse effects include temporary hoarseness, changes in voice/speech, pain, headaches, and insomnia.

RNS is similar to a pacemaker that monitors, detects, and responds to seizure activity by giving small bursts or pulses of stimulation. The device monitors and detects brain waves and responds to activity that looks like a seizure. The device is placed in the bone covering the brain and leads are placed atop the brain in areas where seizures begin and can stop epileptic activity prior to the seizure actually occurring (Yengar & Shafer, 2017).

Insurance mandates frequently require a presurgical neuropsychological evaluation as an important part of the screening process for selection of candidates for these procedures in predicting postsurgical changes in neuropsychological and motor functioning. This usually involves a quality-of-life measure, neurocognitive psychometric testing, as well as an evaluative assessment of their mood and level of emotional stability. Generally, considerations include significant dementia (severe cognitive impairment or cognitive deficits), psychopathology (e.g., multiple suicide attempts, premorbid psychosis, etc.), poor or unrealistic expectations, understanding of diagnosis, ability to make an informed decision (e.g., cost–benefit analysis of various procedures or engages in decision-making if only one procedure), and the ability to care for oneself, adherence to schedules, and managing daily regimens. Additionally, there are other considerations that present as disease-specific, which are summarized in future sections. (See Fig. 6.2 for a recap of aforementioned neurosurgical procedures).

Surgical Intervention	Disorders			
	Parkinson's Disease	Essential Tremor	Epilepsy & Seizure Disorders	Degenerative Disc Disease & Chronic Pain
Deep Brain Stimulation (DBS)	X	X	X	
Globus Pallidus Internus (GPi)				
Subthalamic Nucleus (STN)				
Focused Ultrasound (FUS)		X		
Low Intensity Focused Ultrasound (LIFU)				
High-intensity Focused Ultrasound (HIFU) or MRI-Guided Focused Ultrasound (MRgFUS)				
Responsive Neurostimulation (RNS)			X	
Stereotactic Radiosurgery [formerly, Gamma knife surgery (GKS)]			X	
Ablation			X	
Resection (e.g., Amygdalohippocampectomy; anterior temporal lobectomy; hemispherectomy; corpus callosotomy; multiple subpial transection)			X	
Spinal Cord Simulator (SCS)				X

Fig. 6.2 Diseases, Disorders & Surgical Intervention Techniques

Movement Disorders: Parkinsonism & Essential Tremor

Parkinsonism is the umbrella term used to describe various neurodegenerative conditions that cause involuntary movement-related symptoms, but often also result in non-motor symptoms such as cognitive dysfunction and behavioral changes (Cleveland Clinic, 2022). In fact, up to 90% of patients with Parkinson's meet the criteria for a mood disorder (Nuti et al., 2004). These movement disorders vary in terms of symptom onset or severity, response to treatment, and prognosis. There are four cardinal features to Parkinsonism, often referred to as "TRAP," of which 2 symptoms are required to meet clinical diagnostic criteria:

- **T**remor—a slow tremor that occurs mainly during inactivity
- **R**igidity—increased muscle tone that causes trunk and limb stiffness
- **A**kinesia/Bradykinesia—refers to movement. Akinesia means lack of movement and bradykinesia means slowed movement.
- **P**ostural instability—involves the inability to maintain a stable balanced position and is often accompanied by disequilibrium, which is a sensation of impending fall or feeling of improper "tilt" on the floor.

Idiopathic Parkinson's Disease (PD), the most common type of Parkinsonism, adversely affects dopamine-producing nerve cells in the brain. There are several types of PD, but the most frequently encountered variants include Atypical Parkinson's (Parkinson-Plus Syndromes), Progressive Supranuclear Palsy, Multiple System Atrophy (MSA), Corticobasal Degeneration, Diffuse Lewy Body Disease (DLBD), and Vascular Parkinsonism.

At present, intervention techniques for Parkinsonism utilize medical model practices that aim to counteract diminished dopamine production. The goals of most treatment planning involve medications (e.g., levodopa, dopamine agonists, monoamine oxidase-B (MAO-B) inhibitors, catechol-O-methyltransferase (COMT)-inhibitors, anticholinergics, amantadine, and antidepressants) that either increase the amount of dopamine in the brain, act as a dopamine substitute, stimulate the parts of the brain where dopamine is stored, or block the action of other factors (enzymes) that break down dopamine (Parkinson's UK, 2019).

Available treatment for Parkinsonism varies and not all options are suitable for everyone. Depending upon the patient's clinical presentation, severity of symptoms, medication tolerance, and medication efficacy, each variant of Parkinsonism may require a specific class of pharmacological intervention with tailored dosages and scheduled administration times. Further, patients on dopamine medications may experience motor fluctuations ranging from a state in which symptoms are well controlled, known as "on" periods; to a state in which patients become slower moving, stiffer, and experience difficulty with movement known as "off" periods. These states correspond to highest and lowest plasma concentrations of levodopa ("on" and "off" periods, respectively). In the 1980s it became apparent that patients taking levodopa could develop resistance following years of treatment as well as side effects including dyskinesias (Pycroft et al., 2018).

Brief Overview of the Neuroanatomy of Parkinsonism

The neuropathology of movement disorders involves dysfunction of the basal ganglia and/or cerebellum. The basal ganglia are a complex cluster of subcortical gray matter nuclei that are traditionally associated with initiation and control of motor movements and in cognitive and affective processing. Represented by bilateral hemispheric composition, the basal ganglia are subdivided into several structures including the subthalamic nuclei (STN), dorsal striatum, ventral striatum, and the globus pallidus.

The dorsal striatum (DS) is a region of the brain that is part of the basal ganglia and is involved in executive functions, motor control, and habit formation. It integrates information from sensorimotor, cognitive, and motivational sources to help with decision-making, action selection, and initiation. The DS is comprised of the caudate nucleus, putamen, and caudolenticular (or transcapsular) gray bridges.

In contrast, the ventral striatum (VS) is a large region in the brain that plays a key role in reward processing and is a central site for studying drug reinforcement. It is located deep within the brain and is part of the limbic system and includes the nucleus accumbens, ventromedial caudate nucleus, and ventromedial putamen (Humphries & Prescott, 2010).

The globus pallidus comprises both the globus pallidus externa (GPe) (lateral structure) and globus pallidus interna (GPi) (medial structure) which collectively control conscious, voluntary movement and proprioception. In neurosurgical candidacy consideration, the GPi and STN are two of the main surgical targets for deep brain stimulation (DBS) treatment of Parkinsonism and Essential Tremor (ET).

Surgical Intervention Techniques for Movement Disorders

One of the most common groups of patients with neurological disorders referred for presurgical neurocognitive examination to determine surgical candidacy are those with movement disorders. Patients with treatment-resistant movement disorders such as Parkinson's Disease (PD), Parkinsonism, and essential tremor (ET) are often considered possible surgical candidates for one of two advanced treatments (neurosurgical procedures) that can help to alleviate the tremors that patients or their families often find significantly disconcerting: deep brain stimulation (DBS) and focused ultrasound (FUS).

The Food and Drug Administration (FDA) approved DBS for placement in the thalamus to treat PD and ET in 1997 and the STN and GPi in 2003 (Miocinovic et al., 2013). DBS has since evolved as a revolutionary therapy for other conditions including psychiatric disorders, epilepsy, dystonia, dementia, addiction, and dementia. The two most common sites for placement of DBS are the STN and the GPi. STN is the preferred target, but if patients have language, cognitive, or mood disturbance, placement in the STN can worsen these symptoms. Part of the neuropsychologist's role in presurgical assessment of Parkinson's patients includes recommendations for target placement based on the neuropsychological assessment. A brief summary of that aspect of the neuropsychologist's role is presented as the anatomical and surgical aspects of the procedures are beyond the scope of this chapter (Miocinovic et al., 2013) (see Fig. 6.3).

Eligibility Criteria from a Neuropsychological Perspective

One of the primary goals of such an evaluation is to establish a baseline with which to compare later cognitive performance scores as the procedures have a common risk for decline in several areas of cognitive functioning, especially for those with a more advanced disease course. Empirical evidence suggests that up to one-quarter of people over 75 years of age who have major surgery may experience significant cognitive decline; however, the causes and risk factors are still being explored, and diagnostic criteria are not yet standardized (Subramaniam & Upadhyay, 2020).

Another primary goal of preoperative testing aims to predict neuropsychological outcomes and assess the patient's risk for negative affective changes (e.g., apathy, indifference) or positive mood changes (elevated mood, decrease in anxiety, and apathy), or behavioral changes (impulsivity, disinhibition, or recurrence of a previous impulse control disorder). Determining whether surgical candidates have an untreated mood disorder, significant cognitive impairment, or impulse control

DBS	FUS
• Invasive – 2 inpatient implantations surgeries (i.e., electrodes through the skull, and a battery pack under the skin of the upper chest region) *Wires project from the brain down the neck subcutaneously) • Minimal risk of infection, hardware issues, speech difficulties, and cerebral hemorrhaging • Long-term studies suggest durable tremor control which can be adjusted if tremors become worse • Electrodes can inadvertently reposition over time • Batteries must be replaced surgically	• Less invasive – outpatient treatment under MRI guidance (i.e. beams of ultrasound waves are targeted at the VIM nuclei) • Minimal risk of facial tingling, speech difficulties, and balance issues. *If these do occur, they tend to resolve within a couple of months. • Follow-up studies at three years suggest durable tremor control • No hardware in the body

Fig. 6.3 Adverse Effects in Essential Tremor Surgical Intervention

disorder that may hinder their ability to participate in a cost–benefit analysis of surgical risk and postsurgical expectations can all impact the surgical team's decision-making, not only regarding the patient's general suitability for proceeding with surgery, but also in determining the site of placement or resection (See Fig. 6.4).

Essential Tremor & Other Tremor Disorders

Though it is often confused with PD, essential tremor is distinct in terms of its diagnostic profile, presenting symptomatology, and clinical etiology. It is the most common of all neurologic diseases (except stroke) and even more common than PD (NorthWestern Feinberg School of Medicine Parkinson's Disease & Movement Disorders Center, n.d.). Essential tremor is a clinical syndrome of idiopathic tremulousness (Elble et al., 2013) and action tremor in the upper limbs and occasionally in the head, face, jaw, tongue, voice, trunk, and lower limbs. Patients with essential tremor may also exhibit postural tremors that occur when maintaining a bodily position against gravity, whereas non-motor features include cognitive impairment and neuropsychiatric symptoms. As with many other neurodegenerative conditions, medication intervention (propranolol and primidone) has limits in its ability to alleviate involuntary motor symptoms, so DBS and FUS are commonly used to treat intractable cases (Sperling, 2019).

Cognitive Changes	Behavioral Changes
• Slowed information processing speed	• Severe anxiety
• Slowed psychomotor speed	• Depression
• Visuoperceptual and visuoconstructional deficits	• Apathy
• Deficits in attention/executive functioning	• Agitation
• Memory retrieval deficits	• Psychosis
• Language problems (e.g., hypophonia and micrographic)	• Sexual dysfunction
	• Compulsive and impulsive behaviors

Fig. 6.4 Adverse Changes in Parkinsonism Conditions. *Disclaimer regarding parameters for cognitive deficits: For the purpose of specificity and refraining from ambiguous terminology, the interpretative labels "intact" and "impaired" are based on the criteria provided by the American Academy of Clinical Neuropsychology (AACN) guideline and the Institute of Medicine: Intact Performance= Score falling within one standard deviation (SD) of the normative mean; Impaired Performance= Score falling less than 1.5 to two SD below the normative mean (Guilmette et al., 2020)

Epilepsy and Other Seizure Disorders

Epilepsy is a brain disorder that causes recurring, unprovoked seizures. Seizures are paroxysmal alterations of neurologic function caused by the excessive, hypersynchronous discharge of neurons in the brain (Stafstrom & Carmant, 2015). Seizures involve sudden surges of abnormal and excessive electrical activity in one's brain and can affect individuals' behaviors and comportment.

Although antiseizure medications can suppress seizures, they do not have a long-term efficacious prognosis. About a third of patients have seizures that cannot be controlled by two or more appropriately chosen antiepileptic medications or other therapies (Stafstrom & Carmant, 2015). Resective surgery is the most effective (and only curative) means of attaining long-term seizure freedom. Unfortunately, most patients with epilepsy are not surgical candidates, others have no improvement or only partial improvement with minimal seizure relief.

Per the *Epilepsy Foundation*, resection and ablation are the most common intervention techniques typically considered after patients fail to benefit from pharmacotherapy (Epilepsy Foundation, n.d.) (see Fig. 6.5). More recently, newer neurosurgical interventions are increasingly utilized to help manage seizures including VNS, RNS, and DBS (Benbadis et al., 2018).

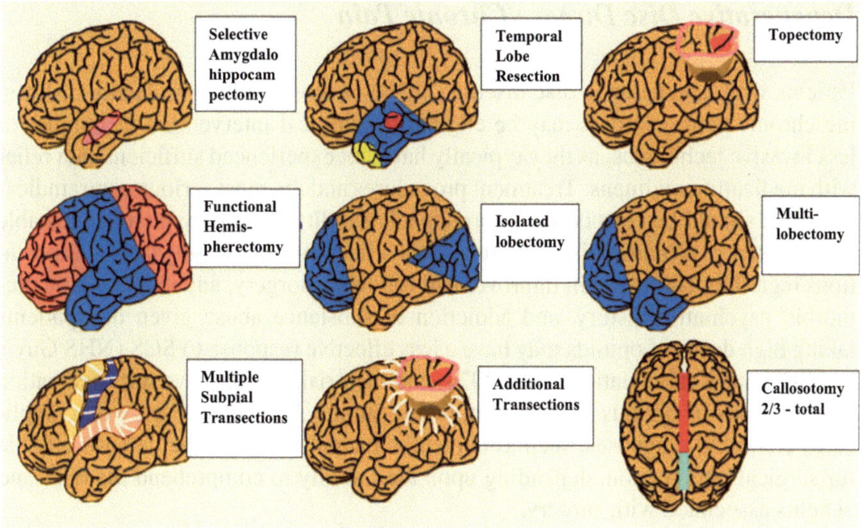

Fig. 6.5 Courtesy of Dr. Christian Elger, University of Bonn

Psychogenic Non-Epileptic Events (PNEEs)

Psychogenic non-epileptic events (PNEEs), formerly known as psychogenic non-epileptic seizures, or psychogenic non-epileptic attacks, are defined as episodes of involuntary movement altered responsiveness, or subjective experiences that resemble epileptic seizures (Lesser, 1996; Reuber & Elger, 2003; Drane et al., 2011). Previous nomenclature included pseudoseizures and psychogenic non-epileptic seizures (PNES). Both terms are now obsolete because these events are non-epileptic in nature, so the word "seizure" has been removed.

It's imperative to note that PNEE patients do not require surgical intervention. However, they are routinely seen by neuropsychologists who conduct presurgical evaluations in a neurosurgical setting. Patients with PNEEs often exhibit dysfunction in emotional regulation and family dynamics (LaFrance Jr. & Devinsky, 2002). Studies have found a higher incidence of reported history of physical and sexual abuse among patient with PNEE than patients with epileptic seizures (84% and 12.5%, respectively) and exhibit more use of immature defense mechanism (denial, repression, reaction formation) and infrequent use of mature defense mechanisms. Patients with PNEEs also reported a dysfunctional family environment (See Fig. 6.5).

Degenerative Disc Disease/Chronic Pain

Patients with degenerative disc disease (DDD) or those with significantly distressing chronic pain disorders may be eligible for surgical intervention techniques or less invasive techniques, as they typically have not experienced sufficient pain relief with medication regimens. Treatment procedures and the most serious contraindications that should be considered before the advisability of surgery include: unstable or untreated psychiatric disorders (e.g., hallucinations and anxiety), poor expectations regarding chronic pain improvement following surgery, any longstanding premorbid psychiatric history, and addiction or substance abuse given that patients taking high doses of opioids may have a less effective response to SCS (NHS Guy's and St Thomas' Foundation Trust, 2024) and their risk of excessive self-medication of high doses of opioids increases following surgery. However, even with complicated comorbid diagnoses, such as dementia, patients may still be deemed eligible for surgical intervention, depending upon their ability to comprehend the risks and benefits associated with surgery.

Spinal cord stimulator (SCS) placement is the most common neurosurgical option for chronic pain patients. Available options include conventional implantable pulse generator (IPG), rechargeable IPG, and a radiofrequency stimulator. [See Fig. 6.6 summarizing each surgical option, courtesy of Eallan Sivanesan, MD (John Hopkins Medicine, n.d.)]

Family Systems Dynamics as a Variable in Surgical Clearance

The limited work done examining family systems in neuropsychology is disorder or disease-specific. We have found that in neurosurgical practice, family systems dynamics play an important role in case conceptualization, especially when the presentation of the patient is not straightforward. We often find that the criteria by which surgical determinations are made become contingent on collateral information from family members but are significantly impacted by the strained familial

Conventional Implantable Pulse Generator (IPG)	Rechargeable IPG	Radiofrequency Stimulator
• Battery-operated • Implanted in the spine • Battery must be replaced with another surgery. • This device can be a good choice for patients with localized pain because it has a lower electrical output	• Similar to the conventional device in implantation location • Battery can be recharged **without** another surgery • Recharge allows for stimulators to put out more electricity • This device may be a better choice for people with pain in the lower back or in one or both legs, as the electrical signal can reach propagate further	• Battery is implanted **outside** the body • Battery can be recharged • This device may be better for people with pain in the lower back and extremities because of the device's power • This stimulator is rarely used today because of newer designs and technological advancements

Fig. 6.6 Spinal Cord Stimulator (SCS): Options for Treatment

relations emanating from the patient's functional limitations, medication effects, and related behaviors. When something has gone awry in the family system, the task of the neuropsychologist to evaluate surgical candidacy from a neurocognitive perspective becomes more challenging; eligibility criteria and contraindications for surgical intervention may collide with family members' expectations or needs and subsequently impact surgical decision-making. Consequently, one of the tasks facing the neuropsychologist is to serve as a type of "broker" between the patient, the family, and the neurosurgery team, creating this complex tetradic interface.

Several dynamics we have observed are summarized in the following paragraph. Some are generally seen across a wide range of neurological dysfunction, irrespective of neuropathology, but others are disease/disorder specific. There are several commonly observed family dynamics in neurologically afflicted presurgical patients such as PD & other movement disorders, epilepsy & other seizure disorders, degenerative disc disease & other chronic pain conditions. However, deficit-based conceptualization and psychopathology alone may not effectively address the needs of the patient and the family as a system. We do not propose a focus away from quantifying the patient's cognitive and behavioral functioning, but rather including family systems dynamics in the conceptualization. In clinical practice, we have observed the following examples of how the disease impacts family members, and how family members impact the assessment and collateral information that they provide when the neuropsychologist is attempting to answer the referral question (s).

Impulsive Behaviors and Hypersexuality in Movement Disorders

Although movement disorder medications may be effective in tremor reduction, they are not 100% efficacious. Treatment with dopaminergic therapy and even DBS intervention can trigger significant aberrant behaviors such as pathological (addictive) gambling, hypersexuality (e.g., compulsive or pathological use of pornography), pathological or compulsive buying/spending, stealing (e.g., shoplifting or robbery), hoarding, or binge eating. Patients with PD, parkinsonism, and ET often present with a prevalence of impulse control disorders and other complexities that draw attention to their risk of not having a favorable surgical outcome.

The medications most closely linked to impulsive and compulsive behaviors in Parkinson's fall under the class of dopamine agonists such as ropinirole and pramipexole. Patients with PD taking dopamine receptor agonist treatment have been associated with a 2- to 3.5-fold increased likelihood of having an impulse control disorder when compared to patients not receiving such treatment (Zhang et al., 2021). The exact mechanism of impulse control disorders in movement disorders is not well-understood, but the reward and inhibition systems are clearly involved.

Often, male patients with PD who have hypersexuality exhibit a propensity for pathological porn watching (Charoenporn & Newman, 2013). Unfortunately, there is a stark paucity in the literature regarding compulsive sexual behaviors. Hypersexuality is one of the most neglected non-motor symptoms of

PD. Neuropsychological complications are unaddressed and poorly understood to be the consequence of a character trait or some perceived disloyalty to the relationship on the part of the marital partner rather than an exceptional result of a physiological process. All of these manifestations clearly impact the patient's quality of life and have significant ramifications for marital and family dynamics.

In our clinical practices, recurring dynamics have been observed in patients referred for neuropsychological evaluation as a preoperative requirement. These are summarized below.

Observed Family Relations (FR) in a Neurosurgery Setting (1–7)

FR #1) Avoiding the Truth & Minimizing Clinical Symptoms

One of the most reliable sources of patient information comes from collateral information received from a loved one of the patient. In a good situation, the informant is a knowledgeable, truthful, and reliable source of information about the patient's symptoms and behavior. However, sometimes the informant is not helpful either because they don't have the ability (i.e., low intellectual ability, cognitive impairment), they share conflicting cultural beliefs, or have their own agenda and may not want to provide accurate information that might affect the outcome, such as having their loved one's driving privileges withdrawn, preventing the patient's admission into a long-term care facility (e.g., assisted living or skilled nursing home); sabotaging the patient's eligibility to have the procedure, or conversely, providing exaggerated or false information in order to ensure that the patient is cleared for the procedure).

In these instances, caregivers will "avoid the truth" either by omission or fabrication and may also minimize behaviors that pose a risk to optimum surgical outcomes (e.g., spouse chooses not to fully report deficits in instrumental activities of daily living as a way to protect his family's image). Although it may be less a dishonest report and more of a distortion, it is aimed at ensuring that the patient is afforded the surgical intervention or to shield the patient from some negative outcome [e.g., placement in an ALF; surgeon refusing to move forward with the surgical procedure; or avoiding a perceived negative label (e.g., cognitive impairment)].

Case Example # 1: DBS Candidate with Hypersexuality/ Excess Pornography

(All identifying information, patient names, and identifying characteristics are disguised to protect patient identity).

Mr. Garcia was an older gentleman who developed PD and was under consideration for DBS surgery. In his presurgical evaluation, it was noted that he engaged in watching pornography for several hours at a time, several times a day. His wife, who was authorized to be present, accompanied him to the interview to provide collateral information. It quickly became apparent that although the patient was an otherwise excellent surgical candidate, his propensity toward pathological watching of pornographic videos was a red flag for clearance.

Presenting Problem
Mrs. Garcia quickly expressed her anger, jealousy, and frustration with her husband's compulsive behavior. What was meant to be an initial consultation to assess him for surgical clearance quickly escalated to a very emotionally charged discussion. After over two hours of discussion, it was clear that Mrs. Garcia experienced insecurity, jealousy, and a strong need to be the only source of attention for her husband. In every other way, the patient was a faithful (by self-report), caring, emotionally expressive, and dedicated spouse, but Mrs. Garcia was ready to file for divorce. It required considerable psychoeducation to explain and help her understand that these compulsive behaviors were the result of dysfunctional brain activity.

Role of the Neuropsychologist
The neuropsychologist's role is to gather information, educate patients and family members about the purpose of the neuropsychological evaluation, and explain the findings, as well as their recommendations. Sometimes it is unavoidable being pulled into a therapeutic role during such a session, even though psychotherapy is not the purpose of the neuropsychological evaluation appointment. During this session, the author described the reason for the patient's compulsive behavior, namely that it is an uncontrollable impulse and a symptom of his Parkinson's disease, and not a character flaw or otherwise "bad behavior."

Outcome
As a result of this assessment, the patient was cleared for the surgical procedure, but the neurosurgery team was advised of the history of compulsive behavior. The neurosurgeon opted for placement of the DBS leads in the GPi, rather than the STN, given that placement in the GPi results in less psychiatric symptomatology.

FR #2) Disclosing Inconsistent Information to Providers

With the use of electronic health records, providers often have access within a health care system to progress notes entered by staff from multiple disciplines and to patient portal communications. This often affords the clinician the advantage of reading through the records and looking for trends in reports of symptoms or behaviors, but there may also be inconsistencies in the records. For many of the same reasons, family members may provide conflicting information to different providers, if they have a specific investment in the outcome. For example, in a case of a patient seen by these authors, a patient's adult child denied and minimized several suicidal gestures made by the elderly patient, but the record revealed several communications to another provider describing the patient's suicidal gestures and the urgency of those communications was in direct contrast to their denial to the author regarding the suicidal gestures. Their family was denying symptoms that would likely reduce the probability that the patient would be cleared by neuropsychology and were motivated to keep the patient out of an ALF, even though the patient was clearly no longer capable of living independently.

FR #3) Medication Non-Compliance

Another behavior often seen among family members is their engagement or support of the patient's non-compliance with medications. They will often disregard instructions, withhold medicines, administer medications as they perceive to be best for the patient, or worse, adjust the patient's dosage to meet their own needs (e.g., having the patient sleep, remain sedated, or stay awake). As part of the neuropsychological assessment, review of current medications and dosages is essential. When there is a discrepancy between the medical record, pharmacy record, or report of the patient from that which is reported by a family member, it is essential to determine what the beliefs and values of the family member are. Education about the importance of adherence to the prescribed schedule of medication is often required.

FR #4) Help-Rejecting Complaining

Frequently family members will be offered recommendations for services, additional intervention procedures and referrals, yet resist the provider's clinical suggestions. They exhibit a dynamic of help-rejecting and complaining as a preferred manner in which to cope with their own stressors when serving as a caregiver or having a health compromised family member. This might involve accepting the suggestion, but then not following up on it or sabotaging the intervention. We often see patients whose family members reject referrals to other disciplines, including psychiatry for pharmacological intervention, or psychology for psychological consultation and treatment. This dynamic may be paired with externalization of blame, in which the patient or family member blames the provider, treatment team, or someone from another discipline for their refusal to follow continuity recommendations.

Case Example # 2: DBS Candidate with Tardive Dyskinesia

Mrs. Smith was an 85-year-old patient with a long history of schizophrenia spectrum or other psychotic disorders and obsessive-compulsive features, who had years of extensive treatment with antipsychotic medications. The nature of the psychotic disorder was not known, as the family was not forthcoming. Her prolonged use of medicines ultimately led to the development of severe tardive dyskinesia. She had never had psychotherapy nor any other cognitive behavior therapy.

Presenting Problem

Her adult children desperately wanted to have her undergo the DBS procedure (as did the patient), but unfortunately, the patient's neuropsychological assessment revealed significant neurocognitive impairment in addition to severe psychopathology (i.e., hallucinations, delusions, non-compliance with medication, and multiple suicidal gestures). During the interview, her grown children minimized the severity of the recent suicidal gestures and reported that they weren't actually suicidal gestures, but rather that the patient simply "forgot" how many pills she had taken; or that the psychiatrist was "exaggerating" or "saw her only a few times," etc. This adult child of the patient was unaware that all of the involuntary hospitalization admissions were visible in her electronic record and that the author had access to that information. The patient had been hospitalized six times over the past five months and made several suicide attempts, including taking an overdose of anxiolytics, antipsychotics, and sleep medication.

Not Providing Truthful Information

Two of her adult children provided collateral information. One was present, the other (living out of state) was available on speaker phone. The informant who was present was providing minimal details, and the informant on the phone contradicted the sibling present. The sibling who was present stated that the suicide attempt was exaggerated as the patient has "only taken a few Xanax," and added that they were "only 0.25 milligrams," all to minimize the gravity of the suicidal gesture.

Minimizing

The informant stated that the most recent hospital admission was not "actually a hospital admission," and noted that she was only in the inpatient psychiatric unit for "a couple of days." She added that the patient didn't actually threaten suicide on another occasion, but only said "I don't want to go on like this." However, hospital records clearly indicated that the patient made suicidal threats and had taken various medications.

Non-Compliance with Medication Instructions

Review of Mrs. Smith's medical record progress notes revealed that the patient's adult child (present informant) had been giving her mother a full dose of one of her medications, in spite of instructions to taper it down. This caused the patient to have several falls.

Patient Expectations

In any presurgical neuropsychological evaluation it is essential to assess and address patient expectations. In the case of Mrs. Smith, neither the patient nor her family had realistic expectations regarding DBS, but rather had an idealized notion that a simple procedure would resolve all her symptoms. The neurosurgery team was advised of these unrealistic expectations and was able to address them in detail during their consultation.

Role of the Neuropsychologist

The neuropsychologist's role is to *inform* the surgical team of his/her findings and not to serve as a gatekeeper who can deny the procedure. Rather, the neurosurgery team was informed of the patient's significant psychiatric history, her neurocognitive status (dementia), the adult child informants' desperate hope to have their mother undergo the procedure at all costs, and their inability to rely on the collateral information provided as it was not consistent with medical record documentation. Further, the neurosurgery team was advised that the patient was probably a poor candidate for surgery given her significantly impaired cognition (inability to make an informed decision and to follow through with recommendations) and her recent instability due to significant mood disturbance and subsequent recurring suicidal gestures. The recommendation was made to consult psychiatry, treat the depression and psychotic symptoms, and if and when the patient exhibited a reasonable period of stability, the question of eligibility could be revisited.

Outcome

Another finding of the neurocognitive assessment was the high level of impairment the patient exhibited not only in terms of neurocognitive ability, but also in terms of activities of daily living. Mrs. Smith's adult children were desperately trying to keep her out of an assisted living facility as she lived alone with an aide who would visit for a few hours daily. The outcome of the neurocognitive assessment was the recommendation that she receive a much higher level of care in light of all of her deficits. The patient was deemed a poor candidate for surgery given her cognitive impairment (dementia), psychiatric symptoms (history of suicidal gestures, psychosis) and history of non-compliance. Ultimately, the neurosurgery team together with the patient and family opted to forego the DBS procedure.

FR #5) Family Wishes to "Mandate" the Procedure

Often a family member does not recognize the discomfort and limitations associated with a neurodegenerative disease. For instance, in the case of DBS or FUS intervention, a spouse may be embarrassed or ashamed of their partner's tremor, speech dysfluency (e.g., stutter or slowed cadence), dysphonic or raspy voice quality, drooling behaviors, or inability to perform tasks involving fine motor functions (e.g., food falling off of the utensil; inability to bring a cup of coffee up to their mouth). We have observed strained intimate relationships exacerbated by a spouse who desired surgical treatment on behalf of his wife for "cosmetic" purposes.

As mentioned earlier, movement disorders often result in non-motor changes including negative emotional symptoms. Some spouses are distressed if the patient no longer wishes to participate in socially motivated behaviors (e.g., doesn't want to drink alcohol; doesn't want to socialize; or to dance, etc.), which can lead to dissolution of a romantic relationship.

Case # 3: DBS Candidate with Parkinson's Disease: "The Trophy Wife"

Mrs. Williams was a 68-year-old female with PD who was referred for presurgical neuropsychological assessment for DBS clearance. Her husband was intent on participating in the interview and was authorized by her permission to be present. It was immediately apparent that Mrs. Williams was not interested in pursuing any type of surgical intervention, but her husband was adamant about her having the procedure.

Presenting Problem

The patient, Mrs. Williams, had Parkinson's disease with worsening symptoms that no longer respond to medication. She was troubled by persistent fatigue, tremors, balance problems, and dyskinesias (involuntary, erratic writhing movements of the face, arms, legs, and trunk). The problem was that Mrs. Williams, 11 years younger than her husband, had always been an outgoing, vivacious, attractive lady. She and her husband were part of a moderate sized group of couples that made up a small club and regularly met for drinks at a place which we will refer to as "the club." She had been a social drinker prior to the onset of her Parkinson's diagnosis and was described by her husband as *"the life of the party."* As her Parkinson's disease progressed and her symptoms worsened, she became less interested in going out as it required considerable effort to dress, apply make-up, and style her hair, and she no longer enjoyed drinking because she would not feel well if she consumed alcohol. She no longer wanted to socialize nor be *"the life of the party"* as described by her husband. Rather, she preferred quite evenings at home, listening to music, or watching television and spending time with her husband.

Relational Dynamics

After Mrs. Williams explained her subjective experience, her husband insisted that he wanted his wife to be the life of the party, to get dressed up and go to the club, to drink and dance, and socialize again. He could not accept that she was older and now had a neurodegenerative disease that was impacting every aspect of her life. The patient could not understand why her husband couldn't appreciate her needs and wishes, and ultimately agreed to have the neurosurgery consultation with the neurosurgeon.

Role of the Neuropsychologist

For the most part, the patient was an excellent candidate for the DBS procedure, as she did not present any neurocognitive deficits, had no history of clinical psychopathology or impulsive/compulsive behavior, and she was able to make an informed decision. However, under the continued pressure and badgering by her husband, she hesitantly agreed to proceed. Given observations of these dynamics, the author (YCL) provided information about the procedure, a list of questions to review with the neurosurgeon, and advised the patient that however she felt and whatever decision she made would be acceptable and every effort was made to normalize her experience. A long discussion followed with a referral to a Family Psychologist to help both parties understand the other's point of view. It was apparent that this patient did not want to undergo the procedure, but also that she would abide by whatever her husband decided. The neurosurgeon was advised of the apparent dynamic and encouraged to explore the husband's expectations to determine whether they were realistic; and to advise that the patient might not have the emotional ability to decline the procedure in light of her husband's insistence.

Outcome

Because the neurosurgeon was informed of the observed dynamics, he was prepared to broach the differences in treatment goals and the patient did not proceed with surgery. This was possible because the neurosurgeon was aware of the neuropsychologist's findings and was able to broach the subject directly.

FR #6) Apprehension Toward the Procedure

Often, family members resist the patient going forward with a surgical intervention because they fear that they will be put into a caregiver role, or that they may have increased tasks and responsibility for an already physically limited family member. They seem to fear that the patient will be different, and in an effort to maintain homeostasis, they resist change. However, this may not be in the best interest of the patient and may keep surgical candidates from the opportunity to dramatically improve debilitating symptoms emanating from the disease and/or disorder.

Cultural Considerations: The ECLECTIC Framework and Complementary "León-Cedeño FAMILIA Model"

Cultural competence is a term that refers to understanding cross-cultural considerations in the context of neuropsychological assessment, including bilingualism, "culturally neutral" tests, and the role of acculturation in cognitive performance (Rivera Mindt etal., 2010). Dr. Rivera Mindt, a pioneer in the field of cultural neuropsychology and diverse neuropsychological assessment, has shed light on the importance of cultural competency in neuropsychology (Diáz-Santos & Hough, 2016; *Navigating Neuropsychology*, 2019; Rivera Mindt et al., 2019). When conducting a neuropsychological evaluation, it is as important for the examiner and personnel involved with test administration to be culturally competent as it is for each assessment to preserve cultural and linguistic validity. Thus, it would be an oversight not to incorporate cultural considerations when assessing patients in a neurosurgical practice setting.

A novel framework coined "ECLECTIC" by neuropsychologist Daryl Fuji (Fujii, 2018) conceptualizes key ethnocultural components that present themselves among diverse neuropsychology patients and does so in a structured, diagrammatic way. Although it originated as a topic of study in Asian American populations, over the last few years it has gained momentum in other ethnic minority groups also leading to a stronger topical presence in conferences and in research publications. Each letter in the monogram signifies a facet in cultural neuropsychology that Fuji argues should be considered when evaluating a patient from a less acculturated or a diverse ethnic background:

- **E** for education and literacy
- **C** for culture and acculturation
- **L** for language
- **E** for economics
- **C** for communication style
- **T** for testing situation
- **I** for Intelligence and conception
- **C** for content and immigration

This framework succeeds in addressing key areas of diverse assessment that are otherwise often ignored in neuropsychological practice. However, despite its major contributions to the field of cultural neuropsychology, the ECLECTIC framework does not adequately address the component of family relational dynamics that play a significant role in the patient's overall clinical presentation and candidacy for neurosurgical intervention.

In our previous considerations for neuropsychologically based case conceptualization, we have explored the interconnectivity between family systems dynamics and neuropsychological dysfunction (i.e., that which arose because of a disruption in healthy family relationships or any observed deficits that were organic in nature and independent of family malfunctioning). Our experience with a neurosurgical population eventually brought us to develop a methodical representation of this interface which views case conceptualization as an element of the consideration of a family systems framework (indicated as the monogram, "FAMILIA") that are shaped by the patient's presenting cognitive dysfunction [(FAMILIA (x)] and the neuropsychological deficits that are independent of said familial frameworks (indicated by "X") (Cedeño et al., 2024).

CC ∈ FAMILIA(x) + X

The acronym for which we define "FAMILIA" includes the following:

F—Family Framework/Structure)

This tier addresses the functional organization of families that determines how members interact. It considers hierarchical relationships (e.g., matriarch vs. patriarch; head of the household vs. more subordinate roles, etc.) and examines the style in which family members socialize and engage interpersonally [e.g., levels of communication (both adaptive and maladaptive); relying on one another for support; and formation of self-concept from an individual (sense of separateness from the family) or self-construal (integrally related to the family) perspective. In culturally diverse families, a self-construal perspective often develops given the typically greater emphasis on familism and the larger family framework.

A—Antecedent/Premorbid Circumstances)

This tier considers circumstances that existed before the neuropsychological consultation. Although these may include pre-existing familial frameworks, this is not an isolated component and may also include premorbid diagnostic conditions or any diagnoses that were present before the patient's referral to neuropsychology and any dysfunction in family dynamics.

M—Medical Considerations/Iatrogenic Factors

This tier aims to cover all medical variables that play an active role at the time of neuropsychological consultation. This may include but is not limited to current diagnoses, symptomology caused by the predominant or secondary diagnostic conditions, strained family dynamics, or iatrogenic factors induced by the medical treatment of the attending physician.

I—Identification of Key Family Relationships

This tier conceptualizes reciprocal active family relations as noted previously (i.e., Avoiding the Truth & Minimizing Clinical Symptoms; Disclosing Inconsistent Information to Providers; Medication Non-Compliance; Help-Rejecting Complaining; Family Wishes to "Mandate" the Procedure; Apprehension Toward the Procedure) as well as formal family dynamics that may be affecting the patient's clinical presentation. The concept of adaptability is one dynamic in family systems theory that must be accentuated. This framework describes the family's ability to adapt to novel situations and stressful events that may threaten the stability of familial networks [i.e., rigid (poor balance), structured (optimum balance), flexible (optimum balance, and chaotic methods (poor balance) (Joh et al., 2013)]. When environmental demands exceed the ability of the family to cope in a healthy manner, the balance between permanence and change operates in greater discord, potentially resulting in another family systems component- homeostasis (Bowen, 1978). This conceptualization reflects that the identification of family dynamics is a fluid process in which one observed dynamic may also give rise to another.

L—Life Quality & Long-term Expectations

This tier considers the patient's quality of life as it pertains to appropriate expectations of the individual's likelihood of recovery of function during the disease course of any neurological disorder. In a functional neurosurgery context, the importance of preoperative hope and managing expectations of postsurgical outcomes is emphasized as it relates to quality of life, psychological distress, and satisfaction. "Family Myths," a set of beliefs based on a distortion of historical reality shared by all family members, can complicate the patient and the family's ability to set reasonable expectations of postsurgical outcomes. Maladaptive beliefs that negatively shape the rules by which the family functions may result in the patient having a substandard quality of life, exacerbated familial strain, and could result in poor candidacy for neurosurgical intervention.

I—Identified Patient

This tier elucidates a concept described in family systems theory in which the patient is identified as the "symptom bearer" or "presenting problem." As defined by Bowen (1966), the identified patient (IP) is the family member who is the least differentiated and most fused to the family collective. Often, the family's method of coping with ancillary stressors that accompany the patient's neurodegenerative condition is maladaptive in nature and opposes problem-focused coping mechanisms, which give rise to this dynamic. In other cases, one person may become the IP due to a resultant process of triangulation, a family systems theoretical framework that describes detouring conflict between two people by involving a third person (possibly the IP) to stabilize the relationship between the original pair. In these instances, the patient may be the first to seek help, not only on their own volition but often at the request of the family. He or she may display aberrant emotional or physical symptoms that reflect their dissonance to help-seeking. In the context of presurgical examinations, this component of the "FAMILIA Model" (Cedeño et al., 2024) may incite perverse family motives for the patient to undergo risky, life-changing, neurosurgery.

A—Agendas (e.g., Legal Considerations and Litigation)

This tier describes scenarios in which ulterior motives are concealed and legal issues typify these complex referrals, that is that there are litigious parameters that would otherwise preclude the patient from a *clinical* neuropsychological evaluation. In other words, though the patient may have a documented neurodegenerative condition that would warrant neurosurgical intervention, family members will often seek neuropsychological consultation not with the purpose of obtaining surgical clearance (from a *neurocognitive* standpoint), but rather as a guide to have neurocognitive concerns evaluated for them to utilize in a *forensic* context. In these instances, it is imperative that the attending neuropsychologist clarify expectations of the evaluation and establish that if a forensic opinion is desired, it is advised that the patient seek a neuropsychologist with forensic training to perform a forensic neuropsychological evaluation.

Collectively, each component of our "FAMILIA" model (Cedeño et al., 2024) constitutes a multidimensional examination of antecedent, existing, and future elements that have the potential to affect the patient's clinical presentation. We strongly advocate this model which incorporates family systems theory in neuropsychology clinical settings for case conceptualization.

Future Considerations

Future developments for the practice of neuropsychology within a neurosurgical setting ideally will reflect incorporation of family systems theory. It is our goal to motivate clinicians involved in neuropsychology to proactively implement the "León-Cedeño FAMILIA Model" (Cedeño et al., 2024) into clinical practice. This should include deliberation about the dysfunction of the family system at the time of neuropsychological consultation, which may increase their capacity to develop into well-rounded neuropsychologists. It is a long-term aim that they learn to appreciate the reciprocal family systems variables that impinge upon the patient, their family, and the disease course that affects the family system and the patient.

References

Amadio, J. P. (2015). Neurosurgery ethics: Perspectives from the field, circa 2015. *Virtual Mentor, 17*(1), 3–5. https://doi.org/10.1001/virtualmentor.2015.17.1.fred1-1501

Benbadis, S. R., Geller, E., Ryvlin, P., Schachter, S., Wheless, J., Doyle, W., & Vale, F. L. (2018). Putting it all together: Options for intractable epilepsy. *Epilepsy & Behavior, 88*, 33–38. https://doi.org/10.1016/j.yebeh.2018.05.030

Bowen, M. (1978). *Family therapy in clinical practice*. Jason Aronson, Inc.

Bowen, M. (1966). The use of family theory in clinical practice. *Comprehensive Psychiatry, 7*(5), 345–374.

Cedeño, K. B. N., León, Y. C., & Kaslow, F. (2024). *FAMILIA: The influence of family systems dynamics within a multidisciplinary neuropsychology clinical setting.*

Charoenporn, D., & Newman, C. (2013). Pornography addiction in a patient with Parkinson's disease receiving deep brain stimulation and cognitive behavioural therapy. *Australian and New Zealand Journal of Psychiatry, 47*, 42–42.

Cleveland Clinic. (2022, April 15). *Parkinsonism: What it is, causes & types*. https://my.clevelandclinic.org/health/diseases/22815-parkinsonism

Díaz-Santos, M., & Hough, S. (2016). Cultural competence guidelines for neuropsychology trainees and professionals: Working with ethnically diverse individuals. In F. R. Ferraro (Ed.), *Minority and cross-cultural aspects of neuropsychological assessment: Enduring and emerging trends* (2nd ed., pp. 11–33). Taylor & Francis.

Drane, D. L., Coady, E. L., Williamson, D. J., Miller, J. W., & Benbadis, S. (2011). Neuropsychology of psychogenic nonepileptic seizures. In M. R. Schoenberg & J. G. Scott (Eds.), *The little black book of neuropsychology* (pp. 521–550). Springer US. https://doi.org/10.1007/978-0-387-76978-3_17

Elble, R., Bain, P., João Forjaz, M., Haubenberger, D., Testa, C., Goetz, C. G., Leentjens, A. F. G., Martinez-Martin, P., Pavy-Le Traon, A., Post, B., Sampaio, C., Stebbins, G. T., Weintraub, D., & Schrag, A. (2013). Task force report: Scales for screening and evaluating tremor: Critique and recommendations. *Movement Disorders, 28*(13), 1793–1800. https://doi.org/10.1002/mds.25648

Fujii, D. E. M. (2018). Developing a cultural context for conducting a neuropsychological evaluation with a culturally diverse client: The ECLECTIC framework. *The Clinical Neuropsychologist, 32*(8), 1356–1392. https://doi.org/10.1080/13854046.2018.1435826

Guilmette, T. J., Sweet, J. J., Hebben, N., Koltai, D., Mahone, E. M., Spiegler, B. J., Stucky, K., Westerveld, M., & Conference Participants. (2020). American Academy of Clinical Neuropsychology consensus conference statement on uniform labeling of performance test scores. *The Clinical Neuropsychologist, 34*(3), 437–453. https://doi.org/10.1080/13854046.2020.1722244

Humphries, M. D., & Prescott, T. J. (2010). The ventral basal ganglia, a selection mechanism at the crossroads of space, strategy, and reward. *Progress in Neurobiology, 90*(4), 385–417. https://doi.org/10.1016/j.pneurbio.2009.11.003

Joh, J. Y., Kim, S., Park, J. L., & Kim, Y. P. (2013). Relationship between family adaptability, cohesion and adolescent problem behaviors: Curvilinearity of circumplex model. *Korean Journal of Family Medicine, 34*(3), 169–177. https://doi.org/10.4082/kjfm.2013.34.3.169

Koay, J. M., Spat-Lemus, J., Cornwell, M. A., Sacks-Zimmerman, A., Mandelbaum, S., Kohn, A., McLean, E., Meli, G., & Bender, H. A. (2023). The evolving need for neuropsychology in neurosurgical settings: Challenges facing transformative care. *World Neurosurgery, 170*, 277–285. https://doi.org/10.1016/j.wneu.2022.09.099

LaFrance, W. C., & Devinsky, O. (2002). Treatment of nonepileptic seizures. *Epilepsy & Behavior, 3*(5), 19–23. https://doi.org/10.1016/S1525-5069(02)00505-4

Lesser, R. P. (1996). Psychogenic seizures. *Neurology, 46,* 1499–1507. https://doi.org/10.1212/WNL.46.6.1499

Miocinovic, S., Somayajula, S., Chitnis, S., & Vitek, J. L. (2013). History, applications, and mechanisms of deep brain stimulation. *JAMA Neurology, 70*(2), 163. https://doi.org/10.1001/2013.jamaneurol.45

McLean, E., Cornwell, M. A., Bender, H. A., Sacks-Zimmerman, A., Mandelbaum, S., Koay, J. M., Raja, N., Kohn, A., Meli, G., & Spat-Lemus, J. (2023). Innovations in neuropsychology: Future applications in neurosurgical patient care. *World Neurosurgery, 170*, 286–295. https://doi.org/10.1016/j.wneu.2022.09.103

National Association of Psychometrists. (2016). *What is a psychometrist?* https://napnet.org/what

Navigating Neuropsychology. (2019, June 1). *21| Cultural neuropsychology: Embracing the mosaic – A conversation with Dr. Monica Rivera Mindt.* https://www.navneuro.com/21-cultural-neuropsychology-embracing-the-mosaic-with-dr-monica-rivera-mindt/

NHS Guy's and St Thomas' Foundation Trust. (2024, February). *Spinal cord stimulation - Overview.* https://www.guysandstthomas.nhs.uk/health-information/spinal-cord-stimulation#:~:text=Traditional%20therapies%20(such%20as%20painkillers

Northwestern Feinberg School of Medicine. (n.d.). *Essential Tremors & Other Tremor Disorders.* https://www.parkinsons.northwestern.edu/get-care-support/programs/essential-tremors-and-other-tremor-disorders.html

Nuti, A., Ceravolo, R., Piccinni, A., Dell'Agnello, G., Bellini, G., Gambaccini, G., Rossi, C., Logi, C., Dell'Osso, L., & Bonucelli, U. (2004). Psychiatric comorbidity in a population of Parkinson's disease. *European Journal of Neurology, 11*(5), 315–320. https://doi.org/10.111/j.1468-1331.2004.00781.x

Parkinson's UK. (2019, August). *Parkinson's drugs.* https://www.parkinsons.org.uk/information-and-support/parkinsons-drugs

Pycroft, L., Stein, J., & Aziz, T. (2018). Deep brain stimulation: An overview of history, methods, and future developments. *Brain and Neuroscience Advances, 2*, 239821281881601. https://doi.org/10.1177/2398212818816017

Reuber, M., & Elger, C. E. (2003). Psychogenic nonepileptic seizures: Review and update. *Epilepsy & Behavior, 4*(3), 205–216.

Rivera Mindt, M. G., Byrd, D. A., Morris, E. P., Tureson, K., Guzman, V., Summers, A. C., Crook, C., Savin, M. J., & Aghvinian, M. (2019). Cultural neuropsychology considerations in the diagnosis of HIV-associated neurocognitive disorders. In L. A. Cysique & S. B. Rourke (Eds.), *Neurocognitive complications of HIV-infection* (Vol. 50, pp. 193–223). Springer International Publishing. https://doi.org/10.1007/7854_2019_121

Rivera Mindt, M., Byrd, D., Saez, P., & Manly, J. (2010). Increasing culturally competent neuropsychological services for ethnic minority populations: A call to action. *The Clinical Neuropsychologist, 24*(3), 429–453. https://doi.org/10.1080/13854040903058960

Schoenberg, M. R., & Scott, J. G. (Eds.). (2011). *The little black book of neuropsychology: A syndrome-based approach*. Springer Science and Business Media. https://doi.org/10.1007/978-0-387-76978-3

Schoenberg, M. R., Soble, J. R., & Osborn, K. E. (2019). Psychometrics of assessment: Understanding what neuropsychology adds to the physician's understanding of the patient. In K. M. Sanders (Ed.), *Physician's field guide to neuropsychology: Collaboration through case example* (pp. 45–60). https://doi.org/10.1007/978-1-4939-8722-1_4

Sivanesan, E. (n.d.). Spinal cord stimulator. *Johns Hopkins Medicine*. https://www.hopkinsmedicine.org/health/treatment-tests-and-therapies/treating-pain-with-spinal-cord-stimulators

Sperling, D. (2019, May 6). Focused ultrasound versus DBS: Which is better for you? *Neuravive - Sperling Neurosurgery Associates*. https://essentialtremortreatment.com/focused-ultrasound-dbs-which-better-for-you/

Stafstrom, C. E., & Carmant, L. (2015). Seizures and epilepsy: An overview for neuroscientists. *Cold Spring Harbor Perspectives in Medicine, 5*(6), a022426. https://doi.org/10.1101/cshperspect.a022426

Subramaniam, B., & Upadhyay, P. (2020, May 22). Reducing your risk of changes in thinking following surgery. *Harvard Health*. https://www.health.harvard.edu/blog/reducing-your-risk-of-changes-in-thinking-following-surgery-2020052219898#:~:text=While%20advances%20in%20medicine%20may

Synofzik, M. (2013). Functional neurosurgery and deep brain stimulation. In A. Chatterjee & M. J. Farah (Eds.), *Neuroethics in practice* (1st ed., pp. 189–208). Oxford University Press. https://doi.org/10.1093/acprof:oso/9780195389784.003.0015

Yengar, S., & Shafer, P. (2017). Responsive neurostimulation (RNS). *Epilepsy Foundation*. https://www.epilepsy.com/treatment/devices/responsive-neurostimulation#:~:text=Tiny%20wires%20or%20leads%20are,when%20anything%20unusual%20is%20detected

Zhang, J.-F., Wang, X.-X., Feng, Y., Fekete, R., Jankovic, J., & Wu, Y.-C. (2021). Impulse control disorders in Parkinson's disease: Epidemiology, pathogenesis and therapeutic strategies. *Frontiers in Psychiatry, 12*, 635494. https://doi.org/10.3389/fpsyt.2021.635494

Yolanda C. León PsyD, ABPdN, earned a doctorate in Clinical Psychology from the Florida Institute of Technology and completed specialty training in Neuropsychology. She is board certified and has over 30 years of experience in Neuropsychology. She is currently an Assistant Professor at the USF Morsani College of Medicine, Department of Neurosurgery and Brain Repair (Tampa, FL), and Co-Director of the Neuropsychology Fellowship training program. She is an ad hoc reviewer for the *Neuropsychology Review* peer-reviewed medical journal. Incorporation of family systems theory is a core practice for Dr. Leon

K. Brianalysse Nicolena Cedeño BA, CSP is a published researcher and board certified Psychometrist in Neuropsychology. She has 10 years of experience administering neuropsychological assessments to cognitively impaired patients of all ages and varying neurological disorders, including Spanish-speaking Latinos and neurosurgical patients. She is currently Lead Psychometrist at the USF Department of Neurosurgery and Brain Repair (Tampa, FL). Under the supervision of respected neuropsychologists, she promotes the study of the robust implications of family systems relations and cultural considerations on neuropsychological assessment and case conceptualization.

Chapter 7
Partners in Time: Multigenerational Family Businesses in the Twenty-First Century

Mark I. Sirkin

First, family businesses are considered by the numbers: Worldwide, FOBs [Family-Owned Businesses] have long played a huge role in the global economy—a role that often goes unnoticed or underestimated. The UN Conference on Trade and Development notes that FOBs "account for more than 70% of global GDP [Gross Domestic Product]…. and are responsible for about 60% of global employment. They play a critical role in supporting education, healthcare, and infrastructure development across their communities around the world" (United Nations, 2021). In the United States, family businesses account for 64% of U.S. gross domestic product, generate 62% of the country's employment, and account for 78% of all new job creation (Astrachan & Shanker, 2003). They are the backbone of the American economy. About 35% of Fortune 500 companies are family-controlled and represent the full spectrum of American companies from small businesses to major corporations (Astrachan & Shanker, 2003).

Some estimates range even higher. According to the U.S. Census Bureau, about 90% of American businesses are family-owned or controlled. Ranging in size from two-person partnerships to *Fortune 500* firms, these businesses account for half of the nation's employment and half of its Gross National Product. They may have some advantages over other business entities in their focus on the long term, their commitment to quality (which is often associated with the family name), and their care and concern for employees. But family businesses also face a unique set of management challenges stemming from the overlap of family and business issues (Hayden, 2021).

Family business succession is often fraught with rivalry, jealousy, or conflict. Estimates on first generation succession, that is, from the founder(s) to their children, suggest that only 30% of these businesses successfully transition from the first

M. I. Sirkin (✉)
Sirkin Advisors, White Plains, NY, USA
e-mail: mark@sirkinadvisors.com

F. W. Kaslow (ed.), *Contemporary Issues in Individual, Couple, and Family Lives and Treatment*, https://doi.org/10.1007/978-3-031-90006-8_7

to the second generation; only 12% successfully transition from the second to the third generation; and only about 3% successfully transition into the fourth generation and beyond (Baron & Lachenauer, 2021). While there are many factors that contribute to longevity and success of the family business, there are also factors which contribute to failures of succession and sale (to non-family) or dissolution of the business altogether. The most successful family businesses are adaptive and resilient. They are conservative with their money, treat their people well, and know their markets and customers well enough to anticipate changes and survive (Asaf & Leke, 2024). The data that suggest that family businesses are short-lived fail to account for the "normal life span" of businesses which are relatively short and getting shorter (Garelli, 2016). Family businesses are at least as viable, if not more robust and personally rewarding, than non-family enterprises.

What are the "secrets" to successful and long-lasting family businesses? A recent review of the literature suggests the ability *to innovate in the second generation, and beyond, may hold some keys* (Baltazar et al., 2023). Television, movies, and some books about corporate succession or dynasties portray family businesses as ugly, nasty places, where family members plot and scheme to steal shares from each other or gain control, and the money that comes with it, through other means. Family businesses, when they succeed, are the stuff of legend: Compare the Rothschilds, the Fords, the Guggenheims (Landes, 2007). When they fail, or struggle, they can also be the subject of condemnation, as in a morality tale gone bad. Recent books about the Redstone family (Stewart & Abrams, 2024) or the Sackler family (Keefe, 2021) illustrate the dark side of family businesses. Such books often present simplistic views of the family business universe, replete with good guys, bad guys, heroes, and villains. However, the truth lies in the middle. Family businesses, like any others, have their strengths and weaknesses. Ultimately, they are a complex interaction between owners, workers, and managers. This chapter discusses the stars, as well as the bit players, of these family dramas, the values that hold these families together and, at times, tear them asunder. It is through an examination of the complex interplay of goals, issues, and personalities that we find the keys to these secrets, which account for much of the drama and are responsible for the great debacles and stunning successes in the world of Family-Owned Businesses.

Definitions, Structures, and Dynamics

What is a family business? Numerous business journals often feature articles about family businesses (*International Journal of Entrepreneurial Behavior and Research* (cf. Jain et al., 2023; *NTU Management Review* (cf. Lee et al., 2017); *Corporate Governance: The International Journal of Business in Society* (cf. Mukarram et al., 2018). Indeed, *Harvard Business Review*, one of the leading business journals in the world, regularly features articles about family businesses (cf. Levinson, 1971; Fernandez-Araoz et al., 2015). Some journals such as *Family Business Review* and *Family Business Strategy* are solely dedicated to research and discussion about family businesses. While multiple definitions may exist, one definition found in a recent article from *Review of Management Science* (Baltazar et al., 2023) defines family businesses as: **Commercial organizations in which various generations of the same family may influence the decision-making processes to achieve objectives defined by the family leadership** [emphasis added] (Lee et al., 2017; Mukarram et al., 2018; Jain et al., 2023). In addition, according to König et al. (2013), family businesses are organizations characterized by the existence of individuals interrelated by their family bonds that deploy their influence in their businesses, whether through their direct participation or as a family member holding executive roles (Baltazar et al., 2023). In other words, family businesses may literally employ family members or family members may serve other functions such as advisors, board members, or in some other consultative capacity. Some family members, particularly in older family businesses where they may represent the third, fourth, or fifth generations, may enjoy the wealth and privileges associated with ownership without any active participation in the company.

More simply, Ernesto Poza (2013), a leading expert in the field, has suggested a multidimensional definition of family businesses, which he says are characterized by:

1. **Ownership control** by two or more members of a family or consortium of families;
2. **Strategic influence** of a family in the management of the firm, whether by being active in management, as an advisor, or board member;
3. **Concern** for family relationships; and.
4. **The dream** of continuity across generations.

   [emphasis added].

Poza's (2013) definition contains the essential elements of the types of family businesses being discussed here. It is not just a legalism about who owns a controlling interest of shares or equity, but how much influence (control) family members exert, their concern for each other *qua* family (and not just business partners or co-owners of assets) and perhaps most importantly, the intent of being a family enterprise and the dream of continuity across multiple generations, and possibly locales as well.

An often used graphic to illustrate the roles and pulls of family business involvement has been offered by Tagiuri and Davis (1992) (See Fig. 7.1). This model, which may be referred to as the Tripartite, or Three-Circle model of family business includes more than just *family*, on the one hand, and the *business*, on the other. It includes *ownership* as a distinct and separate category. Ownership becomes more important over time, when some family members have left the business, and/or new relations have entered; ownership issues become even more important in larger or older businesses that are publicly traded. Often due to the specific nature of the business and how it is structured, controlling ownership may be a relatively small percentage of stock, with control being legally maintained through privileged voting shares owned and controlled by family members; in addition, when these favored owners join together, they may exert an irresistible influence on the activities of the

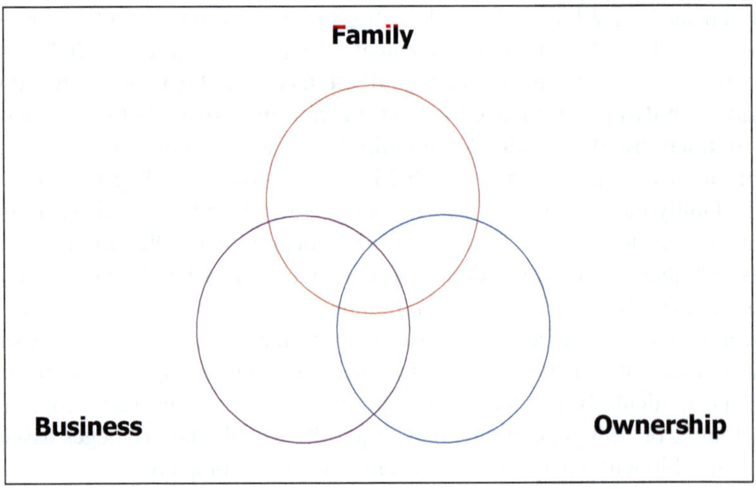

Fig. 7.1 The three-circle model (Tagiuri & Davis, 1992)

business and the distribution of its assets—all quite legal and accepted business practice. For example, as Purdue Pharma started to suffer from negative publicity, Sackler family members were able to legally distribute large amounts of cash, in the form of bonuses, to owning family members (Keefe, 2021); since they controlled the majority of voting shares on the board, there was no legal means to prevent these distributions which only benefitted a select few. Another recent example is when Elon Musk, controlling shareholder of X and Tesla, managed to have the Board of Directors, which included his brother Kimbal Musk, approve a record setting $56 Billion pay package (Reuters, 2024). To be sure, Tesla does not fit our precise definition of a family business (yet), but this story illustrates how families may work together in business environments to help each other achieve greater success.

It is the legal reality of control, whether through shares of stock, assets, or of the entire the company, that is important. There are actually many names for the family enterprise, or FOB, among which are: Family Business, Family Enterprise, Enterprising Family, Entrepreneurial Family, Family Firm, Business Family, or Family Company. These names are roughly equivalent. Thinking of the family business as potentially multiple businesses under a single family's control is essential over time and as assets grow. By the third generation, the average number of businesses owned and/or controlled by the owning family averages around six (Baltazar et al., 2023). Older and larger family businesses come together around the management of assets, often through a family office or by dedicated individuals, hired by or related to the family. Although these "facilitators" are not quite family members, they are thought of as "part of the family" and are seen as stewards and trusted advisors. For example, consider Tom Hagen in the (fictional) Godfather saga (Puzo, 1969) or the (actual) case of Allen Weisselberg, who preferred jail rather than betrayal of the Trump family for whom he worked (Pomerantz, 2023). Typically, as the number of members in the family naturally increases over time, i.e., through marriage and children, there may be more people interested in being involved in the work of maintaining and growing the company or companies.

Each of the three circles in Fig. 7.1—ownership, management, and family—represents its own pull or gravity, and those occupying overlapping roles or responsibilities often experience the greatest conflict, both internally and between family and business colleagues. So for example, a manager whose father is the CEO may want to support Dad but also thinks someone else would be better for the business. While this does not always result in conflict, there is often a natural tension between roles.

Challenges and Opportunities for Owners and Families

Family businesses have distinct advantages that should be maximized so family members experience both the satisfaction of contributing successfully to the family enterprise and engaging in work that is meaningful and rewarding. Family businesses usually are more profitable than their similar sized peers (similar by revenue and/or number of employees) by a small but significant amount; that is, by about 6.65% among the S&P 500 (Anderson & Reeb, 2003). "Large, long-standing, publicly traded family businesses grow faster than non-family companies, are more resilient, and outperform market returns by several percentage points" (Fernandez-Araoz et al., 2015).

Increased Roles for Women

Women have always had more significant roles and power in family businesses than non-family businesses. For a variety of reasons, women seem to fare better in family businesses: They have a better chance of becoming CEO—about 24% of family businesses have women CEOs compared with about 2.5% female CEOs in the Fortune 1000 (as of 2007) (Glavin et al., 2010). More recently, EY Family Business Center (2017) has looked to the future indicating that 70% of family businesses are considering a woman for their next CEO. Women CEOs have better retention of employees than their male counterparts, seem to command greater loyalty, and naturally provide more opportunities for women, both as role models and by providing a more level playing field for women executives (Glavin et al., 2010). New developments in the US tax code also give financial advantages to female-owned and -controlled firms, thereby providing additional incentives for families to place women at the helm of their businesses. The roles of women in family businesses seem to be increasing thereby creating a virtuous circle in which female CEOs provide more opportunities for women, both within and outside the family and the business.

Aging in Place

All family businesses face similar challenges as they navigate the vagaries of time and talent. Founders get older and some release the reins of control gradually and deliberately, while others hold fast until the bitter end, often to the detriment of the business and the people whom it supports. It is essential that leaders and owners plan for inevitable transitions, both expected and unexpected. Family dynamics must be managed, not ignored, as they pertain to issues within and between generations. Everything from salaries to bonuses to roles must be negotiated. In the first generation, it is often the Founder who makes these decisions based on personal preference and the talents and aptitudes of the individuals concerned. But inevitably feelings may get hurt, decisions may be disputed, and grudges may develop and take on a life of their own. Over time, what was once a group of people who were related to each other and worked together becomes a business fraught with disagreements and rivalries. To illustrate consider the development of a single family-farm ranch to *Yellowstone*, the Paramount-produced, neo-Western television drama covering three time periods in a multigenerational story about a single family of Montana cattle ranchers that spans more than a century and a half, and starring Harrison Ford and Helen Mirren in the *1923* portion of the saga, and Sam Elliott in the *1883* episodes of the series within a series; and Kevin Costner in the first, and most chronologically recent series named simply *Yellowstone* (Sheridan & Linson, 2018).

Capital Accumulation: Something Else to Manage

Success breeds its own problems. For example, the CEO or Executive Committee must decide about the best way to divide assets to maximize generational wealth. Are all the assets better off kept in one carefully watched company, or should the mantra of money-managers, who advise their clients to divest and diversify, be followed? And how do those assets get divided? Evenly, to each according to need or to each according to contribution? Without an undisputed leader in each generation, these decisions may not be easily resolved and may lead to family and/or business dissolution. Once attorneys and other interested parties become involved, these family disputes could well mark the beginning of the end of the family enterprise. If the "pie" is the sum total of all the family assets, how does the pie get divided in each generation? Among the many people who may expect a piece of the pie, there are founders, family members who work in the business, family members not in the business but who may have some ownership shares, employees, outside investors, and other combinations of stakeholders; that is, every part of the three circles (see Fig. 7.1).

Naturally Arising Tensions

One way to think about family business tensions has been suggested by Tagiuri and Davis (1996), in their discussion of *bivalent attributes* of such businesses. They point out that the same positive aspects of these businesses also contain the seeds of strife and conflict. For example, they suggest a list that includes: Simultaneous Roles, Shared Identity, Lifelong Common History, Emotional Involvement & Ambivalence, Private Language, Mutual Awareness & Privacy, and Meaning of the Family Business. Each of these attributes of family businesses may be true *and* have both positive and negative elements. For example, a person may be both a father (which is a role in itself) and the founder/owner. In the father role, he may be understanding of a child's lateness to work, but as a boss, he must enforce fairness and discipline (i.e., no special treatment for the boss's son). A shared identity can be a source of pride or embarrassment, depending on the circumstances and history. Private meetings, agreements, or understandings may also be a source of strength and bonding, or a source of confusion and miscommunication for those not "in on the secrets." Nothing is an automatic given nor universally good or bad in a family business. Each attribute, whether as a source of strength or disagreement, must be processed and discussed to enable that attribute to have a positive impact on thc family and the business. The ability to help the business leaders do this may be one factor that differentiates the psychologically informed family business consultant over the many other consultants that family businesses use. We encourage dialogue while understanding there may be no single, "right," answer; other professionals such as lawyers, accountants, or insurance brokers may believe their professions provide them with tools to identify the right answer, while more psychologically informed consultants understand that "right" answers are more situationally relevant.

Dyads, Triangles, and Beyond

Bowen Theory, which undergirds an approach to family therapy developed by Murray Bowen and his students, suggests triangles add stability to small systems, while dyads are inherently unstable (Keller & Noone, 2020). This may be as true of two-person systems as it is of two-group systems. In the early literature about family businesses, they were often seen as small, primitive, and immature (Levinson, 1971). Dyadic family-business systems may be inherently unstable and therefore require a third element to balance them. As Tagliuri & Davis suggest (1992), this third leg may well be ownership. Thus, an incipient or immature family business has two legs, family and business, but may require the third leg of an ownership group to maintain long-term stability. I have referred to the two-legged model of family businesses as the Bi-Polar Theory of this dyadic system and suggested that it is inherently unstable (Sirkin, 2004). By introducing a third dimension to the system, i.e., *ownership*, a stabilizing influence is added. For example, a Board of Directors may legally be created by the owners of a company. It is through the Board that owners exercise their power and authority. Ownership also means accountability, often to third parties, and legal constraints that add an additional element of objective responsibility to the system. It is the "Ownership" circle that represents stability, accountability, and objective evaluation into what may be an unstable bipolar family/business system (Davis, 2018).

The Long Game

Longevity over three or more generations introduces a temporal component. Technically, the Tagiuri and Davis (1992) Tripartite model, even with its added "Ownership" dimension, is still a slice of time, frozen as it were, at some point in the history of the business, even if only in the present. The true complexity of family business only emerges with the added dimension of time (Gersick et al., 1997). As the graphic below illustrates, the Three-Circle model expands geometrically with the dimension of time and the additional complexity it entails (see Fig. 7.2).

While the challenges of family, business, and ownership are difficult enough, they also evolve over time and may be unique to each generation. The generations, or temporal phases, are expressed in Fig. 7.2 as T(time) 1, T2, etc. For example, at T1, we see a controlling owner/founder struggling with a relatively new business. At T0, the owner may be working alone or with a few employees, while at T1, as the children get older, they may begin to enter the business. At T2, siblings may find themselves in business together, making decisions by and for themselves, with the

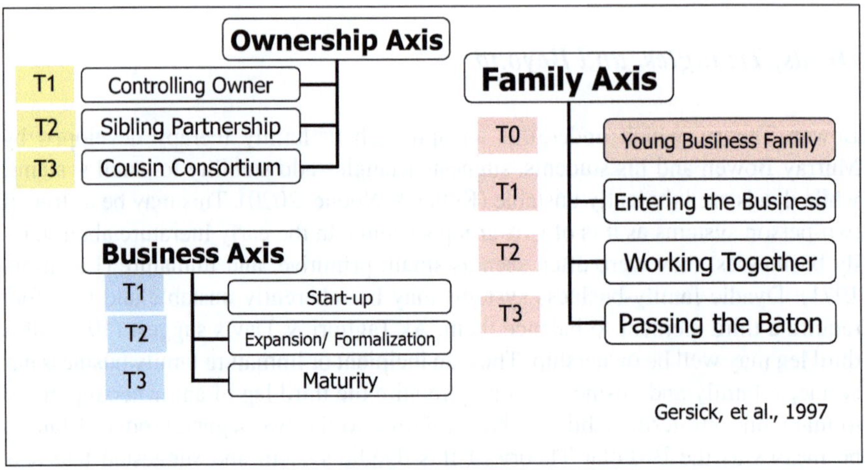

Fig. 7.2 Multi-dimensional Axes Over Time

founder either diminishing his or her involvement or already gone. In T3, Sibling Partnerships often become Cousin Consortiums as the third generation comes in and begins to lead. Over time, one becomes a few, and a few become many. Assuming the business remains financially healthy, it nevertheless has a larger payroll, perhaps has added locations, and often has demanding shareholders to manage. Public companies have even more onerous reporting burdens as well.

How Consultants Help Family-Owned Businesses[1]

Opportunities to assist people in family businesses come at predictable points in the life of a family-owned business which typically correspond to life cycle events: marriages, retirements, deaths, etc. Typically consulting interventions are sought at a crisis point, when the business or the family is being challenged in some way. For first generation family business members, sometimes referred to as G1, the needs are often tied to family: helping children enter the business, smoothing the path to allow children to have meaningful responsibility without destructively challenging the founder, and making room for additional siblings coming into the business are all examples of when family businesses seek consultation. Additionally at this stage, people in two or three systems may struggle to differentiate working relationships from family relationships with the same people. Help with role differentiation is often a critically needed service.

[1]A note about consulting vs. psychotherapy: I use the word "consulting" rather than "therapy" with the realization that many readers of this volume are family therapists. As most systems therapists, I eschew the use of diagnostic labels when dealing with people who are not seeking therapeutic help, and have not been diagnosed, with mental health disorders. The work I do as a consultant presupposes a level of mental functioning that exhibits health and wellness rather than psychopathology. There are many reasons for this emphasis, both theoretical and practical, that would require an additional article to explain. Suffice to say, the work I am describing in this chapter is consulting, not psychotherapy nor family therapy. If I am working with a family in which someone is exhibiting symptoms of mental illness, I will refer them out rather than treat them instead of, or alongside, the family. This is an ethical consideration. Nor will I accept insurance payments for work with non-diagnosed individuals. For the cost-conscious client, I can assure them the work we do is indeed a deductible business expense, however, in my opinion it is not a medical expense per se. In addition to the costs, the model of the work is different. Family business clients struggle with problems in living caused by the fact of being embedded in a family that is embedded in a business. The help I provide, as a consulting psychologist, is on the healthier side of the sickness–wellness continuum: From a developmental perspective, I use psychological constructs (not necessarily related to mental illness) to enhance understanding, lay the groundwork for change, and facilitate communication among and between family members and, when applicable, with employees. Considerations of mental health, while they may enter the picture, are rarely the focus of my interventions. While I may be trained to do such interventions, I consider psychotherapy a different contract than consulting, and I am explicit with every member of the family about the nature of the work we do together.

Role Differentiation and the Evolution of the Business

In G2, as the family involvement in the business expands, new challenges arise. As the founders age, they may lose energy or interest in a business that formerly consumed all their time and energy; this may be a healthy development, but often catches everyone by surprise. More typically, founders often refuse to acknowledge diminished capacity or interest. Short vacations turn into much longer and more frequent vacations, a second home—often far away—becomes a preferred residence. These developments often entail prolonged absence and less involvement with the business. This should be seen as a natural development, but often founders are loath to relinquish control. This may add friction to parent–child relationships, where things run smoothly when parent(s) are away but flare up when one or both return back to the office. Transition planning, for all key people in the business, children as well as parents, is often essential at this stage. Coaching for both generations can be very helpful at this point. Eventually, hopefully through a planned and thoughtful process, members of G2 find themselves in charge and with greater authority. The "kids" are finally running the show. But what they envision may not be the reality.

Eventually G2 is fully responsible for setting direction, making strategic decisions and investments for the near- and long-term. All businesses will face challenges over time: the economy has its ups and downs, industries evolve, technology and globalization affect the business environment, and to be successful the second generation will need to rise to these challenges. As the number of progeny in the business increases and ownership and management structures evolve to reflect more roles and responsibilities, there is greater complexity to manage. This complexity adds challenges: One store becomes several, closely held stock is now dispersed, and if a company has gone public, there are many more rules and reporting requirements. The business environment may demand changes in the business that were unexpected. For example, who could have accurately predicted the impact of AI, social media, and pocket telephones that are more powerful than the computers that guided men to the moon? The world is in constant flux and successful businesses navigate these changes as required. Members of G2 may or may not be up to these challenges and they may need help to adapt the business to grow in new directions. And, before anyone realizes, a new generation is looking for summer jobs and opportunities to work in the business.

Expanding into Philanthropy: A Natural Development

G2, as with G1, must prepare the way for G3. But not everyone in G3 will want to become part of the business. This Cousin Consortium will have varied interests. Some members of G3 will want to work in the business, while others will be content to help manage through serving on Boards and other ownership structures. If the business has been lucky, there may be enough capital to fund a Foundation, which is another way for the family to come together to distribute assets, in this case for a social, or philanthropic, cause. Some family members will simply want to enjoy the wealth that previous generations have made available to them, and not be involved in managing a family business or even a family fortune. Over time, there may be many dozens of people who will benefit, and perhaps want a say in, how the businesses are managed and proceeds are distributed and invested.

Healthy Role Differentiation Within the Business and the Family: Who Does What, Where, and How?

To appreciate the complex interplay of the multiple roles activated by family businesses, consider the Three-Circle (Tripartite) Model, but this time with the addition of roles and overlapping responsibilities (see Fig. 7.3).

One application I often use to demonstrate when training family business consultants is to add Fig. 7.3 which requires deeper thinking about roles and role conflict. I ask them to count off by sevens, to reflect the seven intersections in Fig. 7.3 (as illustrated by each numeral in the boxes). Once the room is done counting off by sevens, we start again. Then I ask all the Ones to sit together, the Twos to sit together, etc. And then I pose the same question to each group: *"The 'old man' is thinking of selling the business. What are your concerns?"* This exercise often leads to a heightened awareness of one's role vis à vis the Tripartite Model. Roles that sit between two slices of the pie (e.g., sections one, three, five, seven) pose special strain as people decide between personal priorities of, say, family loyalty vs. financial gain or career advancement vs. caring for extended family. The strain may become acute among people that have grown up together and spent their lives listening about, and contributing to, the business. What happens in the third, fourth, and fifth generations, and beyond, when a larger group is comprised of people who barely know each other? This distance from the founder and founding events tends to dissolve the (family) ties that bind. Meetings are not so much family get-togethers as they are stock-holder events to vote on policies that may impact personal wealth, but when fewer family members are working in the business. Mechanisms exist to help family members know one another and build common values, such as Family Foundations (mentioned above), or Family Clubs, Societies, Circles, or reunions that offer opportunities for gathering socially, meeting "far flung" relatives, and learning about common history going back generations. One family with whom I have worked, into their third or seventh generation, depending on how one counted, hosted annual meetings paid for by the Family Foundation in the city that was the primary home to the business, where distant cousins met and socialized, and the current patriarch played "happy host." This family had enough capital to fund its members' educational needs from birth through college, making membership benefits more tangible than a family vacation.

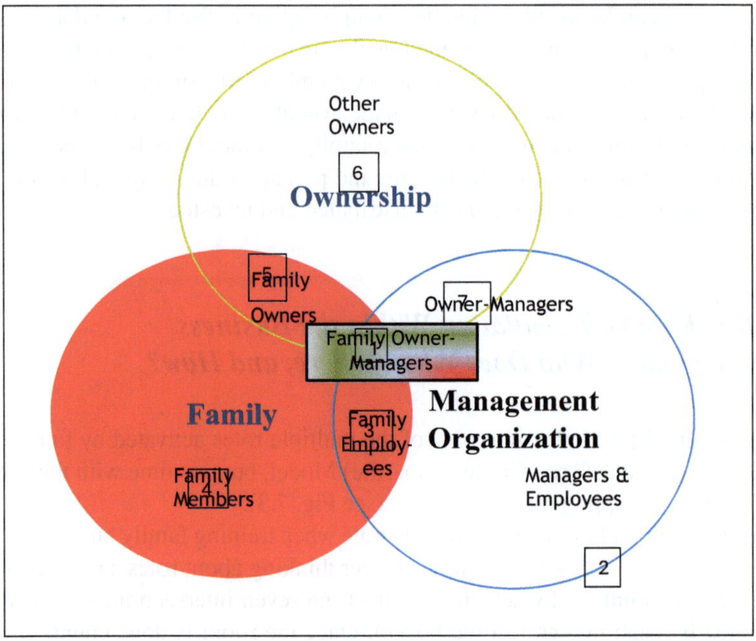

Fig. 7.3 Roles and role-overlap using the tripartite model (Tagiuri & Davis, 1996)

Role Theory: A Closer Look

Roles are, for the most part, sociological constructs (Biddle, 1986). While a person may inhabit a role, the role itself is informed by the social context in which it functions—additionally influenced by culture, ethnicity, gender, SES, and other external factors. Internal factors that affect role include personality factors, genetics, and motivation. In our Tripartite Model, each circle carries its own role expectations: For example, mother, CEO, major shareholder. Each role places its own unique demands on the person. In family businesses, behavior comes down to the salient features, for a given individual, of the role(s) they are enacting. A mother may want to split the assets evenly among all of the children, while a competent CEO may want controlling interest to go to the most capable person, regardless of who is related to whom. By increasing the awareness of these competing demands, consultants help family members make decisions that take as many factors into account as possible. Trying to make one's child happy may compete with the demand to keep the business profitable well into the future. An empathic, well-informed consultant may be helpful in sorting through these competing demands.

Role Suction

How does a social system impact one's choices, attitudes, decisions, and behaviors? Early psychoanalytic thinkers talked about the power of the group to influence the individual, and there is an entire tradition within psychodynamic group theory that reinforces these ideas. This tradition, associated with thinkers such as W. R. Bion (Rioch, 1970), Anna Freud (Freud, 1964), Fritz Redl (Goldsmith & Sanders, 1993) and his close friend, Bruno Bettleheim, and Yvonne Aggazarian (Agazarian & Carter, 1993), explores how people take up, and internalize, role expectations in group settings. The term "role suction" refers to both internal and external mechanisms by which the group affects a person such that the person increasingly conforms, "becomes," or embodies a role cum social expectations. Once those social (external) expectations are absorbed, the person conforms to them, usually without fully understanding or knowing all the ways the external forces have shaped their behavior and inner world.

This is easy to understand, and appreciate, in the case of paid roles. CEOs, Board Members (who are typically compensated), and executives have roles which are often well defined and well remunerated (Barao, 2024). The external incentives are in place and, at times, legally defined (e.g., Board Members and Executives in public companies have clearly delineated duties and responsibilities). On the other hand, family roles and expectations are more variable and less legally binding. This doesn't mean the expectations are any less, but perhaps less enforceable. For example, I worked with a family in which the eldest son built the business well beyond the father's capability, but when the father sold the company (he could because he owned all the stock), and the mother had to distribute the inheritance in her will, she split the money evenly despite the fact that some of their children had never worked in the business. The others benefitted from all the hard work of the first son. The eldest son, my client, shrugged off the injustice, stating, "My Mom doesn't understand business," but it still rankled him and has impacted family relations beyond the first generation. Had the father and mother had the foresight to seek consultation before the sale, they may have realized that a different split would not only have been fairer but would have avoided planting the seeds of resentment that is impacting this family well after the demise of both parents.

Inherent Vulnerabilities in Family Businesses

The preceding pages only scratch the surface of the psychological complexities, pulls, and tensions within the family/business/ownership system. Multigenerational family businesses are typically complex, multifaceted, and a delicate balance of enterprise, values, roles, and capital. In this chapter, the outsized roles that *values* and *capital* may play have not been discussed in depth. And there is more to say about characteristic roles that often emerge within the family business. For example, in our discussion about roles and role suction, it may be possible to specify typical roles elicited in family businesses and how those who take up a role may experience those pressures and successfully navigate them, or not.

The bivalent attributes discussed by Tagiuri and Davis (1996) can expose every family business to potential problems.

Nepotism

This refers to a tendency to hire people, in any business or endeavor (e.g., government, politics, religion), who are related or part of the family. Love can make people blind, especially when it comes to succession. Among the many "best-practices" to deal with the trap of nepotism is to make certain their children have an advanced education and have at least several years of experience working for *another* company in the same industry.

Unprofessionalized

One reason that Harry Levinson (1971) thought family businesses were inferior to non-family businesses was that they often lacked professionalism. Successful growth almost always requires increasing levels of professionalization which suggests that talent may be either trained from within or brought in from the outside.

Family Conflict

This factor often gets the most press and is the most visible aspect of family dysfunction. Conflict is not always destructive, there is such a thing as dynamic tension; however, unchecked conflict can be bad for morale and bad for the business.

Resistance to Internationalization

In a globalized market, such resistance can spell the beginning of the end for the business. The ability to outsource labor and materials, not to mention access to new customers in other countries, may often be a key to growth and success (Kaslow & Friedland, 2021).

CEO Resistance to the Transfer of Power

Founders start a business; it is their vision, it is their blood, sweat, and tears that make the business successful. It is often, especially for men, their most outstanding life achievement. Their self-esteem, sense of self-worth, feelings of pride and accomplishment are often wrapped up in the business. Stepping away from this may feel like an existential demotion, a bit too close to that ultimate demotion—death—and many are not emotionally prepared for it.

Role Confusion

An entitled child doth not a business owner make, and being a family member is not, in itself, a qualification for promotion. People should be held to objective standards of competence, evaluated and mentored on a regular basis. A qualified successor should compare favorably to other (both internal and external) candidates.

Values and Capital: Neglected Components of a Successful Legacy

Human survival is not a solo journey. As I have discussed in previous work (Sirkin, 2020), when families join with other families to enhance their chances for survival, they increasingly specialize and this specialization of tasks creates economies (in the sense that an economy comprises the production, consumption, and trade of goods). For example, having enough to eat in prehistoric times may have meant hunting large animals: Trackers, spear-throwers, skinners, butchers, cookers, servers, cleaners were all specialized roles in small village economies. It is such activity that gives rise to family businesses, as in my father was a butcher, I am a butcher, my daughter is a butcher. Family members are the ultimate "in-group," especially in relation to larger social groups. For example, the family may be a sub-unit of a larger village, or an ethnic group within a city may feel more connected than non-related strangers from the same part of the world. Simply put, familiarity breeds trust, and trust is a core component of any successful working group or team (Hall & Astrachan, 2015; Meinert, 2018). But because they have grown up together, know each other well, understand a shared set of values, they have greater trust with each other than they do with strangers and may operate from a shared set of values. Even in families with high levels of competition within the family, it is more typical for them to band together when faced with a common threat. But sometimes high levels of competition may lead to self-destructive, and self-sabotaging, behaviors. Shared values are a competitive advantage. The importance of values to family businesses is well-captured in the following quote:

> These executives realize something that many family businesses have not: The values, ideals, and sense of purpose nurtured by the owning family are a potentially vast source of strength and energy for business. A healthy owning family with **strong values**, in fact, may be the greatest resource a business can have. (Aronoff et al., 2016)

For most people, the *money* (a less refined term for "capital") is the raison d'être, the first cause and final rationale for the existence of the business. Success is measured by capital accumulation. That is, the money itself exerts a sort of gravitational pull on the identity of these family members that can often be a double-edged sword. In capitalist cultures (where capital accumulation is a significant standard of achievement), the money takes on a life of its own. It solidifies a family identity that is associated with positive local, or even national or international, fame or notoriety. Usually this is positive and a reason to feel special and to feel pride. But it can also be a reason to be hated or envied. Sometimes all of the above. Both the family, and its social circles, sometimes must walk a fine line. This can lead to mixed feelings, ambivalence, or even denial about the role the money plays in the emotional life of the family. It can be a source of pride or entitlement on the one hand, and pain and embarrassment on the other.

- The significant capital that a successful family in business together can accumulate can often seem a parade of opposites: confidence vs. insecurity, entitlement vs. guilt, exploitation vs. philanthropy. Significant wealth is both a burden and a responsibility. Founders, who often began with little and struggled to be successful, often worry that the presence of great wealth will dilute the values of hard work and innovation that led to the fortune in the first place (Rondi et al., 2019). And indeed, how can it not? Being raised in a family of privilege often creates ambivalence in both parents and children. I remember one family with whom I worked that was proud of the way the parents lifted themselves up as penniless Holocaust survivors to become owners of a substantial real estate empire. The three children worked in the business but the father could be emotionally abusive, making disparaging remarks such as "My kids have been on welfare their whole lives." They worked in the family business and he paid them to do so, but he also resented that they had never known hunger, risk, or deprivation. The family fortune was a source of pride but also of irrational jealousy between the generations.

Conclusions

Family businesses are both ubiquitous and a tried-and-true source of family wealth creation and preservation over time. In fact, if we expand our definitions just a bit, family businesses have been with us, literally, since the beginning of history. The pantheons of many religions often evolved into family "businesses," if running the world can be thought of as a family business, and we see similar dynamics in Greek and Roman and Norse mythology. In the Bible, the Patriarchs could loosely be thought of as successful, multigenerational family business leaders. From the founder Abraham who left his hometown of Ur to start a herding business, to Isaac, who grew that business despite conflicts with his brother Esau, to Jacob who worked for, and squabbled with, his Uncle Laban and was able to innovate with novel breeding techniques to grow the business he inherited. Indeed, monarchies too may be considered "family businesses" where the business is conquest or governance or, in their mature state, filling government coffers with tax revenue. In modern times, we have seen the fictional Corleone family demonstrate all the growing pains of a multigenerational (crime) business family (Puzo, 1969) as well as more modern fictional tales such as *Succession* (Armstrong, 2023) or *Yellowstone* (Sheridan & Linson, 2018). We can read about the non-fiction versions of these phenomena in books such as *Empire of Pain* (the Sackler family) (Keefe, 2021) or *Unscripted* (the Redstone family) (Stewart & Abrams, 2024).

Family businesses may influence members to take up certain roles in the service of both the family and the business. These roles result from, and contribute to, the ongoing values that are often key to founding, and continuing, the family business. Whether these values are as prosaic as a strong work ethic or multigenerational as maintaining control at all costs, they contribute to the businesses' continued success. Shared values among family members may be the critical "glue" that holds these families together. As Aronoff et al. (2016) have said, a "healthy owning family with strong values … may be the greatest resource a business can have."

The family fortune itself, whether in the low thousands or high billions, may become larger than life and is somewhat metaphorical, serving multiple functions. It becomes a touchstone, and common grounding, of the family's and its members', sense of self, and self-importance. It is a "gift" from one generation to another, but also a burden. It may represent a complex obligation that is passed from one generation to another.

In summary, this chapter illustrates many of the common aspects or shared beliefs and behaviors that make family businesses successful and viable from one generation to another. Among the most fundamental take-aways for success in family businesses are the qualities below. All successful family businesses demonstrate some aptitude in the following four areas, and consultants can help their family business clients to be better at each.

- Family **communication** reinforces a common purpose, a common vocabulary and shared values. Investments in family unity, in the form of boards of directors, foundations, philanthropic activities, and additional businesses represent a unique resource for family enterprises. Patient family capital (implying a willingness to give the investment time to mature as opposed to short-term investors who want to see a quick turnaround and steady, regular increases), and the values that reinforce it, provide an additional insight into how families leverage wealth from generation to generation.
- A **strategy** for continued growth in revenues and profitability is often central to a continued win–win relationship between family and business. This reinforces the drive, not just for individual success, but for the entire family to participate and work together to be successful. Simplistically, this means they help each

other make money. But more substantially, it reinforces an identity that feeds into a virtuous cycle of industriousness, philanthropy, communal support, and civic pride. Without these, over time, the family dissipates and loses its drive along with its common identity.

- **Governance** of the family-business relationship is key to the continuity across generations to which business families often aspire. Governance relates to the rules and thoughtful means by which families work together. In traditional, established family businesses, governance may be connected to a Board of Directors or Advisors or other controlling interests. These rules and agreements ensure that the way the family operates is not arbitrary or based on favoritism in the moment. Often, lawyers or consultants help craft legal governance rules and structures with input from the family.
- Husbanding **capital**, allowing it to be grown and repurposed, is also a key to businesses that successfully transition from one generation to the next. Capital is both the outcome and benefit of a successful family business—it enables a lifestyle that provides identity and opportunity for generations to come. Yet when care is not taken and capital is frittered away over time, there may be an abiding sense of loss, of opportunities missed, and gifts misused. There may well be a downside and lasting regret about opportunities not taken.

References

Agazarian, Y. M., & Carter, F. B. (1993). Discussions on the large group. *Group, 17*, 210–234. https://doi.org/10.1007/BF01419720

Anderson, R. C., & Reeb, D. M. (2003). Founding-family ownership and firm performance: Evidence from the S&P 500. *The Journal of Finance, 58*(3), 1301–1328. http://www.jstor.org/stable/3094581

Armstrong, J. (2023). *Succession* (American TV Series, Seasons 1–4). HBO Network.

Aronoff, C., Mendoza, D. S., & Ward, J. L. (2016). *Family business values: How to assure a legacy of continuity and success*. Palgrave Macmillan.

Asaf, E., & Leke, A. (2024). *What separates the best family-owned businesses from the rest?* McKinsey & Company: Family Business Newsletter. https://familybusinessmagazine.com/governance/what-separates-the-best-family-owned-businesses-from-the-rest/

Astrachan, J. H., & Shanker, M. C. (2003). Family businesses' contribution to the US economy: A closer look. *Family Business Review, 16*(3), 211–219. https://doi.org/10.1177/08944865030160030600

Baltazar, J. R., Fernandes, C. I., Ramdani, V., & Hughes, M. (2023). Family business succession innovation: A systematic literature review. *Review of Management Science, 17*, 2897–2920. https://doi.org/10.1007/s11846-022-00607-8

Barao, J. (2024). *Guide to board compensation: How much do board members make?* Azeus Convene. https://www.azeusconvene.com/articles/how-much-do-board-members-make

Baron, J., & Lachenauer, R. (2021). *Do most family businesses really fail by the third generation?* Harvard Business Review. https://netfamilybusiness.com/wp-content/uploads/2021/07/Do-Most-Family-Businesses-Really-Fail-by-the-Third-Generation.pdf

Biddle, B. J. (1986). Recent developments in role theory. *Annual Review of Sociology, 12*, 67–92. https://doi.org/10.1146/annurev.so.12.080186.000435

Davis, J. A. (2018). *How three circles changed the way we think about family business*. Cambridge Family Enterprise Press.

EY Family Business Center of Excellence. (2017). *Women in leadership: The family business advantage* (pp. 1–16). EY Family Business Center of Excellence.

Fernandez-Araoz, C., Iqbal, S., & Ritter, J. (2015). Leadership lessons from great family businesses. *Harvard Business Review, 4*, 82–88.

Freud, A. (1964). *The ego and the mechanisms of defense*. International Universities Press.

Garelli, S. (2016). *Why you will probably live longer than most big companies. Big companies used to have a lifespan of 61 years, it's now down to 18*. IMD.

Gersick, K. E., Davis, J. A., Hampton, M. M., & Lansberg, I. (1997). *Generation to generation: Life cycles of the family business*. Harvard Business Review Press.

Glavin, B., Astrachan, J. H., & Green, J. (2010). *American family business survey: MassMutual*. Kennesaw State University, Family Firm Institute. MassMutual https://www.massmutual.com/mmfg/pdf/afbs.pdf

Goldsmith, J. M., & Sanders, J. S. (1993). *Milieu therapy*. Psychology Press.

Hall, C., & Astrachan, J. (2015). Study: Customers really do trust family businesses more. *Harvard Business Review Digital Articles*. https://hbr.org/2015/04/study-customers-really-do-trust-family-businesses-more

Hayden, J. (2021, January 5). *Family-owned businesses*. INC Newsletters. https://www.inc.com/encyclopedia/family-owned-businesses.html

Jain, A., Thukral, S., & Paul, J. (2023). Role of socioemotional wealth (SEW) in the internationalisation of family firms. *International Journal of Entrepreneurial Behavior & Research, 29*(1), 1–26. https://doi.org/10.1108/IJEBR-12-2021-0961

Kaslow, F. W., & Friedland, L. (2021). *Consultation to family business enterprises: An international perspective*. Springer.

Keefe, P. R. (2021). *Empire of pain: The secret history of the Sackler dynasty*. Anchor.

Keller, M. N., & Noone, R. J. (Eds.). (2020). *Handbook of Bowen family systems theory and research methods: A systems model for family research*. Routledge.

König, A., Kammerlander, N., & Enders, A. (2013). The family innovator's dilemma: How family influence affects the adoption of discontinuous technologies by incumbent firms. *Academy of Management Review, 38*(3), 418–441. https://doi.org/10.5465/amr.2011.0162

Lee, C. J., Lee, C. Y., & Wu, H. L. (2017). Entrepreneurial behavior in family business: The investigation on the relationship among steward-like managers, explorative orientation and new product development. *NTU Management Review, 27*(4). https://doi.org/10.6226/NTUMR.2017.MAY.A103-012

Levinson, H. (1971). Conflicts that plague family businesses. *Harvard Business Review, 3*, 21–28. https://hbr.org/1971/03/conflicts-that-plague-family-businesses

Meinert, D. (2018). Why trust matters at work. *Society for Human Resource Management, 24*, 2018. https://www.shrm.org/topics-tools/news/hr-magazine/trust-matters-work

Mukarram, S. S., Ajmal, T., & Saeed, A. (2018). Women directors' propensity towards risk in technology firms. *Corporate Governance: The International Journal of Business in Society, 18*(2), 353–367. https://doi.org/10.1108/CG-09-2017-0213

Pomerantz, M. F. (2023). *People vs. Donald Trump: An inside account*. Simon & Schuster.

Poza, E. J. (2013). *Family business (4th Ed)*. Cengage Learning.

Puzo, M. (1969). *The godfather: Mario Puzo's mafia series*. Fawcett Publications.

Reuters. (2024, June 13). Who is Kimbal musk, the tesla director in cowboy hat? *Reuters*.

Rioch, M. J. (1970). The work of Wilfred bion on groups. *Psychiatry, 33*(1), 56–66. https://doi.org/10.1080/00332747.1970.11023613

Rondi, E., de Massis, A., & Kolar, J. (2019). Unlocking innovation potential: A typology of family business innovation postures and the critical role of the family system. *Journal of Family Business Strategy, 101*(4). https://doi.org/10.1016/JJFBS2017.12.001

Sheridan, T. & Linson, J., (2018, June 20). *Yellowstone* (American TV series, Seasons 1–5). Paramount Network. (Cf. *1883* and *1923* by the same creative team).

Sirkin, M. I. (2004, February). Consulting opportunities with family businesses. In *Half-day seminar for the Society for Consulting Psychology (div. 13, APA), midwinter conference.*
Sirkin, M. I. (2020). *The secret life of corporations: Understanding the true nature of business (2nd Ed.).* iUniverse.
Stewart, J. B., & Abrams, R. (2024). *Unscripted: The epic battle for a media empire and the Redstone family legacy*. Penguin.
Tagiuri, R., & Davis, J. A. (1992). On the goals of successful family companies. *Family Business Review, 5*(1), 43–62. https://doi.org/10.1111/j.1741-6248.1992.00043.x
Tagiuri, R., & Davis, J. (1996). Bivalent attributes of the family firm. *Family Business Review, 9*(2), 199–208. https://doi.org/10.1111/j.1741-6248.1996.00199.x
United Nations. (2021). *UN conference on trade and development*. Author.

Mark I. Sirkin, PhD, is a clinical psychologist and management consultant. He is a senior/board level advisor to several companies and has completed post-doctoral work in organizational consulting. He has written numerous articles and two books, *The secret life of corporations: Understanding the true nature of business* (2004; 2nd Edition, 2020) and *Regain your balance: At work, with family, in life* (2016). He is a past president of the Society of Consulting Psychology, Division 13 of the American Psychological Association (APA); a Fellow of the APA; and a member of APA's Council of Representatives. He teaches at Long Island University where he is Interim Director of the Doctoral Program in Psychology (PSYD).

Chapter 8
Navigating Love Across the Political Spectrum

Nadine J. Kaslow, Samantha C. Patton, and Kallio Hunnicutt-Ferguson

Navigating Love Across the Political Spectrum

Political events can impact people's physical health, psychological well-being, relationships, and engagement in community action (Ford et al., 2023; Smith et al., 2019). The extent to which politics are central in people's lives ebbs and flows and is most evident during divisive periods in history (e.g., Vietnam War, 9/11, Black Lives Matter) and times of societal transformation (e.g., civil rights movement, feminist movement) (Farber, 2018). Several recent events highlight the connection between politics and psychological well-being. The 2016 U.S. presidential election was associated with stress and distress (depression, anxiety, PTSD), political polarization, and civic activism in the United States (U.S.) (American Psychological Association, 2017; Baum-Baicker, 2020; Hagan et al., 2018; Krupenkin et al., 2019; Simchon et al., 2020). This was particularly true for individuals who are Black, Indigenous, and Other People of Color (BIPOC); female-identifying; and/or LGBTQ+ (Hagan et al., 2018; Krupenkin et al., 2019; Lannutti & Paz Galupo, 2019; Mukhopadhyay, 2022). Several subsequent events (e.g., COVID-19 pandemic, 2020 election) similarly impacted the nation, with Democrats and individuals from marginalized groups reporting greater effects (Bock & Schnabel, 2022; Mukhopadhyay, 2022; Olatunji et al., 2022). The physical and psychological difficulties (e.g., exhaustion, hopelessness, anger) and relationship challenges experienced by many in response to these events have persisted (Lee, 2018; Pew Research Center, 2023). Increased political polarization and the related social and traditional media barrage have led to people's political and personal identification becoming more closely aligned, the emotional impacts of the political landscape increasingly

N. J. Kaslow (✉) · S. C. Patton · K. Hunnicutt-Ferguson
Emory University, Atlanta, GA, USA
e-mail: nkaslow@emory.edu; samantha.patton@emory.edu; kallio.hunnicutt-ferguson@emory.edu

F. W. Kaslow (ed.), *Contemporary Issues in Individual, Couple, and Family Lives and Treatment*, https://doi.org/10.1007/978-3-031-90006-8_8

taking center stage, and politics being more focal in individual psychotherapy with youth and adults (Mason & Wronski, 2018; McCarthy & Saks, 2019; Messing & Westwood, 2014; Prout et al., 2019; Solomonov & Barber, 2018; Spangler et al., 2017).

These political feuds and culture wars have challenged couples/families like never before (Lee, 2018; McCarthy & Saks, 2019; Safer, 2019), resulting in problems communicating and both emotional disconnection from and hostility toward loved ones (Lee, 2018; Yu et al., 2023). Many have turned to the media for guidance on navigating partisan politics in their relationships with partners, children, parents, siblings, and extended family (Safer, 2019). Couples/families with major political differences increasingly are presenting to therapy hoping to communicate better, resolve conflicts, regain peace in their relationships, and feel more intimate with loved ones (McCarthy & Saks, 2019). We begin this chapter by reviewing the impact of political similarities and differences on couples/families. After offering an approach for assessing politics and their impact on couples/families, we detail interventions for addressing politics and their consequences on relationships and dynamics, protecting and restoring intimate relationships when possible, and assisting couples/families when restoration is not possible. We then provide a case vignette that highlights key therapeutic strategies. Finally, we explore the effects on couple/family therapists of navigating intrafamilial political discord in their work.

Family Dynamics and Politics

This section summarizes the literature on the association between politics and couple/family relationships, with attention to units characterized by both political similarity and dissimilarity.

Political Similarities in Couples/Families

Many couples have shared political perspectives (i.e., homogamy), a finding explained by theories of assortative mating, assimilation, social homogamy, and mate selection based on politics (Goode et al., 2021; Iyengar et al., 2018). A recent statistic indicated that only 3% of adults in the U.S. are married to a partner who supports an opposing political party, with cross-political marriages accounting for only 6% of all marriages (Fisk & Fraga, 2020, August 13). Some people intentionally seek a partner who shares their political views (Fisk & Fraga, 2020, August 13; Iyengar et al., 2018) and others are less drawn to a potential partner when they discover someone does not share their politics (Mallinas et al., 2018). Some studies demonstrate that over time partners have a bidirectional influence on each other's political leanings (Kan & Heath, 2006), such that differences become attenuated over the course of the relationship. In addition, s*ome recent studies reveal that* *partners who are similar politically are more satisfied in their romantic relationships and more involved politically than partners with politically dissimilar views* (Peacock & Pederson, 2022). However, not all studies find greater relationship adjustment or commitment when both parties vote the same way (Fangmeier et al., 2020).

Politics also affect families. Families in which all members hold similar key political values report better relational quality, more closeness, and less conflict (Buyukcan-Tetik et al., 2023). Family units serve as a major context for political socialization (Goode et al., 2021); 81% of Republican and 89% of Democratic leaning parents have teenagers who describe themselves as aligned with the same party as their parents (Cooperman, 2023). Genetic and environmental factors separately and gene–environment interactions account for young people's development of political attitudes (Willoughby et al., 2021). One major environmental contributor is parental political orientation and beliefs; political discussions within the family promote intergenerational transmission of political views and serve as pressure for children to conform to their parents' political attitudes (Iyengar et al., 2018). In addition, in 2016 as compared to 1958, more Democrats (60% versus 33%) and Republicans (63% versus 25%) wanted their children to marry someone who supports the same political party (Enochs, 2017). Families with some common political ground are more willing to talk about politics than are families with marked differences (Oliphant, 2018).

Political Differences in Couples/Families

Political differences often lay the groundwork for ongoing tension in couples, especially during the past decade when many people's political identities are central to their overall identities (Goode et al., 2021). Even couples that voted for the same candidate or share a political persuasion note distance or tension when their reactions to a political decision or sociopolitical event differ (Gabriele-Black et al., 2021). Voting differently than one's partner in the 2016 election stressed many romantic relationships and made it challenging for couples to prioritize ongoing relationship maintenance, which in turn led to increased conflict and stress (Afifi et al., 2020). Marked political disagreements related to this election led 11% of couples to dissolve their relationships, a statistic that rose to 22% among millennials (Wakefield Research, 2017). Importantly, couples invested in ongoing relationship maintenance, even when they voted differently, had less stress related to Trump's presidency, less conflict and relational strain, and greater communal orientation and relational resilience (Afifi et al., 2020).

Political differences within the family and with extended family members are common and influence family interactions (Afifi et al., 2020; Yu et al., 2023). Recent election outcomes changed relationships among family members who voted differently (Gabriele-Black et al., 2021). Following the 2016 presidential election, 39% of families in the U.S. chose not to discuss politics during the holidays (Oliphant &

Smith, 2016). Similar findings emerged in 2018; 40% of families planned to avoid political discussions at Thanksgiving and those willing to discuss politics often reported common ground with others in their family (Oliphant, 2018). There are countless reports of people being "unfriended" by loved ones and/or "unfriending" people close to them on social media due to political differences following the election (Lannutti & Paz Galupo, 2019; Safer, 2019). Many political differences with family members have longstanding effects, with people distancing themselves often out of anger or pain and some relationships becoming permanently ruptured. *Such ruptures often occur when people conclude others' politics reflect not only their attitudes and beliefs but also their character.*

In families impacted by the political divide, conflicts about other politicized situations may reduce overall levels of communication. For example, young people tend to avoid political discussions with parents and/or friends whose views they perceive to be different from their own (Levinson & Yndigegn, 2015). Further, disagreements related to politics negatively impact communication patterns, leading to greater dysfunction within the unit and a lower sense of shared family identity (Warner et al., 2021; Yu et al., 2023). Themes of power and control often are pervasive in families where there are marked political differences and these interpersonal dynamics further fuel anxiety and conflict (Goode et al., 2021). T*hese communication challenges can be mitigated when family members express love and care, respect divergent political views, and discuss differences openly* (Peacock & Pederson, 2022; Warner et al., 2021; Yu et al., 2023).

Assessment

Interventions need to be informed by best practices for systemic assessment that explore couple/family structure and life cycle stage, social identities and sociocultural contexts, attachment bonds, emotion expression, decision-making, power dynamics, communication styles, relational strengths and family resources, areas of agreement and disagreement, and prior steps taken to resolve difficulties (Gurman et al., 2015; Rajendrakumar et al., 2023). Assessment practices in the current political context should include gathering information about each member's political views and the history of political similarities and differences within the system. When noteworthy differences in political beliefs are present, their relevance to the couple/family's functioning and presenting problems should be explored by examining when differences emerged, the meaning of the political differences to each person, and the impact of the differences on each person and the unit. Areas of political alignment should be identified, the significance and meaning of these areas of common ground should be explored, and the way the couple/family navigates political differences should also be assessed. For example, do they avoid conflict including that related to politics, embrace their differences, debate respectfully, or believe that having similar views is non-negotiable? The impact of political differences on couple/family dynamics and the relevance of these differences to the therapeutic work should be determined collaboratively and goals set accordingly.

Interventions

Although politics typically have been ignored in psychotherapy, political themes are more often emerging in couples/family therapy and more couples/families are seeking therapy when politics cause them difficulties. This section details interventions that can be used to minimize the negative impact of political divides within the couple/family unit and with the community and foster more positive intrafamilial interactions.

Build and Maintain a Strong Therapeutic Alliance with all Members of the Couple/Family

Key to effective couple/family interventions related to love across the political divide is forming and maintaining a productive therapeutic relationship with all members of the system. This requires the couple/family therapist to be attuned to the differential impact of their own intersecting identities (e.g., age, gender, race/ethnicity, sexual orientation, veteran status) on each member of the system (Bodnar, 2018) given that social identities often are linked to politics (West & Iyengar, 2022). Since therapist-client similarity is associated with stronger therapeutic alliances (Solomonov & Barber, 2018, 2019), the therapist must be cognizant of their alignment with members of the couple/family with whom they share similar political views and any biases they may have against those individuals with whom they have more political disagreement. They must be intentional about capitalizing on their similarities with each member of the couple/family and about managing biases that could interfere with progress.

One complex aspect of the therapeutic alliance pertains to abandoning neutrality and sharing one's own political views as a therapist. *The increased focus in therapy on politics has challenged therapists to be more reflective about their own views, assumptions, and reactions and more thoughtful and intentional in their decisions about self-disclosure.* Previously therapist self-disclosure about topics such as politics was rare and decisions about disclosure depended on the therapist's training, theoretical orientation, and personal predilections, as well as the goals of the therapeutic work. However, the intensely personal nature of contemporary politics has challenged traditional therapeutic norms about self-disclosure (Prout et al., 2019). On the one hand, many therapists believe self-disclosure about emotionally charged topics such as politics should be avoided. They often think that such disclosure could hamper the formation of an alliance and/or lead to a therapeutic rupture, particularly with individuals in the system with whom they have the greatest political differences. As a result, they typically decline to share their views and when such topics are raised tend to refocus the conversation on other aspects of the couple/family's dynamics and challenges. These therapists need to recognize the potential negative consequences of their stance; it can inhibit discussions related to politics that are central to the couple/family dynamics and functioning (Farber, 2018) or fuel inaccurate assumptions based on overt characteristics of the therapist (e.g., therapist aligns with oppressive political groups) on one or more members of the couple/family (Bodnar, 2018). These therapists should state their stance on self-disclosure, including political leanings, at the outset of therapy, even if political preferences are not related to the presenting problem.

On the other hand, it has become increasingly common for individual therapists to participate in political discussions and close to two-thirds (63%) share their own political stance (Solomonov & Barber, 2018). Such self-disclosure in individual therapy, when thoughtful and intentional, is linked to a stronger and more authentic therapeutic alliance, serves as a model of open communication about politics, and facilitates emotional growth (Doherty, 2021; Prout et al., 2019; Solomonov & Barber, 2018, 2019). Yet, little is known about self-disclosure about politics in couples/family therapy. When there is strong political alignment between the therapist and all members of the couple/family system, therapists will likely be prone to share their political views if they have a positive bond with the family (Solomonov & Barber, 2019). However, when the therapist's politics do not align with all members of the system, self-disclosure decisions become more complicated and nuanced. While uneven alliances are problematic and should be avoided (Janusz et al., 2023), thoughtful disclosure by the couples/family therapist has the potential to lead to more productive alliances among members and opportunities for growth for all members of the couple/family and the therapist (Katz, 2003).

Given the potential ramifications of either therapeutic choice, thoughtful clinical judgment should prevail regarding the decision to self-disclose. Regardless of the decision(s) made, the couple/family therapist must highlight the strengths of different members of the couple/family unit and emphasize areas of common ground and use the differing views in the couple/family as a vehicle for developing the capacity to navigate disagreements in social relationships within and beyond the couple/family unit.

Strengthen Bonds within the Couple/Family

Before major conflicts about politics and the couple/family's decision to seek treatment, there was likely a period in which the couple/family felt they were in a better place and had positive bonds with one another. Focusing on the strong attachments the unit has already established can be the start to finding or being reminded of common ground and shared values that already exist, and rediscovering joy and pleasure in their interactions with one another. Several strategies can be utilized to strengthen bonds within the couple/family.

The couple/family can be encouraged to prioritize ongoing maintenance of the relationship to reduce conflict and stress and bolster their capacity to navigate challenges (Afifi et al., 2020; Mazur et al., 2023). Relationship maintenance refers to enhancing and repairing aspects of the relationship that threaten each member's sense of relational stability and satisfaction (Ogolsky et al., 2017). Techniques that support relationship maintenance include shifting from an individualistic to a collectivist view, expressing gratitude, communicating effectively, and engaging in joint activities. Below, we detail interventions related to three of these themes; effective communication is elaborated on in a subsequent section of this chapter.

Interventions designed to facilitate a shift from an individualistic to a collectivist mentality aim to move members away from thinking primarily about themselves ("I," "me") to thinking about the "us" and "we" (Ogolsky et al., 2017). The "we" mentality can serve to strengthen bonds that enable the couple/family to rise above their political and values differences and focus on shared goals (Seshadri & Knudson-Martin, 2013). Such bonds require loyalty, a sense of friendship, and an investment in working together and communicating over time. The therapist can convey that such interdependence strengthens the sense of interconnection within the couple/family unit and benefits each individual member. One major intervention to promote the shift to a collectivist mentality involves helping the couple/family find common ground, as a shared reality related to beliefs, feelings, and concerns about the world is associated with more positive interactions (Bar-Shachar & Bar-Kalifa, 2021). The therapist may help them reflect on and understand underlying emotions (e.g., fears of rejection or self-protection) driving offensive or aggressive responses and shift toward connecting on underlying shared values (Fisher, October 2020). Moreover, common ground enables members of the couple/family to communicate more effectively, collaborate, feel closer to one another, and find mutually beneficial ways to navigate differences. Finding common ground can be accomplished by facilitating discussions among members of the couple/family about their shared values rather than specific political views, which can help center areas of agreement and foster connection. With regard to political differences, helping the couple/family differentiate each member from the political figure or party they support may be particularly helpful (Fisher, October 2020). Even if commonalties cannot be found related to political values and experiences, commonalities in other domains based on an appreciation of shared humanity (i.e., deep caring for all human beings) can be identified (McFarland et al., 2013) and then capitalized upon. Clarification of expectations, values, and shared identities can reduce conflict related to political differences (Fangmeier et al., 2020). *Efforts to guide people to find common ground also need to underscore the importance of agreeing to disagree.* The couple/family may need to be reminded that there are times the most prudent course of action is to accept that no one in the system can change anyone else's mind and stop the debate. They can be encouraged to move forward with a respectful recognition that loved ones have the right to espouse a different view and an appreciation of their shared attitudes and viewpoints.

Systemically oriented interventions to increase gratitude can bolster well-being including happiness at the individual and couple/family levels as well as relational satisfaction (Gordon et al., 2011; Kirca et al., 2023; Waters, 2020). Specific interventions from positive psychology that show promise with couples/families are gratitude journaling; writing, sharing, and receiving of gratitude letters; and gratitude visits in which loved ones discuss gratitude letters they received (Gordon et al., 2011; Seligman et al., 2005; Toepfer, 2019). It behooves the couples/family therapist to convey that gratitude is not just a technique, but a way of living and interacting. As such, couples/families should be encouraged to express heartfelt gratitude to one another on a regular basis. Such expressions of gratitude reduce psychological distress and improve life satisfaction for each member of the couple/family and strengthen positive bonds within the unit.

Interventions that emphasize engagement in activities together can lead to increases in communication, relationship satisfaction, and individual well-being (Ogolsky et al., 2017). In couples/families with tension or conflict related to political and associated value differences, creating daily routines in which each person practices self-soothing and relaxation can ameliorate some of the stress. Couples/families can be encouraged to practice mindfulness to the present moment as a couple/family, share in mindfulness practice, and redirect attention away from worries about the future or things that are out of their control (Rajendrakumar et al., 2023). Mindful attunement to each family member's inner states, particularly negative thoughts and emotions, may be helpful for couples/families navigating challenging political differences that are contributing to difficulty with emotion regulation (Brody et al., 2018).

Improve Communication in Support of Meaningful Dialogue

To help couples/families connect across political lines, therapy often needs to prioritize meaningful dialogue that it is supportive and loving, respectful, and authentic (Israel, 2020; Peacock & Pederson, 2022; Warner et al., 2021; Yu et al., 2023). This requires therapists to provide a context for safe, mindfully structured dialogues and offer guidance and skill-building (Israel, 2020; Lee, 2018; Schneider, 2020). This entails providing people the tools to foster productive communication about political differences, as meaningful dialogue enables all parties to feel heard, promotes understanding and flexibility rather than defensiveness, and fosters closeness (Lee, 2018). Interventions to improve the couple/family's capacity for constructive dialogue related to difficult subjects must build on the ways in which they already communicate effectively. With practice, the couple/family can integrate such conversations into their lives. Below we detail a five-step process for promoting meaningful dialogue.

Five-Step Process

The first step relates to preparing for meaningful conversations by creating a safe and brave environment conducive to sharing. This involves facilitating the couple/family's *development of an agreement about ground rules for conversations* so all parties remain civil and respectful, speak from their own experience, do their best to manage their own emotional discomfort, and approach conversations with integrity and grace (Israel, 2020). In the preparation phase, couples/families can be guided in developing a shared appreciation of the facilitators and barriers to effective communication and creating a plan to optimize the facilitators and mitigate the barriers. They can be encouraged to reflect on and articulate their goals for communicating about political differences, which may include fighting about them, persuading others to change their mind, discussing politics respectfully and with an acceptance of differences, and/or seeking common ground (i.e., ascertaining similarities in their personal or political values as well as hopes, fears, goals, interests, likes, dislikes, and experiences) (Israel, 2020). Therapy is only likely to help with the latter goals if all parties can agree, whereas the former goals typically are associated with increased discord and dissatisfaction.

The next step is counseling each person to talk about their differences in a way that promotes listening and breaks down, rather than puts up, barriers (Lee, 2018). One pertinent skillset is modulating one's own emotions, given the divisive political climate and implications of political differences. This may involve pausing and attending to one's own sensations, thoughts, and emotions and processing these experiences internally before sharing them; using grounding techniques to calm oneself and focus; and employing strategies to de-escalate conflict or to pause the conversation when it becomes overwhelming with the goal of returning to the discussion when the emotional intensity has reduced (Israel, 2020). A second critical skill is using "I" statements when sharing internal experiences in an emotionally modulated manner. This skill directs parties away from attempting to mind read or assume what the other may be feeling and instead encourages clear communication of each person's thoughts and emotions. A third skill is storytelling, a powerful way to help other people gain a different perspective (Lee, 2018). Sharing stories related to one's views can break down barriers to communication and closeness and set the groundwork for greater self-reflection and openness to other perspectives.

The third step is emphasizing active, mindful, and compassionate listening to others' thoughts, feelings, and beliefs. This involves teaching people to listen strategically in an effort to understand others' perspectives and help others feel safe and heard (Israel, 2020; Lee, 2018). This entails focusing intently and fully on others' thoughts and feelings, being curious and inquisitive about others' priorities and beliefs in a manner that is sensitive and sincere, being nonjudgmental about others' views and reactions, learning about why others have their beliefs, and assuming others have positive intentions (Stewart & Silvers, 2019).

A fourth step is teaching people to respond sensitively to what others share. This involves focusing on conveying active attention nonverbally, reflecting back what is heard, and asking open-ended questions (Israel, 2020). It entails guiding people to respond to disclosures with curiosity, openness, compassion, grace, and a collaborative spirit rather than with passive agreement, stonewalling, attack, criticism, contempt, or defensiveness (Bar-Shachar & Bar-Kalifa, 2021; Stewart & Silvers, 2019). It helps if the therapist encourages the couple/family orient away from ongoing conflict and distress about politics and toward shared values.

The fifth step is supporting the couple/family in mutual discourse that is respectful, open, and reflects genuine curiosity, key communication accommodation strategies for individuals and systems impacted by political differences (Stewart & Silvers, 2019; Warner et al., 2021). Such discourse can be facilitated by encouraging all parties to pause from their maladaptive communication patterns related to politics; reflect on their thoughts, feelings, and behaviors; and consider the factors shaping their actions, reactions, and perceptions (Schneider, 2020). The couple/family can be urged to share these insights, listen actively to others' views, and become comfortable with being uncomfortable in such dialogues (Stewart & Silvers, 2019). The therapist may normalize differences in political views or values, noting that these do not have to threaten the bonds within the system. If couples/families express concerns that relational bonds have been disrupted, this must be explored, and the couple/family can be guided in protecting the positive aspects of their relationship from areas of strong disagreement. *Interventions fostering respect for different values must help people accept, tolerate, and detach when necessary from views that differ from their own rather than attempt to coerce others to change their minds* (Rajendrakumar et al., 2023). For discourse to support productive communication and positive change, each person must reflect on their contributions and the underlying personal and interpersonal dynamics, use these insights to be more compassionate toward themselves and others, and commit to more genuine and loving interactions (Safer, 2019).

Navigate Conflict

Critical to effective communication is navigating conflicts, including those related to political differences. Conflicts are normal and expectable as no two people share all the same opinions. Conflict becomes problematic when couples/families have too many conflicts, no conflicts, or fail to handle conflicts constructively. Problematic conflict management (e.g., threatening or instituting family cut-offs) negatively impacts individuals within the couple/family system and the system itself. Conversely, couples/families that resolve conflict constructively have more positive bonds, are more cooperative and collaborative, and are more satisfied with their relationships. Thus, therapists need to guide couples/families in managing conflicts, rather than avoiding, getting stuck in them, or trying to eliminate them fully (Gottman, 2015).

These therapeutic efforts most often include the adaptive communication techniques detailed above. They also involve encouraging members of the couple/family to communicate their perspectives as completely and calmly as possible, using "I" statements, requesting that their needs be responded to respectfully, and being open to learning about others' views and diffusing conflict (Fisher, 2020). *Conflict management also entails teaching people to move from gridlock to dialogue, in which people accept their differences and agree to disagree while still keeping lines of communication open* (Gottman, 2015). This requires helping people to alternate as speaker and listener so they each communicate clearly and honestly and listen with interest and without judgment. The couple/family can also be assisted in anticipating and managing strong emotions that hinder productive dialogue and reduce openness to alternative points of view (Weeks, 2015) and encouraged to identify areas for compromise. When couples/families listen actively and communicate openly, they can resolve their conflicts in a healthy manner.

Several additional therapeutic strategies can be employed when the focus is the effective navigation of tensions, including those related to politics. *One critical strategy is learning to protect the positive qualities of the couple/family from the disagreements about politics* (Fangmeier et al., 2020; Gabriele-Black et al., 2021). This might include helping them appreciate that relationship strengths may be best preserved if they can agree upon an approach for handling their political differences, whether that be limiting political conversations, orienting discussions around shared values, addressing political themes in an ongoing manner, or setting boundaries about where/when/how politics will be discussed and determining situations in which such conversations are off limits (e.g., *politics free-zones*). The advantages and challenges of each approach should be examined. Incorporating principles of positive reinforcement in which couples/families deliberately recognize positive interactions with one another may be useful (Scott et al., 2019). Further, couples/families may be reminded of the strong foundation of their relationship(s) and how these foundations outlast any presidential administration. Finally, it can be useful to point out why the difficult work of communicating optimally to manage conflicts related to politics and associated values is worth the effort (Fisher, October 2020).

Pivotal to promoting couples'/families' capacity to navigate conflict is the *use of humility*, which can help bridge conflicts when political disagreements are present and can be a formidable antidote to resentment and animosity (Leary et al., 2017; Porter & Schumann, 2018). There are several ways in which people can be guided to convey such humility. This includes being mindful of their own words, body language, and actions; acknowledging their own fallibility; expressing appreciation for the others' knowledge and points of view; and respecting differences (Porter & Schumann, 2018). It also entails expressing respect, admiration, and gratitude for members of the couple/family unit regardless of political affiliation (Gordon et al., 2011; Warner et al., 2021). Fostering a growth mindset is key to increasing intellectual humility and unlocking the associated benefits (Porter & Schumann, 2018). Those able to recognize the limits of their own knowledge while appreciating their family member's intellectual strengths are more open to learning about opposing views during disagreements (Porter & Schumann, 2018).

Encouraging couples/families to agree to fight fairly (i.e., handle and resolve differences and conflicts so all parties feel respected, heard, and valued) is critical for optimal management of political conflicts. This involves agreeing on ground rules, communicating needs and having these needs recognized, articulating positions respectfully, and problem-solving collaboratively. *The value of fair fighting should be underscored*; such fighting can preserve and strengthen relationships and improve people's well-being. The therapist can provide a structure for allowing all parties to express their needs respectfully that includes determining ground rules for fights such as agreeing upon a time to talk, creating safety, focusing on the present and future rather than the past, coming to a shared understanding, and having a solution oriented focus (Lebow, 2019). These ground rules need to indicate unacceptable behaviors such as criticism, insults, name calling, degrading language, stonewalling, yelling, threats to end the relationship, or violence or threats of violence. Strategies for fighting fairly about political differences can be discussed and practiced. These may include scheduling challenging conversations, setting "fair fight" boundaries, using "I" statements, taking turns speaking and listening without interruption, discussing one issue at a time, taking responsibility for one's actions, agreeing to disagree, repairing ruptures (i.e., something happens and the other person/people feel misunderstood, hurt, angry, scared, or sad and as a result there is relational disconnection), finding a solution best for all parties, and moving forward and forgiving after reaching a resolution. If political disagreements become too intense, couples/families may need to include agreeing to take a "time out" to get physical space and calm themselves down and allow emotions to lessen in intensity before re-engaging in the conversation. The couple/family may need support accepting that healthy relationships do not require perfect agreement, but rather that what is key is compromising or agreeing to disagree and apologizing for mistakes made or harming others in the system.

One final strategy for couples/families invested in in-depth work relates to addressing unresolved past emotional and attachment injuries triggered by politics (Gottman, 2015; Johnson et al., 2001). This means talking about resentments from prior relationships that involved breaches of trust in a manner that allows all parties to better comprehend the perspectives of others involved. It entails taking responsibility and apologizing for the ways they hurt the other person/people and engaging in a path toward relational healing based on the needs of each party.

Moving Forward when Respectful Discourse Is Not a Shared Goal or Attachments Appear Irrevocably Ruptured

Unfortunately, some couples/families seek therapy when a relationship is beyond repair. This typically occurs when respectful discourse and understanding are not a shared goal, bonds have been irrevocably ruptured due to fundamental and irreconcilable differences in political views that feel harmful to one or more parties, and/or one or more parties believes positive change is not possible. In such situations, the couple/family often is engaged in cycles of fighting and conflict that are tearing the unit apart, avoiding political topics and related values in a way that leads to coldness and distance, or vacillating between these poles. For couples, when maintaining or deepening the relationship is no longer the shared goal, the therapist should assist them in the grieving process. This involves honoring the good that came from the relationship and expressing appreciation for what they each received, offering forgiveness for the hurt and pain that has been caused, receiving emotional support outside the relationship, and gaining confidence in moving forward separately. This process needs to be nuanced when there are children as there need to be decisions about coparenting and shared responsibilities. For families that seek therapy under these circumstances, estrangement is an option, but rarely one that is healthy. Family units unresponsive to the strategies detailed above may best be served by setting firm boundaries such as agreeing not to communicate about politics, interacting in ways that can be safe and positive even if limited, prioritizing self-care, grieving the closeness that existed previously, and expanding their social networks or finding a new community for meaningful connection.

Case Study: Keith and Golden

Keith and Golden presented to couples therapy in 2020 after a period of conflict in their marriage. Keith didn't understand why Golden planned to vote for Trump in the upcoming election, especially as a Black man. Keith felt scared for his own future as a man of color, their safety as a Black gay male couple, and their adopted daughter's future as an international adoptee. Golden claimed that Keith was overreactive about their political differences and that they should just agree to disagree. The assessment focused on the couples' sociocultural contexts, power dynamics, communication styles, and areas of agreement and disagreement. It revealed that Keith and Golden were using problematic conflict management tactics when they disagreed. They had grown distant and were struggling to have meaningful conversations or fun together. This had made parenting incredibly difficult. The therapist and couple collaboratively identified the following goals for couples therapy: reducing conflict, increasing communication, and re-engaging in pleasurable activities as a couple and a family.

At the outset of the couples therapy, Keith and Golden agreed to the following ground rules: expressing their own thoughts and feelings using "I statements," asking questions rather than assuming what the other is thinking or feeling, not triangulating their daughter, and not threatening to end the relationship while actively engaged in treatment. To begin to rebuild and strengthen their positive connection with one another, they were encouraged to find a neutral activity to do together weekly as well as an activity to do as a family once per week. They responded well to these assignments and quickly began spending more positive time together.

However, they reported that as soon as topics arose related to political differences, they started arguing or Golden would try to exit the interaction. In response, the therapist encouraged them to schedule times to have these conversations in a comfortable place, give each other their undivided attention, make eye contact, use "I statements" when expressing their perspectives and feelings, invite each other to share their perceptions using open-ended questions, listen to their partner without interrupting, ask clarifying questions, and reflect back what their partner disclosed. During sessions, the therapist invited Keith and Golden to talk about relatively small political differences using these same strategies. In addition, the therapist encouraged them to explore relational issues potentially linked to the political differences that were focal.

As the couple became more facile communicating effectively about their political differences, attention turned to facilitating the couples' efforts to identify areas of common ground and shared values. They both reported caring deeply about their daughter and about the relationship, though both felt their partner had become more radical in their thinking over time and wondered if they "know each other" anymore. Keith and Golden felt closer when focusing on areas of common ground and ultimately decided it was best not to discuss politics and Trump in particular. They agreed to focus on shared values such as contributing to others through acts of service, time with their daughter, and their faith. Having reasonably good success in reaching their goals of improving communication, limiting arguments around their daughter, and feeling closer to each other, they chose to take a break from therapy.

However, as the 2024 election drew near, they recontacted their therapist as they were finding it challenging to keep politics out of their conversations and were feeling more distant. After gathering pertinent information, the therapist offered three options for proceeding: (1) refocusing the couples' attention on shared values and quality time; (2) developing better conflict management skills; and/or (3) strengthening their attachment bonds. Keith and Golden agreed they could easily commit to re-engaging in the positive efforts that had helped before and be more intentional in using the skills they had amassed to fight fairly. They thought multiculturally informed exploratory work would be key to their healing and emotional progress as individuals and as a couple. As of the writing of this chapter, they are embarked on a journey together to understand how their family of origin and prior relationship attachment dynamics along with their experiences of systemic racism and mounting anti-LGBTQ and anti-immigrant sentiments laid the foundation for the negative interactions causing them relationship distress. The therapist is helping them restructure their interactions, including those related to politics, by attending to trust dynamics in their therapeutic relationship based on differences in social identities, appreciating the historic and ongoing oppression and discrimination the couple encounter related to their intersecting social identities, and integrating cultural views about emotion expression and vulnerability. This restructuring involves the couple sharing their attachment vulnerabilities and needs, being emotionally attuned and supportive, and mitigating barriers that impede their being respectful and compassionate. Keith and Golden report feeling more securely attached to each other, more able to share their vulnerabilities and receive comfort from their partner, better able to solve problems creatively, and more positively connected to their family and friends. They are excited to enter the third stage of this course of culturally sensitive emotion-focused couples therapy, which they hope will enable them to be more resilient and feel more empowered in their relationship, their interactions with others, and in the multiple communities in which they are embedded (Johnson, 2004; Nightingale et al., 2019).

The Impact on Couples/Family Therapists of the Current Political Climate

Many therapists experience stress and distress related to politics and feel powerless and helpless in affecting change in policies and practices (McCarthy et al., 2022; Spangler et al., 2017; Winter, 2021). These responses are intensified when working with couples/families with high levels of conflict or disconnection related to politics as the therapist is likely aligned more with one party/subsystem and in conflict with one party/subsystem. In addition, therapists often struggle with ethical challenges such as determining the boundaries related to politics in the context of the therapy, working competently with people whose views differ markedly from their own, addressing discriminatory political views expressed in the therapeutic context, navigating tensions between ethics and the law, and appreciating that therapy is inherently "political" despite its historically limited focus in training or professional circles (Coren, 2018; Winter, 2021). It is incumbent upon therapists to recognize their own political triggers and be attuned to the impact of their associated reactions on therapeutic relationships. Embracing a stance of humility and focusing on the couples/families' strengths can facilitate therapists' efforts to modulate their emotions when providing therapy to couples/families with differing political beliefs from their own (McCarthy et al., 2022). Peer supervision and consultation and personal therapy are excellent mechanisms for gaining relevant self-awareness, understanding how biases influence one's therapeutic work, making decisions about navigating politics in therapy and addressing the related complexities, and ascertaining when political differences make the therapeutic relationship untenable (McCarthy et al., 2022; Spangler et al., 2017).

Therapists need to decide how much conversations about politics are part of the joining process when the couple/family raises the topic, the extent to which the focus should shift from politics to similarities and differences among members' thoughts and feelings about the political topics at hand, and when, if at all, they should discourage discussion about politics. Regardless of the extent to which political content is focal in the therapy, the therapist can validate the fears, desires, and values underlying the differences occurring in the couple/family (Fisher, 2020).

Given the intense nature of political conversations in couple/family therapy, particularly when therapists' views differ markedly from one or more members of a couple/family or views are espoused that the therapist finds to be upsetting or aggressive, therapists must prioritize self-care. Each therapist needs to discover their own balance between engaging in activating self-care (i.e., increases heart rate) such as exercising or learning about/addressing causes that matter versus de-activating self-care (i.e., reduces heart rate) such as unplugging, meditating, or setting boundaries around consuming politically divisive media (Spangler et al., 2017).

Finally, many therapists have discovered that being *citizen professionals* empowers them in the face of stress and disillusionment and gives them a sense of meaning (Doherty, 2020). Citizen professionals are leaders in their communities who contribute to improving the lives and well-being of others in the community (local, national, global) through roles that go beyond their typical work responsibilities

(Henderson Daniel et al., 2021). They find and connect with communities with shared values and engage with them in making a difference. Such engagement is an excellent antidote to the despair and hopelessness experienced by so many therapists.

Concluding Comments

Political polarization is tearing our nation asunder. It is having a devastating impact on individuals, including therapists, as well as couples/families (Spangler et al., 2017). Respect, dignity, and compassion have been overshadowed by anger, hostility, and hatred. Fortunately, we have an impressive armamentarium of practical tools to assist couples/families in protecting and strengthening their intimate relationships.

Couples/family therapy can be invaluable for strengthening bonds and fostering meaningful dialogue across political lines (Lee, 2018). Couples/families skilled at navigating a multitude of differences, including those related to politics, can function well and enjoy interacting. Such effective management of differences occurs when there are strong attachment bonds and a genuine commitment to the relationships within the unit (couple, family) (Fangmeier et al., 2020). Therapists can guide most couples/families to more optimally connect across the political divides that influence their relationships. This involves providing guidance and a framework for couples/families to build upon and improve their positive connections with one another, engage in meaningful and constructive conversations, articulate shared values, find common ground, and acknowledge and accept when common ground cannot be found.

For therapists to provide such interventions, changes need to be made in our training and education systems and professional communities. This requires us to expand our discourse on best practices in navigating politics and associated values in our work as practitioners, educators, and scholars (Spangler et al., 2017). It also means placing greater emphasis on therapists being citizen professionals who partner with members of their community in taking action to address critical problems (Doherty, 2020; Henderson Daniel et al., 2021).

References

Afifi, T. D., Zamanzadeh, N., Harrison, K., & Torrez, D. P. (2020). Explaining the impact of differences in voting patterns on resilience and relational load in romantic relationships during the transition to the trump presidency. *Journal of Social and Personal Relationships, 37*(1), 3–26. https://doi.org/10.1177/0265407519846566

American Psychological Association. (2017). Stress in America: The state of our nation. *Stress in AmericaTM Survey.*

Bar-Shachar, Y., & Bar-Kalifa, E. (2021). Responsiveness processes and daily experiences of shared reality among romantic couples. *Journal of Social and Personal Relationships, 38*(11), 3156–3176. https://doi.org/10.1177/02654075211017675

Baum-Baicker, C. (2020). *Not* fake news: Toxic consequences of the trump stress effect. *Journal of Humanistic Psychology, 60*(6), 730–746. https://doi.org/10.1177/0022167820911757

Bock, S., & Schnabel, L. (2022). Distressed democrats and relaxed republicans? Partisanship and mental health during the COVID-19 pandemic. *PLoS One, 17*(4), e0266562. https://doi.org/10.1371/journal.pone.0266562

Bodnar, S. (2018). November 8, 2016: The day I became a white clinician. *Journal of Clinical Psychology, 74*, 722–729. https://doi.org/10.1002/jclp.22601

Brody, J. L., Scherer, D. G., Turner, C. W., Annett, R. D., & Dalen, J. (2018). A conceptual model and clinical framework for integrating mindfulness into family therapy with adolescents. *Family Process, 57*(2), 510–524. https://doi.org/10.1111/famp.12298

Buyukcan-Tetik, A., Aydin, C., & Eisma, M. C. (2023). Similar minds in the family: COVID-19 centrality and relationship quality. *Personal Relationships, 3*, 806–824. https://doi.org/10.1111/pere.12479

Cooperman, A. (2023). *Most US parents pass along their religion and politics to their children.* Pew Research Center. https://www.pewresearch.org/short-reads/2023/05/10/most-us-parents-pass-along-their-religion-and-politics-to-their-children/

Coren, S. (2018). Mr. trump: How I learned to stop worrying and love the patient-aggressor. *Journal of Clinical Psychology, 74*, 734–742. https://doi.org/10.1002/jclp.22601

Doherty, W. J. (2020). My journey as a citizen therapist. *Journal of Humanistic Psychology, 60*(4), 477–487. https://doi.org/10.1177/002216781989959

Doherty, W. J. (2021). *The ethical lives of clients: Transcending self-interest in psychotherapy.* American Psychological Association.

Enochs, K. (2017). *In US, 'interpolitical' marriage increasingly frowned upon.* Retrieved from https://www.voanews.com/usa/us-interpolitical-marriage-increasingly-frowned-upon

Fangmeier, T. L., Stanley, S. M., Knopp, K., & Rhoades, G. K. (2020). Political party identification and romantic relationship quality. *Couple and Family Psychology: Research and Practice, 9*(3), 167–180. https://doi.org/10.1037/cfp0000141

Farber, B. A. (2018). "clowns to the left of me, jokers to the right": Politics and psychotherapy, 2018. *Journal of Clinical Psychology, 74*, 714–721. https://doi.org/10.1002/jclp.22600

Fisher, L. (October 2020). Empowering relationships despite political divides: How to find and reaffirm shared values. In *Psychotherapy Networker*. Accessed Aug 4, 2024, from https://www.psychotherapynetworker.org/article/empowering-relationships-despite-political-divides/

Fisk, C. A., & Fraga, B. L. (2020). *Til death do us part(isanship): Voting and polarization in opposite-party marriages.* Democracy Fund Voter Stiudy Group. https://www.voterstudygroup.org/publication/til-death-do-us-partisanship

Ford, B. Q., Feinberg, M., Lassetter, B., Thai, S., & Gatchpazian, A. (2023). The political is personal: The costs of daily politics. *Journal of Personality and Social Psychology, 125*(1), 1–28. https://doi.org/10.1037/pspa0000335

Gabriele-Black, K. A., Goldberg, A. E., Manley, M. H., & Frost, R. L. (2021). "life is already hard enough": Lesbian and gay adoptive parents' experiences and concerns after the 2016 presidential election. *Couple and Family Psychology: Research and Practice, 10*(2), 103–123. https://doi.org/10.1037/cfp0000162

Goode, J. R., Knight, K., Denker, K. J., & Cronin-Fisher, V. (2021). Political difference in marriage: Wife's gender linked fate and relational conflict. *Communication Studies, 72*(3), 384–401. https://doi.org/10.1080/10510974.2021.1876128

Gordon, C. L., Arnette, R. A., & Smith, R. E. (2011). Have you thanked your spouse today?: Felt and expressed gratitude among married couples. *Personality and Individual Differences, 50*(3), 339–343. https://doi.org/10.1016/j.paid.2010.10.012

Gottman, J. M. (2015). *The seven principles for making marriage work: A practical guide from the country's foremost relationship expert (Revised edition).* Harmony/Rodale.

Gurman, A. S., Lebow, J. L., & Snyder, D. K. (Eds.). (2015). *Clinical handbook of couple therapy (Fifth edition)*. The Guilford Press.

Hagan, M. J., Sladek, M. R., Luecken, L. J., & Doane, L. D. (2018). Event-related clinical distress in college students: Responses to the 2016 U.S. presidential election. *Journal of American College Health, 68*(1), 21–25. https://doi.org/10.1080/07448481.2018.1515763

Henderson Daniel, J., Rozensky, R. H., Grus, C. L., Brown, K. S., Gómez, C. A., Bruner, L., Crawford, K. A., Hewitt, A., McQuaid, E. L., Mio, J. S., Montalvan, C., Reeb, R. N., Ruiz, A., Sheras, P., Siegel, W., Taylor, J. M., Williams, W., Ameen, E. J., & Andrade, J. (2021). The citizen psychologist curriculum—Preparing psychologists for public service: The 2018 American Psychological Association presidential initiative. *Psychological Services, 18*(3), 328–334. https://doi.org/10.1037/ser0000402

Israel, T. (2020). *Beyond your bubble: How to connect across the political divide*. APA Life Tools.

Iyengar, S., Konitzer, T., & Tedin, K. (2018). The home as a political fortress: Family agreement in an era of polarization. *Journal of Politics, 80*(4), 1326–1338. https://doi.org/10.1086/6989290

Janusz, B., Pawelczyk, P., & Józefik, B. (2023). How therapists respond to "uneven" alliances in couple and family therapy: A conversation-analytic study. *Journal of Marital & Family Therapy, 49*(4), 842–860. https://doi.org/10.1111/jmft.12661

Johnson, S. M. (2004). *The practice of emotionally focused couple therapy* (2nd ed.). Brunner-Routledge.

Johnson, S. M., Makinen, J. A., & Millikin, J. W. (2001). Attachment injuries in couple relationships: A new perspective on impasse in couples therapy. *Journal of Marital & Family Therapy, 27*(2), 145–155. https://doi.org/10.1111/j.1752-0606.2001.tb01152.x

Kan, M. Y., & Heath, A. C. (2006). The political values and choices of husbands and wives. *Journal of Marriage and Family, 68*, 70–86. https://doi.org/10.1111/j.1741-3737.2006.00234.x

Katz, J. M. (2003). Tales of a therapist. *Journal of Couple & Relationship Therapy, 21*, 43–60. https://doi.org/10.1300/J398v02n01_05

Kirca, A. M., Malouff, J., & Meynadier, J. (2023). The effect of expressed gratitude interventions on psychological wellbeing: A meta-analysis of randomised controlled studies. *International Journal of Applied Positive Psychology, 8*, 63–86. https://doi.org/10.1007/s41042-023-00086-6

Krupenkin, M., Rothschild, D., Hill, S. S., & Yom-Tov, E. (2019). President trump stress disorder: Partisanship, ethnicity, and expressive reporting of mental distress after the 2016 election. *SAGE Open, 9*(1). https://doi.org/10.1177/2158244019830865

Lannutti, P. J., & Paz Galupo, M. (2019). *The 2016 US presidential election and the LGBTQ community*. Taylor & Francis Publishing.

Leary, M. R., Diebels, K. J., Davisson, E. K., Jongman-Sereno, K. P., Isherwood, J. C., Raimi, K. T., Deffler, S. A., & Hoyle, R. H. (2017). Cognitive and interpersonal features of intellectual humility. *Personality and Social Psychology Bulletin, 43*(6), 793–813. https://doi.org/10.1177/0146167217697695

Lebow, J. L. (2019). Current issues in the practice of integrative couple and family therapy. *Family Process, 58*(3), 610–628. https://doi.org/10.1111/famp.12473

Lee, J. (2018). *Talking across the divide: How to communicate with people you disagree with and may be even change the world*. Penguin Random House LLC.

Levinson, K., & Yndigegn, C. (2015). Political discussions with family and friends: Exploring the impact of political distance. *The Sociological Review, 63*(Supplement 2), 79–91. https://doi.org/10.1111/1467-954X.12263

Mallinas, S., Crawford, J. R., & Cole, S. (2018). Political opposites do not attract: The effects of ideological dissimiliarity on impression formation. *Journal of Social and Political Psychology, 6*, 49–75. https://doi.org/10.5964/jspp.v6i1.747

Mason, M., & Wronski, J. (2018). One tribe to bind them all: How our social group attachments strengthen partisanship. *Advances in Political Psychology, 39*(1), 257–277. https://doi.org/10.1111/pops.12485

Mazur, A. P., Afifi, T. D., Afifi, W. A., & Haughton, C. N. (2023). The importance of relationship maintenance in marriage at the onset of the COVID-19 pandemic. *Communication Monographs, 90*(4), 522–544. https://doi.org/10.1080/03637751.2023.2235004

McCarthy, K. S., Capone, C., Davidtz, J., & Solomonov, N. (2022). The association between political climate and trainees' supervision experiences and needs. *The Clinical Supervisor, 41*(2), 107–126. https://doi.org/10.1080/07325223.2022.2125918

McCarthy, K. S., & Saks, J. V. (2019). Postelection stress: Symptoms, relationships, and counseling service utilization in clients before and after the 2016 U.S. national election. *Journal of Counseling Psychology, 66*(6), 726–735. https://doi.org/10.1037/cou0000378

McFarland, S., Brown, D., & M., W. (2013). Identification with all humanity as a moral concept and psychological construct. *Current Directions in Psychological Science, 22*, 194–198. https://doi.org/10.1177/0963721412471346

Messing, S., & Westwood, S. J. (2014). Selective exposure in the age of social media: Endorsements trump partisan source affiliation when selecting news online. *Communication Research, 41*(8), 1042–1063. https://doi.org/10.1177/0093650212466406

Mukhopadhyay, S. (2022). Elections have (health) consequences: Depression, anxiety, and the 2020 presidential election. *Economics and Human Biology, 47*, 101191. https://doi.org/10.1016/j.ehb.2022.101191

Nightingale, M., Awosan, C. I., & Stavrianopoulos, K. (2019). Emotionally focused therapy: A culturally sensitive approach for African American heterosexual couples. *Journal of Family Psychotherapy, 30*(3), 221–244. https://doi.org/10.1080/08975353.2019.1666497

Ogolsky, B. G., Monk, J. K., Ric, T. M., Theisen, J. C., & Maniotes, C. R. (2017). Relationship maintenance: A review of research on romantic relationships. *Journal of Family Theory & Review, 9*(3), 275–306. https://doi.org/10.1111/jftr.12205

Olatunji, B. O., Cox, R. C., & Cole, D. (2022). Longitudinal trajectories of coronavirus anxiety and health behavior use before and after the U.S. 2020 presidential election: The effects of political orientation. *Journal of Anxiety Disorders, 92*, 102643. https://doi.org/10.1016/j.janxdis.2022.102643

Oliphant, B. J., & Smith, S. (2016). *How Americans are talking about trump's election in 6 charts*. Pew Research Center. https://www.pewresearch.org/short-reads/2016/12/22/how-americans-are-talking-about-trumps-election-in-6-charts/

Oliphant, J. B. (2018). *Most say their family is OK with discussing politics—but it helps if the family agrees*. Pew Research Center. https://www.pewresearch.org/short-reads/2018/11/20/most-say-their-family-is-ok-with-discussing-politics-but-it-helps-if-the-family-agrees/

Peacock, C., & Pederson, J. R. (2022). Love and politics: The influence of politically (dis)similar romantic relationships on political participation and relationship satisfaction. *Human Communication Research, 48*, 567–578. https://doi.org/10.1093/hcr/hqac011

Pew Research Center. (2023, September). *Americans' dismal view of the nation's politics*.

Porter, T., & Schumann, K. (2018). Intellectual humility and openness to the opposing view. *Self and Identity, 17*(2), 139–162. https://doi.org/10.1080/15298868.2017.1361861

Prout, T. A., Faber, L. J., Racine, E., Sperling, R., & Hillman, R. F. (2019). Clinical encounters with children in the trump era. *Journal of Child Psychotherapy, 45*(2), 191–128. https://doi.org/10.1080/0075417X.2019.1649709

Rajendrakumar, J., Manjula, V., George, T. S., & Wesley, M. S. (2023). The universal dimensions of change: A systematic review of couple techniques. *Contemporary Family Therapy, 45*, 371–393. https://doi.org/10.1007/s10591-022-09645-6

Safer, J. (2019). *I love you, but I hate your politics: How to protect your intimate relationships in a poisonous partison world*. All Points Books.

Schneider, K. J. (2020). *The depolarizing of America: A guidebook for social healing*. University Professors Press.

Scott, S. B., Rhoades, G. K., & Markman, H. J. (2019). Observed communication and relationship quality in female same-gender couples. *Couple and Family Psychology: Research and Practice, 8*(3), 137–151. https://doi.org/10.1037/cfp0000121

Seligman, M. E. P., Steen, T. A., Park, N., & Peterson, C. (2005). Positive psychology progress: Empirical validation of interventions. *American Psychologist, 60*(5), 410–421. https://doi.org/10.1037/0003-066X.60.5.410
Seshadri, G., & Knudson-Martin, C. (2013). How couples manage interracial and intercultural differences: Implications for clinical practice. *Journal of Marital & Family Therapy, 39*(1), 43–58. https://doi.org/10.1111/j.1752-0606.2011.00262.x
Simchon, A., Guntuku, S. C., Simhon, R., Ungar, L. H., Hassin, R. R., & Gilead, M. (2020). Political depression? A big-data, multimethod investigation of American's emotional response to the trump presidency. *Journal of Experimental Psychology: General, 149*(11), 2154–2168. https://doi.org/10.1037/xge0000767
Smith, K. B., Hibbing, M. V., & Hibbing, J. R. (2019). Friends, relatives, sanity, and health: The cost of politics. *PLoS One, 14*(9), e0221870. https://doi.org/10.1371/journal.pone.0221870
Solomonov, N., & Barber, J. P. (2018). Patients' perspectives on political self-disclosure, the therapeutic alliance, and the infiltration of politics into the therapy room in the trump era. *Journal of Clinical Psychology, 74*, 779–787. https://doi.org/10.1002/jclp.22609
Solomonov, N., & Barber, J. P. (2019). Conducting psychotherapy in the trump era: Therapists' perspectives on political self-disclosure, the therapeutic alliance, and politics in the therapy room. *Journal of Clinical Psychology, 75*, 1508–1518. https://doi.org/10.1002/jclp.22801
Spangler, P. T., Thompson, B. J., Vivino, B. L., & Wolf, J. A. (2017). Navigating the minefield of politics in the therapy session. *Psychotherapy Bulletin, 52*(4), 20–25. Retrieved from https://societyforpsychotherapy.org/wp-content/uploads/2018/04/Bulletin52-4.pdf#page=22
Stewart, S. S., & Silvers, B. (2019). *I think you're wrong (but I'm listening)*. Nelson Books.
Toepfer, S. M. (2019). Letters of gratitude as a method for improving family relationship quality. *Interational Review of Modern Sociology, 45*(2), 125–140. https://doi.org/www.jstor.org/stable/48602760
Wakefield Research. (2017). *New Wakefield research study: The Trump effect on American relationships*. Retrieved from http://www.wakefieldresearch.com/blog/2017/05/10/new-wakefield-research-study-trump-effect-american-relationships.
Warner, B. R., Colaner, C. W., & Park, J. (2021). Political difference and polarization in the family: The role of (non)accommodating communication for navigating identity differences. *Journal of Social and Personal Relationships, 38*(2), 564–585. https://doi.org/10.1177/0265407520967438
Waters, L. (2020). Using positive psychology interventions to strengthen family happiness: A family systems approach. *The Journal of Positive Psychology, 15*(5), 645–652. https://doi.org/10.1080/17439760.2020.1789704
Weeks, B. E. (2015). Emotions, partisanship, and misperceptions: How anger and anxiety moderate the effects of partisan bias on susceptibility to political misinformation. *Journal of Communication, 65*, 699–719. https://doi.org/10.1111/jcom.12164
West, E. A., & Iyengar, S. (2022). Partisanship as a social identity: Implications for polarization. *Political Behavior, 44*, 807–838. https://doi.org/10.1007/s11109-020-09637-y
Willoughby, E. A., Giannelis, A., Ludeke, S., Klemmensen, R., Nørgaard, A. S., Iacono, W. G., Lee, J. J., & McGue, M. (2021). Parent contributions to the development of political attitudes in adoptive and biological families. *Psychological Science, 32*(12), 2023–2034. https://doi.org/10.1177/09567976211021844
Winter, L. A. (2021). Swimming against the tide: Therapists' accounts of the relationship between politics and therapy. *Counseling and Psychotherapy Research, 21*, 303–312. https://doi.org/10.1002/capr.12401
Yu, B. Y.-M., Lam, C., & Chan, C. S. (2023). All we need is love? Irreconcilable political incongruence in families after the 2019 social unrest in Hong Kong. *Political Psychology., 45*, 643. https://doi.org/10.1111/pops.12941

Nadine J. Kaslow, PhD, ABPP, is Professor and Vice Chair for Faculty Development, Diversity, Equity, and Inclusion at Emory School of Medicine Department of Psychiatry and Behavioral Sciences and Director of Wellness, Resilience, and Flourishing in the Emory at Grady Dean's Office. Board certified in Couple and Family Psychology, she is past president of the Society of Couple and Family Psychology (Division 43) and former editor of the *Journal of Family Psychology.* A past president of the American Psychological Association, she has expertise in culturally responsive interventions, patient and family centered care, psychology education and training, healthcare worker well-being, and leadership development.

Samantha C. Patton, PhD, ABPP, an Assistant Professor at Emory School of Medicine Department of Psychiatry and Behavioral Sciences, is board certified in Behavioral and Cognitive Therapy. She has expertise in treating substance-related and co-occurring disorders. This includes expertise in problem solving, communication, and conflict resolution skills. She supervises residents and psychology trainees in CBT, DBT, and exposure-based therapies.

Kallio Hunnicutt-Ferguson, PhD, ABPP, is an Assistant Professor at Emory School of Medicine Department of Psychiatry and Behavioral Sciences. Board Certified in Behavioral and Cognitive Therapy, she has expertise in range of evidence-based therapies for mood, anxiety, and trauma and related disorders including problem solving and Dialectical Behavior Therapy (DBT)-based communication skills. Dedicated to psychology education and training; she directs the Emory psychology practicum training program and supervises residents and psychology trainees learning cognitive behavioral therapy (CBT), DBT, and exposure-based therapies.

Chapter 9
Twenty-First Century Relationship Trends and Norms in Psychotherapy

Michael S. Broder and Arlene Goldman

Twenty-First Century Relationship Trends and Norms in Psychotherapy

Couple's therapy has been a crucial form of psychotherapeutic intervention for many decades, but in this new millennium: who, what, and how we treat couples have in some ways shifted dramatically. Aspects of evidence-based treatment and awareness of gender, cultural sensitivity, and neurodiversity now are routinely being addressed in treatment. One of the greatest impacts on couple's therapy has been the proliferation of the Internet, which has affected practically everybody in just about all aspects of their lives and in almost every possible way. This chapter will explore new trends, norms, and challenges for therapists who treat couples: what's new, what's the same, and what's merely going by a different name.

The Internet

How has the Internet impacted couples' lives? The Internet can be used to save time and help people be more efficient with communication, work tasks and community building, and obtain a wealth of information in an instant. Anyone with a laptop or smart phone has access to an infinite amount of information and resources, more than ever before. And if information or knowledge automatically converted to wisdom, as so many mistakenly think it does, humans would be wiser than ever! However, there's also the downside, where people are mesmerized by and thus preoccupied with the Internet, resulting in less quality time spent with their partners.

M. S. Broder (✉) · A. Goldman
Media Psychology Associates, Philadelphia, PA, USA
e-mail: mb@michaelbroder.com

F. W. Kaslow (ed.), *Contemporary Issues in Individual, Couple, and Family Lives and Treatment*, https://doi.org/10.1007/978-3-031-90006-8_9

For example, a couple could be in the same room watching TV together, while one or both are texting or surfing on their smart phones. Thus, many couples (one or both partners) often feel disconnected from each other and even lonely, due to this situation.

An important question is whether smart phones have become this century's most common paramour or even a new (virtual) appendage to our bodies. Often couples come to understand this effect on both their relationship and each other's lives, by realizing how things improve, if only they adhere to the rules regarding phone use, for example, like they set for their children. One challenge for the therapist is to help couples with basic behaviors, such as turning their phones off during dinner, and not looking at them when out together, rather than "phubbing," which is snubbing someone by moving one's attention from them to the smart phone (Al-Saggaf & O'Donnell, 2019). Feeling a constant need to respond to texts from friends or regarding non-urgent work-related matters is an issue that many find difficult to navigate.

Forms of Excessive Internet Use and Abuse

What all forms of excessive Internet use and abuse (such as excessive scrolling, shopping, gambling, and gaming, extreme preoccupation with social media and such things as sports, politics, celebrity news, etc.) have in common is that they can often interfere with a relationship by giving the illusion of partners being together, while one or both are mentally "somewhere else" and mindlessly unavailable to each other. In addition, pornography, which is often used initially as an alternative form of sexual arousal and/or gratification, can become addictive and even replace a couple's healthy sexuality. This may gradually result in the porn involved partner needing more intense forms of stimulation to become aroused, and in many cases, the need to spend more and more time alone, to achieve the same or a greater level of sexual satisfaction, by masturbating, which was once enjoyed with his or her partner.

What sets porn addiction apart is that it may train the brain to need higher and higher levels of arousal than do more conventional forms of sex (de Alarcón et al., 2019).

Case #1: Rebecca and tom

Rebecca (37) and Tom (40) were married for 10 years. They had two children. One day, Rebecca asked Tom if she could use his computer to check something for the children's school. When she went on, she accidently touched something that brought up Tom's browser history and discovered several pornographic sites. When she asked him about it, he initially denied it, but eventually admitted using porn when she was asleep. They shared a bed, but rarely went to sleep at the same time. This was the case for several years, as she got exhausted, "due to working outside the home and taking care of the children" and thus went to sleep early, while he stayed up much later and sometimes slept on the couch. Their sex life was minimal (birthdays, anniversaries, and other rare occasions). Even when together and watching TV, one or both scrolled on their phones, feeling like they were not communicating and had little in common anymore. (In recent years, most therapists have seen versions of this couple in their practice.) In treatment Rebecca accused Tom of being a "sex addict."

To properly set a strategy for a couple like Rebecca and Tom, some questions need to be answered. For example, is this an Internet pornography addiction or compulsion? Internet pornography addiction is not a specific DSM 5 diagnosis, but it is one form of Internet addiction, which like all addictive behavior can impact one's relationships, actual sexual response to one's partner and thus interfere with practically any aspect of life, especially one's primary love relationship.

In addition, the role of dopamine in porn addiction (Hilton, 2013) is a factor that is receiving some much-needed scrutiny. Dopamine, a neurotransmitter, plays a significant role in the brain's reward system and is released during activities that are felt and experienced as pleasurable. When engaging in these activities (such as watching pornography, for those who find it arousing) dopamine is released and creates an often-intense sense of pleasure and reward. Over time, excessive consumption of porn can lead to a tolerance for dopamine, meaning that more and more intense stimuli (e.g., explicit material) is needed to achieve the same degree of pleasure.

Tom admitted to having had an attraction to pornography for much of his life. However, he reported that as Rebecca's sexual responsiveness to him had decreased, the intensity of his desire to engage in porn increased. It was important to assess whether or not Tom's behavior could now be considered an addiction. After Tom agreed to stay away from pornography sites, Rebecca admitted that Tom did not turn her on the way he used to. Both agreed that they would like this issue resolved. This involved using many time-tested couples therapy techniques to work on their intimacy and communication skills (Broder & Goldman, 2004). The first step involved having them turn off their devices (phone, iPads, computers) for one hour a night after the children went to sleep. They also committed to having one date outside their house every week as well as going to bed at the same time together to reestablish the physical connection they had at the beginning of their relationship, as much as they could. The key to establishing a solidly positive outcome existed in how committed Tom was to drastically reduce or stop his porn use. If Tom couldn't do that, the addiction itself would need to be addressed, before going any further. Then there was the issue of whether Rebecca and Tom truly still had (or could have) sexual desire for each other.

This couple exemplifies several issues that are being seen more and more in treatment. In evaluating their relationship, it becomes clear that they make minimal time for each other. Rebecca believes she's "over-functioning" in the relationship. However, while Tom is either playing video games or watching porn, Rebecca was often on Instagram or playing word games with friends. What was important was that neither felt that the other one was "there" for them. Rebecca viewed Tom's pornography use as "a betrayal." This also created feelings of insecurity about her own self-image of attractiveness. Sexual desire (or lack thereof) for one's long-term partner does not happen in a vacuum. In fact, couples in general now report having less sexual activity than previous generations (Twenge et al., 2017). Could this be because partners are spending more time with their phones than their partners?

Tom committed to staying away from porn sites for a month. He noticed, after the first week that his desire for porn greatly decreased. The couple committed to spending time together without any technology, and they began having very honest talks about what they liked and did not like terms of their sex life together. As a result, both reported feeling more connected and less lonely.

Outcomes for a case such as Rebecca and Tom could range from creating a better marriage and sex life together (which is what they stated in their initial session they wanted to do), each "doing their own thing" (which would mean Tom engaging in the pornography he desires and Rebecca accepting it as part of their marriage with both partners blessing) or divorcing, by simply realizing that the marriage had run its course (Broder, 2002).

Pornography and certainly other kinds of distraction have always been an issue in working with couples. The Internet and smartphones seem to engage people in a way that may change their brains. In addition, this certainly allows one to lose track of time. It is also offering people a "new and shiny object" just one click away. In the past, when couples were engaging in the same activity, such as watching a TV show or listening to music together, they were at least having the same shared experience.

Other Effects of the Internet on Couples

The Internet has had a positive effect on couple's therapy as well. Some couples report becoming more educated through podcasts and online courses on a variety of relationship issues and self-help approaches for making their lives better, both individually and as a couple. Clients often report that learning about such things as ADHD and autism spectrum disorders, by taking credible online courses, offers a new perspective that they would be unlikely to find elsewhere or that could be missed in a couples' evaluation. Also, tests that measure traits like introversion–extraversion can answer questions that may have prompted one or both partners to fear that they are incompatible, when simply understanding personality differences (without judgment) can trigger an entirely new and more positive perspective toward each other and the relationship.

Neurodiversity is a framework for understanding brain function that recognizes neurobiological differences in such things as sensory processing, motor abilities, social comfort, and cognition; and often re-identifies such things as autism, for example, as a difference in functioning that is not necessarily pathological. Once this concept is understood, the recognition of a couple's neurodiversity can trigger a reframing that saves a relationship where chronic incompatibility is feared (Sicklels, 2023). However, this also increases the likelihood of partners "misdiagnosing" each other, as well. For example, it is not uncommon for one or both partners who are in the middle of a dispute, to characterize the other one as narcissistic, a borderline personality, or sociopathic. This can lead to gaslighting (manipulating one's partner into questioning his or her own perception of reality) and other forms of avoidance in addressing an issue that could be more easily resolved without this type of misinformation or mischaracterization.

On the other hand, the newest technology can be extremely distracting, and many couples report having less time to spend together, despite having the technology to enable them to do many of the mundane things that heretofore took up their time.

Often, couples enter treatment after one partner discovers (either accidently or on purpose) what they consider an "inappropriate relationship," which the other partner may be having, by reading his or her texts, email or entries on social media, and finding out what they would least wish to uncover. Examples include evidence that a sexual liaison, full-blown affair, parallel relationship, or an emotional connection that threatens the primary relationship is taking place. Negative information that a partner is inappropriately revealing to someone such as financial or family secrets can be of an extremely threatening nature to the discovering partner. Thus, partners tracking each other through their smart phones often lead to unpleasant surprises.

Life is full of paradoxes. Thus, it should be noted that for some couples, an argument could be made that even what many people would consider excessive smart phone usage (regardless of the nature of the use) can enhance the relationship, by optimizing the amount of time partners spend together. In other words, excessive Internet usage may in some cases prevent relationship burnout, in cases where too much time together would put a strain on the relationship. This was especially true during the Covid pandemic, which many couples in treatment reported.

These are but a few examples of how the Internet impacts the lives of couples in ways that would have been unimaginable just a few decades ago. The actual underlying issues themselves have not changed as much as how they have seemed or become more prevalent and thus even normalized, as a result of this new technology.

Treating Couples Virtually, Via Zoom, Online or Even by Telephone

While virtual telemedicine and other forms of virtual approaches to doing psychotherapy for both individuals and couples have been around for quite a while, during the Covid pandemic the use of virtual techniques was at its zenith. Unexpectedly, many psychotherapists, as well as clients, discovered that they preferred virtual sessions to in-person sessions, even when the pandemic ended and that these were no longer necessary. However, virtual couples' therapy has its pros and cons. For example, here are some of the pros:

- Easier accessibility, especially for those with mobility difficulties.
- There is more opportunity to choose the right therapist for a given situation, without distance posing a negative factor.
- Time is saved, by not having to travel.
- For many, there is no need for childcare in order to attend sessions.
- Some report that there is less negativity generated during a virtual session than would take place in the office. (This could be a positive or negative factor.)

And cons:

- Many therapists report subjectively that they do not feel as engaged (Hardy et al., 2021).
- Therapists report that they often miss non-verbal and physical cues that they see as essential, for an optimal couple's therapy climate (Hardy et al., 2021).
- Couples often report that following a virtual session they did not take the time to process what went on during the session, as they might have when commuting to or from home or the therapist office.
- With distractions at home (children, ringing telephones, pets, etc.), many couples report simply not being able to be as present and concentrate as when in the office without such distractions.
- Issues of privacy and security, which characterize any Internet activity, are sometimes a concern for clients when deciding to bring up certain concerns during a virtual session.

With virtual sessions, each therapist must assess their own comfort level. Whether it is a net plus or minus requires further research now that virtual sessions are here to stay. However, preliminary research shows that there is not much difference in initial therapeutic outcome, but after 12 weeks, there are differences; it takes longer to create a positive therapeutic alliance with couples seen virtually as compared to in person (Bradford et al., 2024a, 2024b).

New Lifestyle Norms

Couples now have a greater tendency to realize that they can make their own types of "designer arrangements" for their relationship that fly in the face of tradition but work for them. *A new challenge for therapists is to become more conscious of their own biases, and not let these interfere with the treatment of a couple whose values and practices differ from what therapists would want or accept in their own relationships.* Couples' therapists have always been trained to be as unbiased as possible. In other words, couples' therapists often need to make a greater effort to not pathologize the lifestyle choices of a couple whom they are treating has made (Broder, 1993).

By the same token, therapists often find it difficult to accept the challenge of learning about cultural and lifestyle differences that their clients display, which are not similar to theirs, such as: gay marriage, unique ethnic or political norms, sexual preferences that have become more normalized, and socioeconomic differences. These can be underlying factors with almost any issue a couple presents in treatment (Broder, 2022). What follows are several examples of presenting issues that many couples' therapists were not trained to handle.

Ethical/Consensual Non-Monogamy (CNM)

Ethical or consensual non-monogamy defines an arrangement that allows a varying degree of sexual and/or romantic involvement outside of the primary relationship by either or both partners, or with more than one partner. The foundation of this type of open relationship is allegedly based on the full knowledge, consent, and benefit of all parties involved.

Different forms include polyamory (meaning "many loves," but not necessarily being married to more than one person), swinging or open relationships, which have been a widely discussed part of our culture for over a half century. There are many forms it can take on (Broder, 1993). The explosion of information about these kinds of arrangements on the Internet has allowed couples to read about others' experiences in private and has normalized many of the ideas that were once considered much less common than they truly were. There is research to suggest that a small, portion of the population is living this lifestyle— perhaps 0.6% to 5% of the overall population presently, and over 20% at some point in their lives (Ruben, 2020). More couples are bringing up the issues connected to this overall concept in therapy. For some couples, the issue is "how do we do it?" in a way that strengthens our primary relationship. Other couples seek help when issues of jealousy arise or when "rule violations" occur, and others seek help in navigating more than one primary relationship.

The challenge for couples who wish to engage in ethical non-monogamy is to customize an arrangement that works for both partners. *The "both partners" aspect of this cannot be emphasized enough.* One partner trying to talk or coerce the other one into agreeing to an arrangement that is counter to their values of what a marriage or love relationship should be, rarely, if ever, leads to a workable situation.

Moreover, what makes a non-monogamous relationship "ethical" is the dynamic of transparency, consent, and honesty between the primary relationship partners. One could argue that non-monogamy is as old as relationships themselves. Polygamy has been around since biblical times, when men who had more than one wife generally held a large power advantage. On the other hand, infidelity is usually accompanied by some degree of deceit. In 1972, when the extremely popular bestselling book *Open Marriage* came out (O'Neill & O'Neill, 1972), the concept was seen by many as scandalous. In fact, even today, according to a study by Sprott and Randall (2017), over 25% of clients who engage in alternative sexual practices do not even report this to their therapists. This finding makes a strong case for therapists to avoid the assumption that a client is monogamous, regardless of the therapist's personal view toward such practices (Broder & Goldman, 2013). Thus, it is incumbent upon all therapists who work with couples to educate themselves about this rapidly evolving phenomenon. This includes forgoing the assumption that a couple is monogamous, as well as the tendency to assume that if they are not, it is a symptom of some form of pathology or difficulty with intimacy or attachment (Edwards et al., 2023) and Moors et al. (2019).

Case #2: Jayne and Chris

Jayne and Chris, a couple in their late 30 s, reentered therapy after they had been married for 7 years. Their previous therapy, years before, had focused on issues each had regarding whether to get married. Both partners were trained as attorneys. Jayne had just left her full-time job, with Chris's blessing, to spend time pursuing her passion of writing historical fiction. This also gave her more time to think about what she wanted to do with her life and with their relationship.

They were considering ethical non-monogamy and wanted some guidance as to how to make it work for each of them. Jayne had brought up the issue to Chris, and both began researching it, which also brought them closer together, and allowed them to open up to each other with some honest conversations about their sex life as well as their sexual desires that they hadn't previously discussed.

Jayne valued her marriage and very much-admired Chris. However, she never felt as emotionally close to him as she wished to. Chris admired Jayne's creativity, and the fact that she was always coming up with new things for the two of them to do, and ways they could know and express their feelings. Chris came from a culture where individual expression was not highly valued. He was quite driven to achieve and had done very well by putting long hours into his work. Jayne realized she was not going to change Chris, and now that she was home more, she was looking for someone with whom to share more emotional and sexual closeness. She had engaged in several same-sex experiences in college, which she enjoyed, but had felt uncomfortable exploring them more than she did, at that time. The idea of having more options now was very appealing to her.

Their sex life had been somewhat monotonous for a while, according to both of their accounts. Chris was now experiencing some physical difficulties with his erections and wondered whether having new partners and new experiences would be helpful to him. While exploring possibilities such as swinging (which most commonly involves switching partners to have sex, often at the same time and in each other's presence)—both individually and as a couple—was thoroughly discussed.

Therapy helped them to examine the issues that could be problematic; including jealousy, honesty, time commitment, safe sex, and how much they wanted to know about each other's sexual life outside the marriage. Neither was interested in seeing their partner with someone else. Also, of concern was how they would handle jealousy, as well as what would happen if one got more involved with another person than the other did. They decided that as they separately sought out other partners, they would both remain committed to making their marriage the primary relationship. Also, they would let each other know when they had dates and give each other any information needed to keep them both safe and to prevent inaccurate assumptions from forming.

They drew up a written contract around what they needed from each other, including what they were comfortable sharing about other sex partners, and agreed to check in with each other weekly to share feelings and assess how it was working for each of them. They also established a regular date night with each other.

Chris went to websites to find partners who would be accepting of an open relationship. Jayne had met Gary in one of her writing groups and was interested in an emotional as well as sexual connection with him. Chris and Jayne agreed to a couple's session at least every 2 months, as this new arrangement began, or more often, if either partner needed or desired one.

As Jayne got more involved with Gary (who was also in an open relationship), and she began wanting to change the rules, for example, seeing Gary on weekends and sleeping over, Chris was uncomfortable, but initially agreed to the changes. Then she wanted more changes in their agreements. The couple began moving further apart, losing even more of the intimacy they once had. Jane had broken several dates with Chris. When they did check in, it was primarily about their arrangement, and very little about the two of them as the primary couple. Chris was feeling very lonely, which ironically Jayne had been previously in their relationship.

They also began to understand that some of her behavior was more about holding on to old resentments than this new lifestyle. The couple talked openly about their feelings and renegotiated some of the rules they had set in their agreement, in order to work again on making their relationship the primary one.

During this time, Gary ended his relationship with Jayne. Chris became Jayne's major source of support. Jayne continued to explore ethical non-monogamy and to have several short-term partners. She reported that this lifestyle worked for her. Chris continued to explore sexual encounters with other women, which he found to be satisfying.

Several issues came up in working with this couple. Chris initially thought that given their lifestyle, he needed to go along with everything Jane asked for. Teaching them how to hear each other's feelings and negotiate what would work for the relationship they were committed to was important. At one point Jayne thought that she would want to move out if Chris did not go along with her needs; and many therapists might have seen this as a natural progression, rather than looking at the underlying feelings—unrelated to their lifestyle—that Jane was experiencing. This couple continues to reassess how their lifestyle is working for each of them and will continue to periodically check in for therapy as needed.

As challenging as it can be to work with couples in traditional relationships, the case of Chris and Janes remind us how the complexity of treatment intensifies when the dynamics of polyamory becomes a factor. Most importantly, couples' therapists need to be aware that this is not unusual in today's world (Broder, 2002).

Sprott and Schechinger (2019) recommend that therapists spend some time and energy self-reflecting on their biases related to their own “internal narratives” about non-monogamous relationships. This includes their view of emotional and sexual intimacy, whether one or both partners need to engage in similar types of behavior that constitute this lifestyle, internalized cultural messaging about monogamy and non-monogamy, and learning about various forms of CNM, as well as what their internal responses are to each. They especially recommend getting some supervision with a couples’ therapist who is familiar, comfortable with, and even affirming of CNM. This is an excellent way to enhance skills, provide support, and work through biases. Couples’ therapists may also benefit from such intensive experiences as attending a support group or conference that focuses on education and awareness of CNM with respect to individuals and relationships.

Living Together Versus Marriage

More people are now choosing to live together, rather than marry. While living together is certainly nothing new, what has now become normalized is unmarried couples buying homes, and having children together, as well as intertwining their finances in every way that was once considered a norm for only those in traditional marriages (Horowitz et al., 2019).

Many therapists have tended to look at such couples, or either partner who may prefer this lifestyle, as being unwilling or unable to commit. As in the case with non-monogamy, therapists best serve couples who fit into this category by avoiding the “temptation” to impose their values or be blinded by traditional norms, and thus creating a therapeutic issue where none may exist.

DINKS (Double Income no Kids)

Traditionally, there was an assumption that when a couple married, it was not a matter of if, but when they would have (or at least try to have) children. Often, that decision hinged upon when they would be able to financially afford one partner giving up an intense full-time career and/or stream of income to become involved with having children and expanding the. Family.

In the twenty-first century, there has been a subtle shift in thinking about the decision of whether to have children. The question “why not?” have children, has for some couples morphed into “why” have them at all?

In many cases, there is great ambivalence. For example, one partner could decide he or she wants children while the other does not. In couples therapy, often both partners we see are ambivalent. Working through this ambivalence can be extremely complex but it can be argued that there are few (if any) issues that are more crucial for many couples (Broder, 1993). After all, in reality, it’s not so much who one marries, but who one has children with that in fact has a lifelong impact. Once a couple has a child together, regardless of where life may take them individually or as a couple, there is an important part of them that will be connected for life, even if there is a complete end to their relationship as a couple.

Some areas that need to be explored in treatment include guilt (as a reaction to the idea that "selfishness" is the culprit for not wanting children), one or both partners desire to please their parents by delivering grandchildren, and a lack of understanding of the intense responsibility and profound lifestyle changes that come with bearing and rearing children.

Case #3: George and Judy—Gray Divorce

George and Judy, a couple in their mid-60 s had been married 35 years. They had three grown children and had been in couples therapy several times during their marriage. Therapy seemed to help for a while with addressing such issues as communication and sexual compatibility.

Judy, who had stayed at home to raise their children, started a new career 5 years before they entered couple's therapy and had become very involved in her work. George, an accountant, was beginning to think about retirement. Two of the couple's three children lived nearby them. Judy's mother had recently died at age 95.

When the couple came for treatment, Judy was ambivalent about continuing their relationship. During their initial sessions, what had worked in their past therapies and why they had not continued making progress once therapy ended was discussed. Judy was very ambivalent about entering couples therapy this time, and after several sessions, the couple decided to initiate a trial separation. George stayed in their house and Judy got a short-term rental for 6 months.

They agreed that they would not date others during this time but date each other if and when both desired. During this time, they dated each other about once a week and also attended therapy sessions together. Judy enjoyed her newfound freedom, but George had a more difficult time. Gradually, he began to feel comfortable living by himself and started reaching out to others. He even started playing pickleball.

Dating was generally initiated by Judy, and the couple had several sexual encounters with each other during this time. Judy had concerns about moving back into their home, but for both financial and emotional reasons agreed to do so. They quickly fell back into old patterns, and after another 6 months, the couple decided that they would both be happier if they divorced. Their divorce was amiable, as both felt that their marriage had run its course (Broder, 2002).

While the rate of divorce is decreasing for younger couples (perhaps because they are more reluctant than previous generations to marry in the first place), it is on the increase for couples, in which the partners are over 50 (Brown & Lin, 2012). Whether this is a function of the Baby boomer generation, or the fact that we are living healthier and longer lives, remains unclear. Marriages that worked when the focus was on child rearing don't always work when the partners become empty nesters. Moreover, interests and priorities change with age, making it more common for incompatibility to set in as people live longer. For example, one partner may wish to start or continue in his or her satisfying career, while the other wants to retire and travel the world or simply live a post career lifestyle.

Conscious Uncoupling

We believe that *marriages and other love relationships that end don't fail, they run their course.* This concept was considered by both the media and many professionals involved in all aspects of marriage and love relationships to be an extremely controversial statement to make when the author Broder (1990) first wrote *The Art of Living Single*. However, as people live longer and divorce becomes a much more acceptable part of our culture, couples who entered into what they once considered a lifelong commitment have tended to realize that they do not have to be enemies in order to end a marriage or change the nature of their relationship.

New strategies such as discernment counseling (Doherty et al., 2015), which is a short-term approach that is appropriate for "mixed agenda couples"—where one partner wants to end the relationship, and the other does not—help clarify why divorce is being considered now. This helps each partner first to understand their role in the present crisis, and then whether a more traditional couple's therapy can and/or should take place. Divorce mediation along with a general acceptance of the concept of growing apart has eliminated much of the pain that was once considered inevitable when uncoupling. This also permits the type of optimal coparenting that benefits children of all ages as well as their parents. The concept of remaining something between lifelong friends and being cordially civil once a marriage has ended is now a norm that, when genuine, has little downside and can benefit everyone involved.

Conclusion

Many of this era's couples' therapists face challenges that did not exist when they were trained to treat couples. The new challenges are not only unique but continue to change rapidly. It is vital that therapists to stay up to date in incorporating new knowledge and treatment strategies in their thinking and practice.

References

Al-Saggaf, Y., & O'Donnell, S. (2019). Phubbing: Perceptions, reasons behind, predictors, and impacts. *Human Behavior and Emerging Technologies, 1*(2), 132–140. https://doi.org/10.1002/hbe2.137

Bradford, A.B., Banford-Witting, A., Anderson, S.R., Johnson, L.N., Hunt, Q. A., Miller, R.B., & Bean, R.A. (2024a). *Lost in translation: Therapeutic alliance as a mediator in the relationship between teletherapy and marital satisfaction*, https://doi.org/10.1111/famp.13004.

Bradford, A., Johnson, L. N., Anderson, S. R., Banford-Witting, A., Hunt, Q. A., Miller, R. B., & Bean, R. A. (2024b). Call me maybe? In person versus teletherapy outcomes among married couples. *Psychotherapy Research, 34*(5), 611–625. https://doi.org/10.1080/10503307.2023.2256465

Broder, M. (2022). *Helping adults to grow up: A practitioner's guide to stage climbing*. Springer.

Broder, M., & Goldman, A. (2013). The role of maturity in the cognitions that govern love relationships and sexual satisfaction. *Journal of Rational Emotive & Cognitive-Behavior Therapy, 31*(1), 75–83. https://doi.org/10.1007/s10942-013-0159-y

Broder, M., & Goldman, A. (2004). *The secrets of sexual ecstasy*. Penguin Books (Alpha).

Broder, M. (2002). *Can your relationship be saved? How to know whether to stay or go*. Impact Publishers.

Broder, M. (1993). *The art of staying together*. Hyperion.

Broder, M. (1990). *The art of living single*. Avon Books.

Brown, S., & Lin, I. (2012). The grey divorce revolution: Rising divorce among middle-aged and older adults 1990-2010. *The Journals of Gerontology: Series B, 67*(6), 731–741. https://doi.org/10.1093/geronb/gbs089

de Alarcón, R., de la Iglesia, J., Casado, N. M., & Montejo, A. L. (2019). Online porn addiction: What we know and what we don't—A systematic review. *Journal of Clinical Medicine, 8*(1), 91. https://doi.org/10.3390/jcm8010091

Doherty, W. J., Harris, S. M., & Wilde, J. L. (2015). Discernment counseling for "mixed agenda" couples. *Journal of Marital and Family Therapy, 42*(2), 246–255. https://doi.org/10.1111/jmft.12132

Edwards, C., Allan, R. A., Marzo, N., Wynfield, T., & Hicks, R. (2023). The use of emotionally focused therapy with polyamorous relationships. *Family Process, 62*(4), 1362–1376. https://doi.org/10.1111/famp.12934

Hardy, N. R., Maier, C. A., & Gregson, T. J. (2021). Couple teletherapy in the era of COVI-19: Experiences and recommendations. *Journal of Marital and Family Therapy, 47*(2), 225–243. https://doi.org/10.1111/jmft.12501

Hilton, D. L. (2013). Pornography addiction—a supernormal stimulus considered in the context of neuroplasticity. *Socioaffective Neuroscience & Psychology, 3*(1). https://doi.org/10.3402/snp.v3i0.20767

Horowitz, J., Graf, N., & Livingston, G. (2019). *The landscape of marriage and cohabitation in the US*. Pew Research Center. Microsoft Word–PSDT_11.06.19_marriage_cohabitation_FULL.final.docx.

Moors, A. C., Ryan, W., & Chopik, W. J. (2019). Multiple loves: The effects of attachment with multiple concurrent romantic partners on relational functioning. *Personality and Individual Differences, 147*, 102–110. https://doi.org/10.1016/j.paid.2019.04.023

O'Neill, N., & O'Neill, G. (1972). *Open marriage*. M. Evans and Company.

Ruben, A. (2020). Counting polyamorists who count: Prevalence and definitions of an under-researched form of consensual non monogamy. *Sexualities, 23*(1–2), 3–27. https://doi.org/10.1177/1363460718779781

Sicklels, L. (2023). A how to guide to emotional support for neuro diverse couples. *Autism Spectrum News*, (October 2023).

Sprott R., & Randall A. (2017). Health disparities among kinky sex practitioners. *Current Sexual Health Reports, 9*, 104–108. https://doi.org/10.1007/s11930-017-0113-6

Sprott, R., & Schechinger, A. (2019). Consensual non-monogamy: A brief summary of key findings and recent advancements, *The Family Psychologist Newsletter*.

Twenge, J., Sherman, R. A., & Wells, B. E. (2017). Declines in sexual frequency among American adults, 1989-2014. *Archives of Sexual Behavior, 46*, 2389–2401. https://doi.org/10.1007/s10508-017-0953-1

Michael S. Broder, PhD, is a psychologist, bestselling author, and acclaimed expert in cognitive behavioral therapy (CBT) who specializes in dealing with both relationships and high achievers. He has written numerous audio programs as well as eight books, including the bestselling *Art of Living Single* and *The Art of Staying Together.* His latest book is for professionals—*Helping Adults to Grow Up*: A *Practitioner's Guide to Stage Climbing* (Springer, 2022). Dr. Broder is past president of APA's Media Psychology Division; and was a radio host for 17 years in Philadelphia, NYC, and for NBC *Talknet* and ABC *Talkradio*. He has trained thousands of mental health professionals.

Arlene Goldman, PhD, is a psychologist, who for the last 40 years has specialized in the treatment of sexual dysfunctions and relationship issues. She has served on the faculty of Jefferson Medical College in Philadelphia where she coordinated the Sexual Function Center. She has served on the faculties of Widener University, Chestnut Hill College and has trained professionals at all levels in the treatment of relationship and sexual issues. She is co-author of *The Secrets of Sexual Ecstasy* and has written numerous book chapters and articles for professional journals.

Chapter 10
Handling Couples Issues Pertaining to Relocation and Finances

Florence W. Kaslow

Handling Couples Issues Pertaining to Relocation and Finances

In past centuries in the United States (U.S.) and much of Western Europe and Latin America, the majority of traditional couples presumed that the husband/father worked, and the wife/mother would stay at home and bear and rear children. This changed for a few years in the 1940s when so many men were in the Armed Forces and many women went to work in factories producing war equipment and filling other essential jobs; many liked working and earning a salary. In the twenty-first century as an increasing number of women went to college and sometimes on to graduate or medical school, the earlier prototypical expectation shifted. Many women became gainfully employed, held responsible well-paying positions, and supervised others. Some husbands began helping with childcare and after-school chauffeuring. Either partner might be asked to relocate to be promoted or might want to expand their business out of their home area.

As a result, many couples are now confronted with such life-altering decisions. Does the *partner* automatically agree to move? What about uprooting the children from their friends and activities? What if one is in the military and is transferred—does the other move with him/her, if it is possible? What if the relocation is necessitated because of a natural disaster, such as a major hurricane, earthquake, or tornado, and has destroyed their home, and perhaps community, and it is impossible to remain where they are. They are faced with urgent relocation issues that are addressed in this chapter.

In addition, in individual, couple, and family therapy or consultations, issues about finances are often raised. Do they have joint or separate bank and investment

F. W. Kaslow (✉)
Kaslow Associates, Palm Beach Gardens, FL, USA

F. W. Kaslow (ed.), *Contemporary Issues in Individual, Couple, and Family Lives and Treatment*, https://doi.org/10.1007/978-3-031-90006-8_10

accounts, check books, credit cards, savings accounts? Is the current arrangement working for both or are some adjustments needed? The therapist must be conversant with these high priority issues and skilled in handling them to bring about the best resolution for all family members. This chapter also addresses the kind of financial issues families face. It is based on actual cases I have handled directly in therapy or that I have consulted on to other therapists when they were stymied, as well as from a review of recent relevant literature. These cases illuminate the complexity of the issues that are the focus of this chapter. Identities have been carefully camouflaged.

Relocation Issues

Case #1: The Carters

Mr. Carter (Mr. C), the Branch Manager of a large bank in a medium-sized city on the East Coast was asked to transfer to a much larger branch in a major midwestern city. This move would represent a big promotion and entail a large increase in salary. However, his wife, Dr. Carter (Dr. C), was an Associate Professor at a prestigious local University and enjoyed her teaching and other university involvements. She did not want to relocate. This serious stressful emergency problem led them to seek me out for a consultation. Mr. C's firm wanted an answer within 2 weeks.

We had three sessions. Both stated that they did not want to live separately and take turns commuting every other weekend. Dr. C stated, "There is no way that I can obtain a University Professorship in any city for the next semester quickly nor would it be fair for me to give only a few weeks' notice of resignation where I am currently a full-time faculty member. In addition, I do not think it is fair to suddenly uproot the children just a few weeks before their fall term begins. They are already involved in their sports' practices and games, choir, marching band, etc., and do not want to leave their friends."

Although Mr. C. acknowledged understanding her objections to relocating so hurriedly, he posited that this promotion signified a big boost to his career and a sizable increase in his salary. He very much wanted to accept the promotion he had been working toward for several years and thought it would be an error to turn it down. As they poured their hearts out to each other, it was apparent they loved each other and had a great deal of mutual respect. But neither wanted to budge.

I asked some questions before making a few suggestions for them to consider to break the deadlock. Might Mr. C accept the position, rent a large enough apartment or home for himself and his wife and children to visit him once a month, just as he would return and visit them once a month and give himself time to see if he enjoyed the new position, his colleagues, and the community before uprooting his wife and children? If after several months he did like his new situation in the large, more prestigious bank (and locale), then Dr. C could reconsider her decision and investigate job possibilities at several prestigious universities in her husband's new environs and they could discuss with the children the larger range of activities and exposure to all the advantages a more metropolitan area has to offer. They left the session saying they would mull over this suggestion.

Four days later they returned and stated they had given the suggestion a great deal of thought. Mr. C was determined to move ahead and was investigating more about the community and where the best location might be to rent not too far from his bank branch nor from either of the two local universities. He had also done some checking into the local public and private school systems and obtained information that they were both highly rated. In the interim, Dr. C made inquiries at the local universities, and both had departments in her area of expertise. She agreed to begin exploring the possibilities for the following academic year—after her husband had been in his new position for several months and knew he wanted to remain. Clearly, neither wanted this situation to precipitate a divorce or a prolonged separation.

A few days later we held the third session in the evening so their 12-year-old son and 10-year-old daughter could attend. Their wise parents had done well in keeping them abreast of what was transpiring. Both agreed to the temporary plan and were willing to fly back and forth several times to see how they liked the area and visit the schools they might transfer to.

When Mr. C was "back home" for a long weekend visit several months later, he and his wife came in for another consultation session. He indicated how much he was enjoying everything about his new position and the exciting metropolitan area in which he was residing, but emphasized how much he missed his wife and children, and that he did not want the being apart to continue indefinitely. He thought the children would thrive in his new "hometown." Dr. C. missed her husband more than she had expected to and had decided that keeping their marriage and family together was a more important value than staying in her current position. She had begun the application process for a teaching position at both nearby universities and realized she could expand the search area, if needed. Dr. C and the children moved to join their dad at the end of the school year. She was able to obtain a professorship at one of the two universities—the better of the two in her estimation.

Case Summation

The Carters showed a great deal of mutual respect and love for one another. The decision to move or not to move never disintegrated into a power struggle. Their desire to spend their lives together was very strong and so they found a way they could each pursue their career paths without having to live separately or get divorced. They had kept the children involved in the decision-making process and they had begun looking forward to the relocation as an adventure.

Unfortunately, not all couples faced with this type of potentially highly conflictual situation are as mutually respectful and put the well-being of the entire family above the need of one member to engage in a power struggle and force the others to "give in."

Gender Dynamics

Erlinghagen (2020) in an article entitled "Love in motion: Migration patterns of internationally mobile couples," framed his analysis within the so-called "*trailing wife hypothesis*" that suggests clear, *gender-related migration patterns* following traditional gender roles with the husband taking the lead and exploring the forthcoming relocation and deciding the "couples timing of emigration." However, in contrast, his research revealed that women are more likely than men to be the leading partner (and force) for remigration. This study, which highlights the complexities of family-related inequalities in migration and remigration patterns was based on couples emigrating from Germany to a different country. This work sheds some light on issues that arise when couples are considering relocating to a different country, basically because the husband has a good job transfer offer with a promotion pending, as well as factors that may determine whether the couple returns to their homeland such as unknowns and uncertainties distressing the wife and the presence of young children and availability of childcare and suitable schooling.

Ulrich et al. (2015) investigated gender differences in family-relatedness vis-à-vis decisions about relocation decisions among a sample of 1234 employees. They concluded that spousal willingness to relocate mediates the "negative effect of the spouse's community ties, and the positive effect of the spouse's job alternative." Their findings suggested that (most) employees consider various partner factors in their career relocation decision-making and that the concern about numerous family issues is particularly strong among female employees offered a job requiring relocation.

Dual-Earner Couples

Van der Velde et al. (2017) in an article entitled "Dual-earner couples' willingness to relocate abroad: The reciprocal influence of both partners' career role salience and partner role salience" revealed that employees' willingness to relocate internationally depends a great deal on their spouses' willingness to make the transition, go along with it, and is determined by both career importance and partner role salience (i.e., the level of importance attached to performing a specific role). Their research further highlighted that it is essential for employers to engage both partners in decision-making about an international relocation and being available to assist in planning and supporting such moves to support their success.

Case #2: How Can she Do this to me?

A local psychiatrist, Dr. G., called me for a consultation on the case of a couple he was seeing. He was concerned that subjectively he was siding with the father, and he wanted to regain his objectivity. In his first appointment he said the wife in the case was a nurse at the Naval Hospital near their home. She had been asked to relocate to a different Naval hospital out of the geographic area in which they resided and was offered the position of Director of Nursing there. It would amount to a major step up in her career and a big boost in her salary. She was delighted and eager to accept the offer.

The husband was chagrined and angry that she would even consider accepting the offer and accused her of being selfish and inconsiderate. He had articulated that "if you really loved me, you wouldn't even be tempted." He had worked his way up from being a salesman in a department store in their hometown to being the store's manager. He liked his work, and he was adamant about not being willing to move. They had two children, a son, and a daughter, who were away at college and neither had not given much thought to where they wanted to live after graduating so they had chosen not to get involved on either side of the conflict. Both said, "we just want you both to be happy with your decision and we don't know where our future jobs may be located."

As Dr. G. related the case dilemma to me, he realized he had been unconsciously siding with the husband, probably because subconsciously he believed if a husband was a good "breadwinner," a devoted husband and father, such a decision should be his choice. He realized he would not want to close his practice and relocate for his wife's career.

I pointed out that the situations were not analogous. The husband in the case could no doubt be transferred to another store of the large chain with which his store was affiliated, and there were probably various options within that firm, whereas *if Dr. G were to relocate*, he would have to terminate his current analysands, which is very disruptive to treatment and counterindicated, unless absolutely necessary (Deutsch, 2014), such as if the analyst becomes seriously ill (Freud, 1970). He or she can rarely continue the relationship with his current analysands. A termination for this reason often feels to the patients like an abandonment (Goldner, 2016). Also, he would have the arduous task of rebuilding his/her practice from scratch in a different vicinity, where he would be unknown. He gradually relaxed as he realized why he had over-identified with his patient, that he told me he was projecting his personal preferences onto his patient. He told me how very grateful he was for the insight-producing consult. He called me about 6 weeks later to tell me he was able to help his clients resolve their dilemma and they were going to relocate. The firm the husband worked for had offered him the manager's position in a larger store in the city to which his wife wanted to accept her wonderful sounding new position.

Perhaps the main lesson to be derived from this case consult report is that many therapists and analysts occasionally need to consult another therapist or analyst when something in transference is blocking their ability to intervene effectively for and with their patients or clients.

There is so much to address when the client or patient is relocating. The therapist should be neutral enough to help them make the best decision for both members of the couple, their children and perhaps their own parents, if they live near the current residence and have a close relationship.

In the two cases presented in the foregoing, the choice to relocate belonged to the couple. It entailed weighing the pros and cons for them each individually, as a couple, and with their children (and perhaps the impact on their parents) as a family.

Forced Relocation After a Disaster

Sometimes a family doesn't have a choice; a horrendous disaster, like a crushing tornado, a fierce hurricane, flood, or earthquake destroys their home and community—and in one fell swoop, everything they own is lost or destroyed. The whole situation is mind boggling. Whatever they have spent years accumulating and building is gone—through no fault of their own. Most people who experience such unexpected (natural) disasters must act quickly and the options in such emergencies are limited. Everything they owned like cash, jewelry, savings bonds, etc., that may have been in the house may have vanished in the sudden catastrophe. Those who have insurance on their homes and/or cars, or other liability insurance, may recoup some of their losses, but it will take time, once the agents are notified, for any payment to be forthcoming? If their credit cards were lost in the occurrence, they will need to push for rapid replacement and to have the cards canceled in case someone finds them and tries to use them.

Hopefully they have relatives or friends who live outside the stricken areas where they can live for a short time, until they get their bearings. If not, where can and should they go? FEMA and local agencies like the Red Cross and Salvation Army might become involved in helping them handle their immediate needs for food and shelter. Other agencies (governmental) may have emergency funds available and hopefully, where to apply for aid will be publicized in the local media.

Four or five times in recent years I've been asked by acquaintances and friends on email to "chip in" (Go Fund Me requests) immediately as they have set up a fund to give to the uprooted family. If the request comes from someone I know and respect for people I also know and have high regard for, I have contributed as much as I can at that moment and periodically for a while afterwards until they are resettled. I also suggest to others that they do so if they can. Those who have good coping skills and a large, strong financial and emotional support system fare much better than those who were "loners" and have a small, if any, support system.

Relocation necessitated by such a tragic, "unexpected" occurrence in the area in which the family lived catapults peoples' lives into turmoil, and they must relocate quickly, probably temporarily at first, until they recoup a little emotionally and financially and can consider where they want to go. Unlike with the couples discussed earlier in the chapter, in Cases #1 and #2, there isn't time to weigh options and investigate various possibilities. These people need to deal with the shock and uprooting, obtain safe *temporary housing* (which FEMA may provide) or some sort of a shelter. It is helpful if they can cling to the fact that they all survived (if they indeed did). This all may take weeks or months and is further complicated in terms of the children's school situation—temporary or permanent. How will they get them enrolled quickly and settled in temporarily? Will the teachers understand the trauma the children have survived and make them welcome in the middle of the term? Will their new classmates reach out to them?

If the adults were employed, are they now out of work? What will they rely on for immediate income? Were the homes or businesses of other members of the family also affected by this event? If not, can they help temporarily, either financially and/or by providing temporary housing?

This is a very different kind of scenario undergirding relocations than the ones of moving by choice. Therapists working with these families need to be sympathetic and perhaps take more initiative and do quicker guiding than is usual for them and should encourage them to apply to Community, State, and Federal disaster relief programs for which they may be eligible. Such programs usually mobilize quickly and go to help in the stricken areas and therapists should direct them to these.

It can take many months or more for family members to recuperate enough to make plans for a complete rebuilding of their homes or apartment or to relocate, especially if it is out of the geographic area in which they had resided. In teaching couple and family psychology/therapy, it is highly advisable that instructors include a unit on families stricken by the kinds of disasters discussed in the foregoing material.

Couple and Family Income and Handling of Finances

In centuries gone by, as the men were often the only wage earners in the family in many vicinities, it was customary that they handle the finances. Of note, the situation was and is different for single women who earn their own salaries and decide how to use what they earn and the interest that accrues on any bank accounts, investments, and brokerage accounts they have. The men often kept their saving accounts, checking accounts and brokerage accounts in their name only. Many gave their wives a weekly or monthly allowance to cover household expenses, perhaps to pay the mortgage and for her own needs, like clothing, the beauty salon, social activities, etc. Her allocation might also cover giving the children their allowances, or he might prefer to give it to them himself, so they know it comes from him. But, as mentioned earlier, more and more women started working out of their homes in the 1940s during World War II, earning salaries and contributing to the family income. As this trend continued in the last half of the twentieth century and accelerated in the twenty-first century, women often now had their own pension plans where they worked, opened separate savings and checking accounts, and acquired credit cards in their own names. This meant each couple had to work out a "yours, mine, and ours" financial plan—unless one member of the couple was domineering and needed total control, or one just wanted to be given money by the other, when and as needed.

Gash and Plagnol (2021), in an article entitled "The partner pay gap: Associations between spouses' relative earnings and life satisfaction among couples in the UK" reported that despite women's relatively recent gains in education and employment, men still tend to out-earn their wives. This *partner pay gap* has relevance to one's overall life satisfaction. Specifically, these investigators found that men endorse a more significant positive change in their level of life satisfaction when their earnings increase proportionately more than their wife's earning, however, for women there did not appear to be an association between changes in proportional earnings and how satisfied they are with their lives. They also found that husbands who earned less than their wives reported lower levels of life satisfaction than did husbands who earned more than or equal to their wives. They concluded there is compelling evidence of the continued role of gendered norms in sustaining the partner pay gap. They hypothesized that this is similar to the situation in the U.S. and other Western countries. There was no mention of any "gender-related psychology of envy" in such pay gap situations in the articles on this topic in the U.S. literature reviewed for this chapter.

One's gender and amount of earnings and other income still play a key role in how stature, power, and influence operate in many families. Most of the current research from the U.S. and Western countries abroad substantiates that because many wives either earn no income or earn substantially less than their husbands do, they are not truly deemed equal in the relationship. The complex interaction of gender and financial stature in the marriage cannot be underestimated, although at a social level in the U.S. the underlying disparity is more often overlooked or denied. Still, the children in many families subtly learn these attitudes and values and incorporate them into their own thinking and behaviors. A toast to those couples where real equality exists—not related to one's gender, amount of salary or inherited wealth but to their overall contributions to their marriage, children, parent family and society.

Today, although many men keep their brokerage accounts in single name, others have them in joint names with their partner. Many investment advisors in major prominent *FINRA* regulated investment firms may suggest he or she meet periodically with both members of the couple and sometimes with members of several generations of the family so they can discuss issues like setting up trusts, specifying beneficiaries in their wills, and educating the children in understanding money, investments, and inheritances. *FINRA*, the Financial Industry Regulatory Authority, was founded in July 2007. It is a private American company that acts as a major organization regulating member brokerage firms and exchange markets. It enables firms and investors to participate in the market with full confidence by safeguarding its integrity with great expertise.

The couple's financial advisor may suggest the couple parallel these discussions with their attorney handling their Will. Since state laws concerning Wills and transferring of wealth vary, if the grandparents and parents live in different states, the provisos worked out will have to be acceptable across state lines.

Case #3: The Kline Family

Although Mrs. Joanne Kline had worked as an Executive Secretary to the Chairman of a midsized corporation after finishing college for a few years before she married and had children, when they came in to see me, she had not worked in 8 years. She was eager to return to the work-a-day world, at least part time, while the children were in school. Besides being eager for more stimulating time with adults during this day, she wanted to model for their children that some women who want and/or need to can successfully balance marriage and a career. Her husband, Jerry, was opposed to it, stressing he earned more than enough to support the family. She emphasized this was not about insufficient income, that he was a fine provider, but about her own needs and self-image and how the children viewed the various additional roles married women could play, adding volunteer and paid work into the mix.

His other reasons for objecting were: (1) none of his friends' wives worked for pay and this would make him look inadequate to his friends; (2) his mother hadn't "embarrassed" his father by working, (3) that she should be home if the children were sick or on vacation. I suggested that perhaps she could find and try out a job for three-half days a week and see how it worked out for the four of them, and as tactfully as possible, that maybe he might read some twenty-first century literature about the needs and right of today's women, especially intelligent and energetic ones who want to be Mrs. X and *also* have their own separate identity, just as her husband does. With reservations, but because Jerry cared deeply for his wife—he agreed. They came in for 6 weekly sessions and kept dealing with the situation in and out of therapy. Finally, he said, "ok, let's give it a try" after talking to some of his buddies who were comfortable with and supportive of their wives working.

Joanne and Jerry also did some refiguring of their budget and she indicated she now would pay for her own expensive wardrobe, the visits to her beauty parlor and occasional theater tickets. After six sessions, we took a break for a month. When they returned, both agreed the new arrangement was working well and the marriage was probably "better than ever."

Case Conclusions

Making major changes like those just discussed can be challenging to one's self-image and self-esteem. When it is done over time by (almost) mutual consent, it can be very gratifying. Unfortunately, when it happens because either the husband or wife becomes incapacitated and their partner has to perhaps take on double responsibility, perhaps quit work, hire a nurse and/or housekeeper, the situation often has with more serious consequences.

With all the emphasis placed on gender roles in the literature, I found no reference to those identified as LGBTQ couples in any of the publications from the U.S. or several other countries. This seems a strange oversight at this point in historical time.

In an article on household financial organization, Hu (2019) reported on his research exploring the role played by the specific household's financial organization in configuring the participation in housework of both the men and women in moderating the impact of earnings on housework. He found that women's individual earnings often reduce their time available to spend doing housework. He concluded that "household financial organization is a key premise" undergirding how and when gender equality in the public sphere helps promulgate gender equality at home.

Importance of Financial Planning

Compared to relatively high-income and high-net-worth individuals, people who are wealthy are less likely to avoid money and financial stress and are more satisfied with their life and finances and have a more internal locus of control (Klontz et al., 2015). They are more likely to report workaholic behaviors and having made some "significant investment mistakes." They also enjoy being wealthy and all the pleasures and status this can entail, have a stronger drive to increase their wealth, and are more committed to following their passions.

Compared to financial planners, therapists often are money avoidant and espouse anti-rich beliefs, especially when they experience financial pressures. Their own unresolved issues about money result in many therapists avoiding the topic in therapy, feeling envious of people who are wealthy, and having a more difficult time forging a strong positive rapport with wealthier patients (Klontz et al., 2015). Thus, it is often advisable to include people's financial planners and accountants into the picture when addressing complicated financial matters or even tasks such as filing tax returns. Therapists capable of addressing the psychological component of how their clients view and handle money and their overall financial health may find this improves their clients' overall psychological well-being.

Williamson and Schouweller (2023) found that shared spousal time is an important component of maintaining a good relationship and reported that over the past few decades many couples are spending more time together. They also found that divorce rates have risen much more for lower than higher income couples. They posit that lower income couples may face more time-consuming stressors which limit the amount of time they have to spend together and experience more stress when they are together than high-income couples do. Their results support the theory that the quality and quantity of shared time is a critical variable in explaining differential relationship outcomes between higher and lower income couples. They suggest that the therapist might encourage couples to figure out how to have more time to spend together by realigning their work schedules to match better. (And I would add, to enjoy activities and friends they both like). Their study further provided evidence that "constraints on time use" may be one contributing factor to poorer relational outcomes among lower as compared to higher income couples as they experience higher levels of stress when they are together. They posit that the lack of enjoyable time spent together may be a contributing causative factor to higher divorce rates among lower income couples.

Conclusions

In sum, both the making of relocation decisions and the handling of finances can be a compatible joint venture and be conducive to generating acceptable and workable short-term and long-term decisions about where the couple/family should reside and regarding financial planning from which all family members will benefit. Or it can be an ongoing source of contention, sometimes leading to divorce and numerous complications regarding alimony in a divorce settlement. How people allocate their time and their spending of money is also contingent upon their values as to what is important in life.

Thus, when dealing with both relocation decisions and financial issues, present and future, the therapist needs to help the couple disentangle what the disagreements are about—are they related to issues of power and control, dominance and submission, or is one partner saying the equivalent of "you understand and handle the finances better than I do, so I'm happy to let you do it. I know you are smart and will be fair?" Either the therapist, the financial advisor, and/or their accountant, might raise questions about this, if only one is knowledgeable about family finances. If that one dies, how does the other quickly learn how to manage the finances and who can he or she turn to be taught money management and investing. The financial consultant can make suggestions but can't be a long-term tutor.

Suffice it to say relocation issues and "money matters" are subjects most couples must deal with during their lives together. Therapists can deal with relationship aspects and sometimes with financial issues and need to be careful to keep discussions in the realm of reality, not fantasy or conjecture.

References

Deutsch, R. A. (Ed.). (2014). *Traumatic ruptures: Abandonment and betraual in the analytic relationship*. Routledge.

Erlinghagen, M. (2020). Love in motion: Migration patterns of internationally mobile couples. *Population, Space and Place, 27*(2), e2382. https://doi.org/10.1002/psp.2382

Freud, A. (1970). *The ego and its mechanisms of defense (The writings of Anna Freud)* (Vol. 2). International Universities Press.

Gash, V., & Plagnol, A. (2021). The partner pay gap: Associations between spouses' relative earnings and life satisfaction among couples in the U.K. *Work, Employment and Society, 35*(3), 566–583. https://doi.org/10.1177/0950017020946657

Goldner, L. (2016). Therapists' self-perceptions, attachment, and relationship: The role of selfobject needs. *Psychoanalytic Psychology, 33*(4), 535–553. https://doi.org/10.1177/0950017020946657
Hu, Y. (2019). What about money? Earnings, household financial organization, and housework. *Journal of Marriage and Family, 81*(5), 1091–1109. https://doi.org/10.1111/jomf.12590
Klontz, B., Sullivan, P., Seay, M., & Conale, A. (2015). The wealthy: A financial psychological profile. *Consulting Psychology Journal: Practice and Research, 67*(2), 127–144. https://doi.org/10.1037/cpb0000027
Ulrich, J., Pluut, H., & Buttgen, M. (2015). Gender differences in the family-relatedness of relocation decisions. *Journal of Vocational Behavior, 90*, 1–12. https://doi.org/10.1016/j.jvb.2015.06.003
Van der Velde, M., Jansen, P., Bal, P., & Van Erp, K. (2017). Dual-earner couples' willingness to relocate abroad: The reciprocal influence of both partners' career role salience and parter role salience. *European Journal of Work and Organizational Psychology, 26*(2), 195–207. https://doi.org/10.1080/1359432X.2016.1241768
Williamson, H., & Schouweller. (2023, June). Household income differentiates quantity and quality of shared spousal time. *Journal of Family Psychology, 37*(4), 528–537. https://doi.org/10.1037/fam0001078

Florence W. Kaslow, PhD, ABPP, is in private practice as an individual, couples and family psychologist and Family Business Consultant in West Palm Beach, FL. She has been a Professor at a Medical School in Philadelphia and a former Dean of a Psychology graduate school in Florida. She has guest lectured in over 50 countries, is the author or editor of 32 books, and a contributor to over 100 other books.

Chapter 11
The Rewards and Challenges of International Adoption

Karyne B. Wilner

The Rewards and Challenges of International Adoption

International adoption involves several parties: the adoptee, the adoptive parents and their extended family, the birth parents, and the agencies, lawyers, and governments that make it happen. This chapter focuses on the experiences of those who will live and grow together, the adoptive parents, and the children they adopt. It emphasizes what adoptive parents need to know and what they can expect, how international adoption will affect the emotional context of the family and the emotional health of a child paired with parents with whom they aren't matched genetically, culturally, or sometimes racially, and the types of therapeutic help available to them (Baden et al., 2015, 2017; Kim et al., 2024; Kim, 2021; Lee, 2003; Melosh, 2002; Pertman, 2011; Selman, 2009).

Families Desiring to Adopt Internationally

By 2011, one out of every five adopted children were from another country, and of those under the age of 2 years, two out of five were international adoptees (Selman, 2009; Tessler et al., 2011). At the end of the Korean war, in the early 1950s, Korea was the main source of internationally adopted children. However, since the 1990s, most international adoptees have been born in China. Seventy-eight thousand children, mainly girls, were adopted from China between 1992 and 2010 (Koh et al., 2022). Although they have been adopted by parents living around the world, many of them came to the United States (U.S.). International adoptions to the U.S. peaked

K. B. Wilner (✉)
Core Energetics Academy, Newtown, CT, USA

F. W. Kaslow (ed.), *Contemporary Issues in Individual, Couple, and Family Lives and Treatment*, https://doi.org/10.1007/978-3-031-90006-8_11

at twenty-three thousand in 2004 (Jones, 2019). Since then, they have significantly declined (Budiman & Lopez, 2017; Koh et al., 2022; Mignot, 2015), but China provided the most children until recently. In 2022, due to the covid outbreak, Chinese adoptions stopped all together, but were resumed during the summer of 2023. However, on August 28, 2024, China officially ended its inter country adoption program with all foreign countries, including the United States. Other Asian countries that American parents adopt children from include South Korea, Viet Nam, and India. Latin America has also been a major source of international adoptees, particularly Columbia, Guatemala, and more recently, Haiti. Additionally, some people wishing to adopt have turned to Ethiopia, Africa.

Due to unethical and immoral behavior on the part of people in some countries, the number of countries offering children for adoption has shrunken, as has the number of countries opening their borders to receive international adoptees. Whereas 23,000 intercountry adoptions took place within the U.S in 2004, by 2017, the number had fallen to 4000 (Koh et al., 2022). Because domestic adoptions have increased within countries from which U.S. citizens have adopted children in the past and policies have been put in place to halt child trafficking, fewer international children have been available for U.S. families to adopt (Mignot, 2015; Montgomery & Powell, 2018). According to the Child Welfare Information Agency's (2022) research data, by 2019 the total number of international adoptions per annum to the U.S had dropped to a low of 3000.

The Path that Leads to International Adoption for Families

Couples and families adopt internationally for some of the same reasons that people adopt nationally (Pertman, 2011; Siegel, 2008; Soares et al., 2023). Some feel a strong need and desire to have a child, a deep biological urge, that calls to them all hours of the day or night. They have not been able to conceive, having experienced painful and disappointing failures, and they may feel desperate. For others, the strong desire to nurture, love, and guide a little one from infancy to early adulthood is strong, although they do not wish to conceive themselves. This need, often attributed to women, is also felt by many men. Some people adopt because they are alone and lonely and building a family would give purpose to their lives. Others want to share the holiday rituals, the opportunity to make cookies, wrap presents to place under the tree, dye and hide Easter eggs, or have the children ask the four questions at the Passover Seder. Sometimes couples adopt for social-political reasons. They know the world is overpopulated and wonder "why have children when so many who are already here need a home?" Others adopt to maintain family continuity. When they're gone, someone will carry on their family name or their life's work. Religious and spiritual reasons can motivate people to adopt. Adoption is regarded as an act of kindness and generosity, and fulfillment comes from giving those in need a home, education, and family life.

People who chose to adopt internationally have some additional reasons (Dubinsky, 2010; Freundlich, 2000; Schwartz & Kaslow, 2003). In some cases, they are attracted to a particular country due to their ancestry, prior travel experiences, places they were stationed while serving in the armed forces, to answer a spiritual calling, or perhaps a book or author left a deep impression about what a wonderful experience it can be. Many want to be assured of a confidential adoption, which is more likely to occur outside of the U.S., given that open adoptions have become popular in the U.S. Confidentiality is important to those who want to avoid disagreements with birth parents over how to raise the child, steer clear of being challenged in court about the right to raise the child, and trust that their children will not feel emotionally torn between two sets of parents given that the two sets of parents are in different countries.

Those who adopt internationally may also believe that the children they receive will be physically and emotionally healthier than those available in the U.S., since children placed for adoption in the U.S. often have suffered prior neglect or abandonment (Cohen & Farnia, 2011; Groza et al., 2003; Johnson, 1999–2024). Additionally, children are not always available for adoption nationally, because women have chosen to abort unwanted fetuses rather than carry them full term, and because of lower birthrates. Waiting for a child without being certain of the outcome has not made sense to those desperate for a child when other countries have children available. When couples adopt internationally, they may have the opportunity to receive children who look like them—which is important to some people. Those who are white can look to Eastern Europe and people of color to Africa or Asia or Latinx countries. Finally, adopting internationally may feel morally sanctioned. After the holocaust, the author's great aunt and uncle adopted a boy from Germany whose parents died in a concentration camp. He became an integral part of the family.

Adoption May Not be for Everyone

Not everyone who fails to conceive should adopt. Sometimes the family of origin pressures a couple to adopt without considering if it is right for them. Those who do not want to parent should not feel shame or be pressured. Many people have a wonderful and fulfilling life without children of their own. People may choose not to adopt because they fear taking on emotional or physical problems that are beyond their capacity to deal with, problems that may not show up until the child is older. They may fear the financial stress of raising a child. Feeding, educating, socializing, and clothing a child can be a financial burden. According to U.S. statistics, raising a child will cost approximately $235, 000.00 over a lifetime (Holten, 2023). Additionally, international adoptions are expensive, loaded with fees for agencies, attorneys, governments, and orphanages.

Other couples love their freedom. They want to have fun, work long hours, or live spontaneously without planning ahead. Adopting may not fit their lifestyle. Children have to attend school, limiting the couples' travel for a number of years to come, and they need parents to be available to spend time with them. Finally, some couples dislike or are uncomfortable with children. For them, adoption would be inappropriate. The decision to adopt or not should depend on what is best for those involved and couples should not be swayed or persuaded by the opinions of others, no matter how well-meaning their intention.

Preparing for International Adoption

Doing the Necessary Homework

Whether the adopting families are a couple, single, straight, or gay, if choosing to adopt internationally, it is important for them to gather information (Pertman, 2011). Families need to research which agency will best serve them and which countries are most likely to meet their needs (Pavao, 2005; Schwartz & Kaslow, 2003). Some countries, but not all, are open to same-sex couples and/or single parents adopting their children. Countries have different rules concerning age; many set the upper limit for adopting a child between 50 and 55 years, but this can be as low as age 35 in other countries. Older parents often receive older children.

Because agencies differ, potential adoptive parents may feel more comfortable working with one more than another. Some will seem too rigid, and others too laid back. Some have too much paperwork; others will seem less interested in the parents than in their ability to pay. Some will have high fees for their services. Others will lack connections with the country the family is interested in adopting from, making it more difficult for them to be matched with a child. Cost may also be a factor in choosing an agency. An international adoption can be expensive, although there may be government subsidies and tax breaks when the child becomes part of the family. Adoptive families may also have personal preferences concerning whether the agency is small or large, and its location, whether it is local or at a great distance.

It is suggested that families considering an international adoption ask friends, family members, and colleagues who have experienced successful international adoptions in the past to recommend an agency. People should query their contacts and find out what they liked and did not like about an agency. Those wanting to adopt may want to interview several agencies, asking about their procedures both in the U.S. and then later when the family is preparing to travel abroad. They should look for an agency that will guide them through the entire process, preparing them for the initial interview and home study, making the referral, helping with travel arrangements, guiding their stay in the adoptive country, aiding in the bonding process if help is needed, and organizing the trip home. It is important to find an agency that will support the family through the first year or two after the adoption if they desire this assistance.

If the family chooses to adopt from another country, they will be paying more than if they were to adopt nationally, because the U.S. government subsidizes in-country adoptions (Pavao, 2005; Pertman, 2011) and if they adopt a child in foster care, there would be little to no cost. On average, an international adoption can cost from $20,000 to $50,000 because of fees to the agency, the lawyers involved, and the placing orphanage if there is one, as well as fees levied by the child's home country, and travel and food costs (Holt International, 2024). Once they return to the U.S., families may need to pay doctors who specialize in any health issues their new child has, and child psychologists, family therapists, or social workers, if there are emotional or behavioral problems. One's health insurance company may cover some but not all these costs. The adopting couple will also have to pay for childcare if both parents work outside the home.

Building a Network

Before the family hoping to adopt internationally is matched with a child, they should begin to build and organize their team (Adamec, 2005; Johnson, 1999–2024, Pertman, 2011). The team should include a pediatrician, preferably one with experience with children from the country from which they are adopting or at minimum one familiar with health issues common in global adoptions (e.g., malnutrition, rickets, fetal alcohol syndrome, and lead poisoning). It should also include a lawyer who understands adoption law and who knows whether readoption is necessary (i.e., legal process by which an international adoption, completed in another country, is recognized and validated within the U.S., ensuring that the child has full legal rights). An attorney can also help the family obtain a U.S. birth certificate and passport for the child, as well as help ensure and protect both the parents and the child's rights. Childcare professionals also may be an important part of the team. Adoptive parents who both work need to make childcare arrangements (e.g., nanny, au pair, willing relative, day care) for when they return with their internationally adopted child. Because families compete for good childcare, the parents should start this process early, so that the child can be put on a waiting list. Some adoptive families hire a nanny or au pair from the same country as the child they are waiting to receive to facilitate the child's transition from their homeland to the U.S. When relationships with the nanny or au pair work out well, friendships develop that last for years.

Participating in the International Adoption Process

Once an agency is selected, the first meaningful step involves a home study. Usually, a social worker visits the home, interviews the family, and ascertains if they have an appropriate living space to house a child and whether they can nurture a child. Prior to and during this process, the family may feel anxious and wonder if they will be evaluated and found lacking. They may be concerned that some small snag could upend the process, a candle in the wrong place, a cooking smell, dog hair on a sofa, or words that sound harsh or unfriendly. Potential adoptive parents experience relief upon approval and then prepare their home to welcome the international child who is to become part of their family.

Between 6 months to a year after the home study, the family usually receives a packet of information about the child who will become a member of their family. The envelope includes a photograph, medical history, name, age, list of words the child can say, and developmental milestones met, such as standing and sitting. With this information in hand, the author recommends that the family consult with a doctor who specializes in adoption. In the U.S. and Canada there are international adoption medical clinics, often associated with universities or large hospital systems that can be good resources. They can help parents who have been matched with a child decide whether they should go forward with the adoption based on the health information included in the packet. After reviewing the medical facts, the doctor can make a recommendation about whether the child is healthy enough to become a responsible family member. If the health history indicates potential problems, the doctor can advise whether they would be too costly to treat, either emotionally or financially, for the family to move forward in adopting this particular child. Additionally, adoption medical clinics can help resolve any outstanding medical issues and attain the vaccines that may be necessary for the child once he or she returns with the family to the U.S.

When the time comes to meet their child, excited and nervous, the family sometimes travels to the child's country with other families represented by the same agency. During the time spent together at airports, hotels, restaurants, and in government offices, families bond. Some communicate for several years once they return to the U.S., becoming a support system for each other, comparing notes, and offering solutions for common problems.

A few days after arriving at the city where the families are to meet their child, their children are literally placed in their arms. In China the "mamas," aides from the orphanage, bring each child to their new parents. Tears may be shed as the children and the helpers say their goodbyes. Many families receive an infant; however, some receive an older or special needs child. In some cases (e.g., Case # 1 below), children are flown with representatives from their country to the U.S. and meet their new family at the airport. Family life begins as soon as the child is placed in the parents' arms. At this point the guardians say goodbye and return to their country.

Although it is unusual, in some countries the child the family receives may not be the child with whom they were originally matched, (see Case Example # 2 below.) The child who has been promised for placement by an orphanage and government becomes sick, has an accident, or dies. Another child is released to the family instead. If this occurs, the family should report the exchange to the guide within the country who represents their agency. That person will then negotiate with the orphanage to find the best solution for the family. Even though the family has traveled a great distance and bonded with the picture of the child they are about to receive, the options they are given include keeping this child, returning to the

U.S. and waiting for another referral, or taking a different child from the same orphanage.

Case #1: Hilary, a Single Adoptive Mother and her New Daughter

Hillary, an adoptee herself, and a single mother, was in the process of adopting an international child from a country in South America. Her agency reported one hold up after another and she began to wonder if it had to do with the fact that she was adopting as a single woman. Single people sometimes face more scrutiny related to questions about their ability to provide a stable and supportive environment without a partner. Some countries may have biases or misconceptions about a single person's ability to raise a child, questioning whether one has the financial resources necessary and the network of friends and family to offer support. Some agencies may prioritize couples, even though they may not admit it. Hillary had become increasingly frustrated and upset, since she had been waiting to receive the child that she was matched with for over 2 years. The wait was so painful that she contacted a therapist to help her deal with her feelings. With the therapist's help, she was able to be more confrontational with the people who ran the agency and a few months later her daughter arrived. On that happy day, her daughter, now a toddler, flew from her home country to the U.S., escorted by nannies from the orphanage, and she was handed over to Hillary at the airport.

Case # 2: An Older Couple Adopting a Chinese Child

The adopting couple was in their early fifties, both divorce attorneys. They traveled to China with several younger couples adopting from the same agency. A year earlier, the adopting mother had experienced a deep yearning for a daughter, and her husband suggested that they try to adopt internationally. Since her favorite books from childhood, *Old Buddha* (Der Princess, 1928) and *The Good Earth* (Buck, 1959), were based in China, she knew immediately that she would like to adopt a daughter from China. Luck was with them, because that year, 2000, China allowed couples up to age 55 to adopt, although the child they received would be age two or older. A few hours after receiving their child, they realized that this beautiful little girl who had a full set of teeth couldn't speak, stand, or walk, all behaviors which the child they were told they were getting had mastered. The slight indentations on either side of the child's forehead made them wonder if lead poisoning was a factor. Knowing they did not have the bandwidth or support to care for a special needs child, they called their agency in the U.S., explaining, "This child doesn't look or act at all like the child we were referred" and asking, "What should we do?" The adoption counselor reminded them that they had missed the meeting warning families that situations like this do occur. She told them to explain the situation to their group's leader in China immediately. They were then given the option of returning home to wait for another referral from Beijing or taking another child from the same orphanage. Since they did not want to make such a long trip again, they opted for another child, asking for one who had been recently abandoned, because they were concerned about children being institutionalized too long (Cohen & Farnia, 2011; Tan et al., 2010). The orphanage director introduced them to four children and when one smiled at the mother-to-be in such a way that a beam of energy like a current seemed to cross between them, she knew she was to be her daughter. Although most families who adopt internationally do not have the opportunity to choose their children, sometimes it seems as if synchronicity is at play because many families receive a child who is right for them (Gammage, 2007).

Preparing Family and Friends Ahead of Time

Generally, when adopting internationally, one will need the support of others. The author, who adopted a child from China in the early 2000s, appreciated her father's assistance, valuing his support and encouragement when other people in her life were questioning the wisdom of adopting at her age. She also appreciated her aunt's willingness to be a substitute grandmother, taking on that role because her own mother was deceased.

If the adopting parents are a couple, they still need other people to talk with about the challenges that face them so they do not overwhelm each other with complaints and concerns. It is helpful for new parents to have friends or relatives they can talk to the first time their child uses a bad word or has to be rushed to the hospital after a bee sting or fall. Hillary Clinton, in *It Takes a Village: And Other Lessons Children Teach Us,* (1996, Simon & Schuster) emphasized that parents need support from their community and that it takes multiple people and relationships to raise a child.

In the U.S., family members often live far apart and are not nearby to help welcome the child and visit or available to assist in care giving. Instead, the couple may turn to networks of others who will replace the roles extended family members assumed in earlier time periods. These others consist of church groups, community groups, friend groups, play groups, book groups, neighbor groups, adoptive parent groups, and family therapists (Gray, 2011, 2012; Johnson, 1999–2024; Tan et al., 2012). However, one perk current technology offers is the ability to communicate with family members residing at a distance. Using the internet or smartphone, parents can share baby's first steps with a grandmother who lives thousands of miles away. Families can still be involved, but their role is passive, rather than hands-on.

When international adoption is being seriously considered, family members are not always supportive (Baden, 2016; March, 1995; Suter & Ballard, 2009). They may have negative attitudes and beliefs about adoption; ask intrusive questions (e.g., "Can you afford it?"; "What if the child has mental problems?"); or make critical statements (e.g., "You're still a child yourself"; "You don't have the patience to raise a child"). It may take time for some family members to accept the changes in the parents-to-be and in the family as they know it. The negative beliefs and attitudes they hold may be out of concern for the parents because they fear that they may be hurt and suffer disappointment during the adoption process. It is important for the prospective parents to let friends and relatives know of the plan to adopt as soon as they feel comfortable sharing the news, so that they have time to adjust to the idea (Gray, 2012). However, it may be necessary to hold back from telling certain family members if their hostility is such that they are likely to sabotage the adoption. In one case I am familiar with, a spiteful sister expressed concerns about the couples' ability to parent to the adoption agency they were working with, almost jeopardizing the adoption.

Because one's life will change, it is important that family and friends accept changes in the parents-to-be, recognizing that parenting an international child will require them to behave and act differently. For instance, they will no longer be available to pet sit on weekends or to do most of the cooking for Thanksgiving. Instead, they may be attending a Chinese New Year's celebration with other adopting families or an Ethiopian dinner with friends. When friends and family cannot adjust, the adopting family may have to temporarily distance themselves from them, so as not to create stress in their home. Some couples attend counseling sessions to process their feelings and get advice on dealing with resistant and negative relatives. Using role-play and other techniques, couples learn to communicate under stress and to de-escalate highly emotional situations (Wilner, 2024).

Those who adopt want their family and friends to celebrate their newly adopted international child whose need for positive reinforcement will be strong. If compliments come from the parents only, the child may not believe them, thinking, "parents say that because they have to." But compliments and warmth coming from a close community of people will help the child trust that what is being said is indeed true. Supportive communities of extended family and friends will help internationally adopted children adjust to their new lives and feel a greater sense of belonging.

Welcoming Internationally Adopted Children

Welcoming the international adopted child home requires some emotional work. It is important to resolve as many differences as possible between the parents and other family members before bringing the child home. Many couples are poles apart concerning what is involved in effective parenting, because they were raised differently. It's not unusual for each person to model their own parenting after their parents' behavior, even if they disagreed with some of what their parents had done at the time. Disagreements about how to parent can lead to anger and disapproval that creates a negative atmosphere in the home. By accepting these differences, without judging or demeaning each other, the parents will create a supportive environment in which the adopted child can flourish (Wilner, 2024). If the differences between the parents are large, by working with a family therapist they may be able to resolve these problems in a timely way (Gottman & Gottman, 2008; Johnston, 2012). Tools couple and family therapists use to help parents resolve differences include trust building exercises, psychoeducation that emphasizes common challenges and provides information about developmental stages, and sharing emotions triggered by adopting a child. A family systems approach looks at the roles each parent takes, and a problem-solving approach teaches skills that encourage team building (Gottman & Gottman, 2008).

Integrating the newly adopted international child into the family calls for forethought to prevent negative events (Schwartz & Kaslow, 2003). Deciding where the child will sleep and ensuring that the room is warm and age appropriate is key. It is also necessary to schedule time with the child, which may require the parents to put some of their favorite pursuits on hold or reduce the prioritization of them until the child is older. Children need their parents during this emotionally difficult transition period, as they deal with the loss of all that was familiar. If there are biological or adoptive children in the home, they need to be prepared for the upcoming adoption, so they can be part of the welcoming committee and deal with whatever issues the adoption triggers in them. Although sibling rivalry is normal, it should not get out of hand or turn hostile. Some parents bring their older children with them when they travel to the country of the child's origin so the entire family is involved in the process. If that is not possible or feasible, the parents need to devise ways the older children can participate (e.g., decorating the room, planning a welcome home party) (Eldridge, 1999, 2009; Gray, 2011, 2012: Melina, 1989, 1998; Steinberg & Hall, 2013). Most important is developing a strong attachment between the newly adoptive child and the family and promoting their sense of belonging, which may be challenging when skin color, language, tastes in food, and lifestyles differ (Baden et al., 2012; Lee, 2003; March, 1995; Montgomery & Jordan, 2018).

Attending to the Impact on the Couple

In addition to exploring differences concerning how they view parenting, each member of the couple may discover new aspects of themselves and of the other when they adopt an international child. One may learn that their serious spouse can be extremely playful and enthusiastically build sandcastles on the beach or one may come face to face with a jealous part of themselves that arises when the other hugs the child or makes smiley faces to entertain them. When a new child enters the home, intimacy also changes. The couple's sex life may diminish until they figure out how to attain some private time (Gottman & Gottman, 2008). The couple may have to contend with differences in the way their new baby relates to each of them. For instance, in China, the author noticed one adoptive couple struggling with their baby's strong negative reaction to her new mother. Whereas she lay peacefully in her father's arms, she would scream as soon as her mother touched her. Communicating with this family later, the author learned it took a year for their daughter to bond with her mother; international adoptees' gender preferences may result from their earlier experiences with birth parents or orphanage employees.

In a similar situation, a client of mine who was traveling with her church group in Africa met an orphan girl she wanted to adopt. Phoning her husband, he agreed to the adoption, but because he was not there, the child did not develop the same rapport with him. It took longer for her to accept him. With enough love, compassion, and patience, attachment eventually occurs (Gammage, 2007). If the bonding process is slow or not happening, couple and family therapists who specialize in adoption can help internationally adopted children bond with their parents. Therapeutic Parenting Training can help internationally adopting parents build trust and relationships and Trauma Informed Care can provide tools to help internationally adopted children heal from their past traumas (Purvis et al., 2007).

Telling Internationally Adopted Children Their Story

When internationally adopted children display enough cognitive development to understand concepts, usually between ages three and five, the adoptive parents should begin explaining adoption to them (Smalley & Schooler, 2015). There are many good books written by professionals to help with explanations such as: *Our own: Adopting and parenting the older child* (Maskew, 2003); *Adoption is a family affair! What relatives and friends must know* (Johnston, 2012); and *Talking to young children about adoption* (Watkins & Fisher, 1995). Additionally, children's books supporting adoption are plentiful, such as: *Tell me again about the night I was born* (Curtis, 2000); *A mother for Choco* (Kasza, 1996); *We belong together: A book about adoption and families* (Parr, 2011); and *I wished for you: An adoption story* (Richmond, 2008). The main points in explaining adoption are:

1. Make the explanations simple, direct, and honest.
2. Tell the children that they were born to other parents who could not take care of them. Since they may ask, "why not," be prepared with an answer.
3. Talk about how much you (you and your partner) wanted them, and briefly explain the process you went through to adopt them.
4. Have ongoing conversations, often repeating the story.
5. Use age-appropriate language when you tell their story.
6. Give them your full attention, so that you are not distracted with phone calls, cooking, or other children's requests for attention.
7. Validate their feelings: they may feel sad, happy, or angry.
8. Normalize adoption. Tell them that many people adopt children and tell them some of the reasons why. Also explain that birthparents cannot always keep their children—because of such problems as poverty, war, and illness.
9. Speak about international adoption positively.
10. Explain that adoption is forever. You will be there for them through difficult and happy times.

Here is a sample conversation: *Your mommy and daddy loved you very much, but they couldn't take care of you. Because they wanted you to have a great life and a permanent home, they took you to a place that would find a new set of parents and a new home for you. We were looking for you. We wanted a baby girl or boy just like you. So we went to a wonderful agency and asked them to help us find you. They found you at the place your parents left you and we went to your country to meet you. We loved you immediately, upon first sight, and brought you home to live with us and be part of our family. Now you are here with us, and we are so thankful and have so much gratitude.*

Challenges Families Who Adopt Internationally Experience

Initial Stresses

No international adoption is without challenges from the beginning. Such challenges may include expecting to receive an infant and leaving with a toddler who needed a seat on the plane not previously arranged, having an older child run out of their new parents-to-be hotel room and escape, dealing an infant who won't stop crying or screaming even when picked up and rocked for hours, dealing with airline personnel expressing annoyance over last minute changes in bookings, or arriving back in the U.S. and learning that friends and family are afraid to meet your new child believing they might be bringing a disease into the country. Initially, these experiences are fraught with anxiety, but years later they become fond, friendly memories worth a chuckle (Gammage, 2007). These initial challenges are a central part of the adoptee's story and their successful navigation becomes the building blocks of creating a vibrant family life.

It is not possible to predict how newly adopted children will behave in the beginning. For some children, the adoption may be exciting and joyful, and for others it may be overwhelming (Purvis et al., 2007). Some will have temper tantrums and others will express curiosity and delight. There is so much that is new to them—the atmosphere, the people, smells, foods, and sounds—and each child will cope differently. The bombardment of new stimuli is stressful for some, creating tension and unpleasant sensations in the child's body. Others will enjoy being taken care of, wearing clean, fresh clothing, and being fed enough in a timely manner. It's a time of change and uncertainty and the child may wonder, *"Will this good stuff last?" "Will I be abandoned again?" "Will I see the friends I made in the orphanage?"*

Internationally Adopted Children Need to Feel Safe and Secure

Often upon arriving in the U.S., internationally adopted children are grieving (Boss, 1999). They miss prior caretakers, the food, the scents, the sounds of their home country and their language (Gammage, 2007). Research has shown that even babies who are only two or three days old can grieve the loss of their birth mother. The nine-month bond that develops while they are in the womb—the biological mother's smell, feel, taste, and sound—are all gone. This loss can be traumatic (Siegel,

2012; Verrier, 2015; Wilner, 2020). On an unconscious level, internationally adopted children feel the loss, the rejection, and the abandonment. The separation from the biological mother can imprint on the infant a sense of futility of ever receiving the love it needs. Prenatal memories that live in the unconscious can be reactivated during stressful time periods. In fact, early wounding can be so deep that some adoption theorists suggest not adopting children over the age of one (Rampage et al., 2011) as it effects their ability to build relationships. Others disagree, explaining that primal wounds do not always translate into developmental problems. Research supports this latter theory and shows that international adoptees who have experienced loss of their birth mothers attach to their caregivers as well as non-adoptees do, especially when they are adopted at a young age (van den Dries et al., 2009). However, both points of view may be correct, as some international adoptees do face difficulty in creating successful attachments, and they will often seek counseling at a later time from family therapists who are able to help them work through issues of early loss and confusion about their identity (Brodzinsky, 2013; Gray, 2011; Tan & Yi, 2019).

In response to leaving the orphanage—the only home some international adoptees have ever known—they may act out or have tantrums. These physical manifestations are short in duration and indicate that the children had attached to their caretakers at the orphanage. To decrease these incidents and help the children feel secure, it's important for adoptive parents to take steps to bond with their children, a topic discussed earlier in this chapter (Brodzinsky, 1987; Lifton, 1995, 2009; Pavao, 2005; Verrier, 1993; Verrier, 2015).

Because it takes time to adjust to new and different circumstances, internationally adopted children experience more safety if they feel seen and heard. Communication is important and they need their adoptive parents to listen, be attentive, and to ask them questions about themselves. They are also very sensitive to discipline and if punishment is too harsh, they can possibly see it as a sign of not being wanted or loved, or they can interpret it to mean there is something wrong with them. Although it is important for parents to keep clear boundaries, if the child perceives their adoptive parents as overly authoritative or too strict, the parents will risk losing the child's affection (Foli & Thompson, 2004; Gray, 2012; Kupecky & Keck, 2009; Post, 2010).

Sound advice to adoptive parents is to be accepting and even tolerant of unusual behaviors, such as hiding food, refusing to undress or get dressed, crying for no reason, or not eating. The child is dealing with loss and much anxiety about change. It takes time to adjust. Children need their parents to be patient and remember that time heals. Therapeutic approaches that help families whose adopted children are struggling with loss and lack of bonding include attachment counseling, exercises to facilitate trust, and psychoeducation focusing on adoption issues, such as loss of identity and culture, grief counseling, and trauma-based counseling.

On the surface, internationally adopted children may look like they have adjusted well and indeed many do. They have friends at school and in the neighborhood, good grades, and they have set future goals, like attending college. However, they may struggle with issues around being adopted internally. For instance, there is empirical evidence that international adoptees do not feel comfortable talking with their adopted parents about these feelings and instead they are prone to suppress them (Brodzinsky et al., 1993; Verrier, 1993). Many internationally adopted children view adoption as a sign of being less desirable than other people. They may think there's something wrong with them because they weren't wanted, and therefore, they feel like second class citizens (Grotevant & von Orff, 2011; March, 1995).

Additionally, there can be shame around skin color, especially when non-white children are being raised in a white family (Baden et al., 2015; Baden et al., 2012; Montgomery & Jordan, 2018; Steinberg & Hall, 2013). Prior to the year 2000, international adoption was color blind. Adoption counselors and adoptive parents thought that the color of one's skin was less important than growing up in a warm nurturing family. Therefore, racial socialization did not exist. Instead, parents sent their internationally adopted children to language and cultural schools when they were in kindergarten and elementary school, but ethnic and racial socialization decreased by the time their children reached adolescence. This may be because fewer services that emphasize culture and language are available to older children. Additionally, many, but not all, white parents are unable to discuss issues of bias, microaggression, and racism, lacking familiarity with these behaviors. Being members of the more dominant culture in the U.S., they are not as likely to have experienced them. When internationally adopted children of color leave their white homes to attend college or take a job in a different town, they may suddenly have to grapple with people's responses to their skin color and many are not prepared to do so.

Bonding

In part because of the aforementioned experiences that are common among internationally adopted children, one significant challenge in their adoption process is bonding. It is critical for the parents to bond with the child as quickly as possible. According to developmental studies, there are particular times when learning takes place. If those windows are missed, then children may never learn that particular skill or if they do, it will be deficient in some way, which is why some internationally adopted children have trouble with close relationships (Brodzinsky, 1987; Brodzinsky et al., 1993; Brodzinsky et al., 1998; Groza et al., 2003; Groza & Rosenberg, 2001; Tan et al., 2010, 2012). To foster bonding with older children, families can try to connect over food, because these children are often undernourished and hungry. By taking advantage of the many restaurants in the country being visited, older adoptive children will enjoy eating with their new families and having them experience the traditional foods that they enjoy. The White Swan Hotel in Quangzhou, China, is a place where many families bond with their children. Families who adopt from China stay there while they wait for their child's U.S. passport. The hotel is child friendly, with lovely grounds and game rooms. Its restaurants serve delicious food, and it is located near interesting shops from which families can make their final purchases before leaving China. Parents often buy traditional Chinese outfits for their children to wear later to holiday parties. China is used as an example in this case, because around 2000, it replaced South Korea as the most popular country outside of North America from which to adopt (Koh et al., 2022).

Another bonding technique involves sleep. Initially sleeping in the same room, and sometimes in the same bed, if the child is old enough, helps cement emotional attachment, connection, feelings of safety and security, and belonging together. Generally, becoming parents to active and curious children brightens families' lives and brings a greater level of happiness and fulfillment than they can rationally explain. Yet, this may not be the case for all adoptive parents. If the challenges are greater than the family expects, it may make sense for them to seek counseling (Baden et al., 2017; Lee, 2003; Tan & Yi, 2019). Families who adopt internationally, similar to families who give birth to their children, will have a myriad of experiences—both positive and negative—some that will bring them closer together, some that will create distance between them and their children, and some in which seeking help from family therapists who are knowledgeable about adoption and can suggest appropriate interventions may be warranted.

Emotional Difficulties Experienced by the Internationally Adopted Child

Most international adoptions work out well. Research, particularly on adoptions from China, shows that children make a quick adjustment during the first year. They do as well as their non-adopted peers in school, make friends, and plan to attend college and get good jobs (Brodzinsky et al., 1993; Verrier, 1993). However, some children have problems adjusting and discontent may be displayed in ongoing temper tantrums or other symptoms of distress (Kim, 2021). In these cases, parents need to seek help from adoption counselors, child psychologists, psychiatrists, or family therapists (Brodzinsky, 2013). Although this can lead to unexpected expense, treatment methodologies such as Attachment-based Therapy, Narrative Therapy, Family Systems Therapy, Cognitive Behavioral Therapy, and Play Therapy can be very helpful in addressing dysfunctional patterns, raising self-esteem, and enhancing family cohesion.

Over the course of development, all foreign-born adoptees are not the same. For instance, one internationally adopted client of mine, age 27, reported that although she struggles with her identity, she knows many other international adoptees who do not. Because international adoption offers many opportunities and challenges, adjustment is unique to the individual (Liu & Hazier, 2015). Some, but not all, yearn to know their birth family (Grotevant & von Orff, 2011; Hagood, 2021; Koskinen & Book, 2019; Tieman et al., 2008). They may love their adopted parents but grieve the loss of their biological parents. Others, but not all, struggle with low self-esteem, transracial challenges, difficulty forming emotional attachments, and frustration with not knowing more about their genetic risk of developing certain diseases. These issues may come and go throughout their lives, depending upon their stress levels.

In addition, research shows that international adoptees are more vulnerable to eating disorders, depression, and anxiety than non-adoptees (Brodzinsky et al., 1998; Verrier, 1993). However, Chinese adopted girls, who have accounted for one fourth of all international adoptions through 2012, have demonstrated fewer behavioral problems than non-adopted girls of the same preschool ages, stronger bonding and attachment to their adoptive parents, and better social-emotional development (Tan et al., 2012). They appear to grow rapidly in the first 6 months after coming to the U.S. and their academic performance is appropriate for their grade and age. Adoption counselors believe their social-emotional adjustment is due to the sociopolitical climate in China. China's implementation of the one child policy in 1979, and cultural preference for boys, means that 90% of the children they export for adoption are girls. Little girls seem to have fewer behavior problems and a stronger desire to please than little boys of the same age). Many also believe that Chinese adoptees are healthier than children from Russia and Eastern Europe whose birth mothers have been found to struggle with alcoholism and substance abuse (Kreider & Cohen, 2009).

Children who have spent more time in an orphanage before being adopted also are believed more likely to suffer a greater number of emotional-behavior problems because of that experience than those who spent a shorter amount of time in institutions (Johnson, 1999–2024). Since 85% of all international adoptees have been institutionalized for some period in facilities where their needs were not met due to shortages of food, clothing, water, and toys, they have suffered some emotional and behavioral consequences (Kreider & Cohen, 2009). China has tried to prevent these problems by offering a family-type atmosphere in its orphanages. The aides are called "mama" and "papa" and seem to have close relationships with the children. More crying and distress can be observed when they separate and the aides say goodbye to the children, a sign that bonding had occurred (Gammage, 2007).

As explained earlier in this chapter, better mental health outcomes can be expected when international adoptees experience bonding and attachment (Cohen & Farnia, 2011; Tan et al., 2010). Attachment to one's caregiver or parents facilitates normal brain development. Lack of attachment, when a child is unable to trust and feel safe and close with another person, is associated with learning disabilities, social withdrawal, somatic complaints, behavior problems, and emotional dysregulation. Internationally adopted infants who are overly rejecting of their new parents or unnecessarily clingy demonstrate attachment issues, have a poorer prognosis, and most likely will need mental health interventions as soon as possible (Tan et al., 2012). Future mental and emotional health can also be predicted by the level of stress in the adoptive family at the time of adoption. High stress in the adopting family correlates with the experience of emotional problems later in life for the international adoptee. Learning more about these experiences can help adoptive parents and mental health professionals better support these children (Huff, 2023). Statistics show that internationally adopted children, even those who bond well, receive more mental health services then both non-adopted children and nationally adopted children (Brodzinsky et al., 1998; Verrier, 1993). This may occur because international adoptees lack places, other than a counselor's office, where they can express their confusion, pain, anger, sadness, and frustration without being seen as ungrateful.

Many people believe that international adoptees should feel gratitude because they have been rescued from fates such as death by drowning, starvation, lives of crime, and being homeless or living in institutions. Thus, knowing that gratitude is expected of them, a large percentage of internationally adopted children don't want to rock the boat at home or at school. Therefore, they suppress their negative feelings, which can lead to more anxiety and more depression (Brodzinsky et al., 1993; Henderson, 2007; Lifton, 2009; Rampage et al., 2011; Verrier, 1993). This is why objective and empathetic counselors and therapists can be a great help to these children (Baden, 2007).

International adoptees seek mental health treatment for different reasons and at different times in their lives (Baden et al., 2017; Brodzinsky et al., 1998; Brodzinsky et al., 1993). Of course, there are some who never seek treatment, either because they are resilient, cope well, are private, or don't believe it will help. Clinicians who work with international adoptees understand the complex sets of feelings that they struggle with internally, including carrying the "ghosts" of their biological family in their imaginations and in their hearts (Lifton, 2010). Since every adoption story includes loss and grief, therapists can help adoptees express these feelings and learn to deal with their loss (Rampage et al., 2011). Acknowledging the trauma that occurred prior to the adoption, along with the love and compassion they have been receiving, opens the door to empathy, understanding, good communications, and fulfilling relationships.

Family Dynamics

Sometimes the problem occurs with the adopting parents. They can't get along and divorce. Then the child experiences more loss. After a divorce, one or both parents may remarry, and new people come into the child's life, creating more change and a lack of stability, all outside of the child's control. Occasionally there's toxic sibling rivalry creating situations where the adopted child has to be concerned with surviving abuse in the family home, in addition to the other challenges. Feelings of emotional safety and security are lost or diminished when this occurs (Boss, 1999). Additionally, older children, who formerly lived in dormitory situations with many other children, sharing a few caretakers or nannies, may feel like an outsider in their new home, experiencing jealousy or insecurity when they observe the close relationship their parents have with each other or with other members of their new adoptive family. They have not yet learned skills that will allow them to trust others, let down their defenses, open up, and feel safe with other people (Verrier, 1993).

Open Adoption

One challenge that may become more common in the future related to international adoptions is open adoption. Open adoption means that contact exists between the biological and adoptive families (Grotevant et al., 2011), which can range from an exchange of letters or pictures, online videos, email communications, phone calls, to in-person visits. Domestically, open adoptions have increased in the last two decades, however although other countries are considering open adoption, it remains rare outside of the U.S. (Koskinen & Book, 2019; Pertman, 2011; Seymore, 2015; Tieman et al., 2008). In fact, many families choose international adoptions so that they will not be challenged at a later date concerning who is entitled to raise the child (Bartholet, 1995; Freundlich, 2000; Kim et al., 2024; Pertman, 2011). They will not have to deal with "intrusions" from the birth parents: letters, photographs, gifts, and opinions about how to raise the child. On the other hand, genetic information is lost and this information can be helpful in diagnosing specific conditions that have occurred or that could occur in the future. Due to the lack of genetic data, as well as the rights of children to know their birth parents, interest in open international adoptions is now growing (Seymore, 2015). There is increasing interest in connecting international adoptees with their birth families (Hagood, 2021; Koskinen & Book, 2019; Tieman et al., 2008). Some families who adopted internationally in the past are now in the process of seeking out the birth parents for their children, looking for DNA matches online. They believe that once their children get to know their birth parents, they will develop a more secure sense of identity. However, for some of the reasons given above, not all parents who adopt internationally want their children to know their birth parents.

Meeting birth parents can be a mixed blessing (Hagood, 2021). For instance, some Chinese adoptees, who have attempted to find their birth parents, after spending much time and energy, have experienced disappointment. The birth parents may not have wanted to meet them due to shame about giving them up or not wanting to upset their other children. If they do meet their Chinese birthparents, who abandoned them most likely because of the one child rule in China, the birth parents may want money or gifts that the adopted child and adoptive parents are unwilling or uncomfortable providing. This becomes more complicated in other countries, where the birth parents may have been paid well for the child at the time of the adoption. Understandably, the adopted family does not want to pay more than it already has paid.

Adopted children, themselves, may have mixed feelings about searching for birthparents, especially if they have bonded well with their adoptive parents. They may feel disloyal or guilty, not wanting to betray the people they love. On the other hand, some will feel relief; it is like a breath of fresh air, *"I'm meeting people who look and sound like me."*

Special Addition After Completion of this Chapter

The Associated Press released a statement on September 6, 2024, saying that the Chinese government is ending a program that allows international families to adopt children from China. It will no longer process any adoptions, including those that are close to completion. The position China is taking will cause confusion for adoptive parents who have been currently assigned children and for those who were expecting to adopt from China in the future. The State Department is asking China for clarification of this new policy in writing. These circumstances offer proof that international adoptions continue to be tenuous and lawyers and agencies in the U.S. need to warn potential adopting parents of possible complications.

Conclusion

International adoption is a gift. For the adoptive parents, it is an honor to raise internationally adopted children and see them flourish and develop as full functioning human beings able to contribute to society and live fulfilling lives. Yes, there are struggles, but not necessarily more than parents have with their own biological children, particularly when they become adolescents. The difference is that internationally adopted children, in contrast to children living with their natural parents, have unique concerns, such as grief for someone they only knew for 9 months in the womb, racial identity concerns if they are being raised by parents of a different race, and self-esteem issues if they have a negative view of adoption. In most cases, adoptive parents, the extended family, support systems in the community, and family therapists have been able to help these children grapple with these issues. In conclusion, the lives of both the international adoptees and their adoptive parents become deeply intertwined, and the love they share with each other helps to bring about healing and fulfillment.

References

Adamec, C. (2005). *The complete idiot's guide to adoption* (2nd ed.). Alpha.

Baden, A. L., Kitchen, A., Mazza, J. R., Harrington, E. S., & White, E. E. (2017). Addressing adoption in counseling: A study of adult adoptees' counseling satisfaction. *Families in Society, 98*(3), 209–216. https://doi.org/10.1606/1044-3894.2017.98.26

Baden, A. L. (2016). "Do you know your *real* parents?" and other adoption microaggressions. *Adoption Quarterly, 19*(1), 1–25. https://doi.org/10.1080/10926755.2015.1026012

Baden, A. L., Alvarado, S. B., Malott, K. M. & Multi-Racial/Ethnic Counseling Concerns (MRECC) Interest Network of the American Counseling Association Taskforce (2015). Competencies for Counseling the Multiracial Population, *ACA Competencies*. htpps://www.counseling.org/docs/default-source/compatencies-for-counseling-the-multiracial-population-2-2-15-final.pdf?sfvrsn=10

Baden, A. L., Treweeke, L. M., & Ahluwalia, M. K. (2012). Reclaiming culture: Reculturation of transracial and international adoptees. *Journal of Counseling and Development, 90*(4), 387–399. https://doi.org/10.1002/j.1556-6676.2012.00049.x
Baden, A. L. (2007). Putting culture into context: The impact of attitudes toward the adoption of Chinese adoptees. In R. Javier, A. Baden, F. Biafora, & A. Camacho-Gingerich (Eds.), *Handbook of adoption: Implications for researchers, practitioners, and families* (pp. 117–133). Sage.
Bartholet, E. (1995). Race separatism in the family: More on the transracial adoption debate. *Duke Journal of Gender Law & Policy, 2*, 99–106. https://scholarship.law.duke.edu/djglp/vol2/iss1/7
Boss, P. (1999). *Ambiguous loss: Learning to live with unresolved grief.* Cambridge University Press.
Brodzinsky, D. M. (2013). *A need to know: Enhanced adoption competence among mental health professionals*. The Donaldson Adoption Institute. https://njarch.org/wpress/wpcontent/uploads/2015/2013_08_ANeedToKnow.pdf
Brodzinsky, D. M., Smith, D. W., & Brodzinsky, A. B. (1998). *Children's adjustment to adoption*. Sage.
Brodzinsky, D. M. (1987). Adjustment to adoption: A psychosocial perspective. *Clinical Psychology Review, 7*(1), 25–47. https://doi.org/10.1016/0272-7358(87)90003-1
Brodzinsky, D., Schechter, M., & Henig, R. (1993). *Being adopted: The lifelong search for self.* Anchor.
Buck, P. (1959). *The good earth (11th printing)*. Cardinal Books, Pocket Books.
Budiman, A., & Lopez, M. H. (2017). *Amid decline in international adoptions to U.S., boys outnumber girls for the first time*. Pew Research Center.
Child Welfare Information Agency. (2022). *Numbers and trends.* http://www.childwelfare.gov; https://cwig-prod-prod-drupal-s3fs-us-east-1.s3.amazonaws.com/public/documents/adopted2010_19.pdf
Clinton, H. R. (1996). *It takes a village: And other lessons children teach us*. Simon & Schuster.
Cohen, N. J., & Farnia, F. (2011). Social-emotional adjustment and attachment in children adopted from China: Processes and predictors of change. *International Journal of Behavioral Development, 35*(1), 67–77. https://doi.org/10.1177/016502541037160
Curtis, J. L. (2000). *Tell me again about the night I was born (L Cornell, illus.)*. Harper Collins.
Dubinsky, K. (2010). *Babies without borders: Adoption and migration across the Americas*. University of Toronto Press.
Eldridge, S. (2009). *Twenty things adoptive parents need to succeed: Discover the unique need of your adopted child and become the best parent you can*. Jessica Kingsley.
Eldridge, S. (1999). *Twenty things adopted kids wish their adoptive parents knew*. Delta.
Foli, K., & Thompson, J. (2004). *The post-adoption blues: Overcoming the unforeseen challenges of adoption*. Rodale Books.
Freundlich, M. (2000). *Adoption and ethics: The role of race, culture, and national origin in adoption* (Vol. 1). Child Welfare League of America.
Gammage, J. (2007). *China ghosts: My daughter's journey to America: My passage to fatherhood*. HarperCollins ebooks.
Gottman, J., & Gottman, J. S. (2008). *And baby makes three: The six-step plan for preserving marital intimacy and rekindling romance after baby arrives*. Harmony.
Gray, D. (2012). *Attaching in adoption: Practical tools for today's parents*. Jessica Kingsley.
Gray, D. (2011). *Nurturing adoptions: Creating resilience after neglect and trauma*. Perspectives Press.
Grotevant, H. D., Rueter, M., Von Korff, L., & Gonzalez, C. (2011). Post- adoption contact, adoption communicative openness, and satisfaction with contact as predictors of externalizing behavior in adolescence and emerging adulthood. *Journal of Child Psychology and Psychiatry, 52*(5), 529–536. https://doi.org/10.1111/j.1469-7610.2010.02330.x
Grotevant, H. D., & von Orff, L. (2011). Adoptive identity. In S. J. Schwartz et al. (Eds.), *Handbook of identity theory and research* (pp. 585–601). Springer Science and Business Media.
Groza, V. K., Ryan, S. D., & Cash, S. J. (2003). Institutionalization, behavior and international adoption: Predictors of behavior problems. *Journal of Immigrant Health, 5*(1), 5–17. https://doi.org/10.1023/A:1021096028003

Groza, V. K., & Rosenberg, K. F. (2001). *Clinical and practice issues in adoption: Revised and updated, bridging the gap between adoptees placed as infants and as older children*. Bloomsbury Publishing.
Hagood, W. O. (2021). *Searching for your Chinese birth family*. Heritage Books.
Henderson, D. B. (2007). Why has the mental health community been silent on adoption issues? In R. A. Javier, A. L. Baden, F. A. Biafora, & A. Camacho-Gingerich (Eds.), *Handbook of adoption: Implications for researchers, practitioners, and families* (pp. 403–417). Sage,. https://doi.org/10.4135/9781412976633.n25
Holt International. (2024). *Families in process*. A step-to-step guide to your adoption. https://www.holtinternational.org/adoption/families-in-profcess/
Holten, K. (2023). *The true cost of raising a child*. Institute for Family Studies.
Huff, C. (2023). Behind the international adoption journey. *APA monitor, 54*(7), 52.
Johnson, D. H. (1999–2024). *International adoption: Sensitive advice for prospective parents*. Adoptive Families Magazine. https://www.adoptivefamilies.com/transracial-adoption/5-ways-talking-about-racism/
Johnston, P. I. (2012). *Adoption is a family affair!: What relatives and friends must know*. Jessica Kingsley Publishers.
Jones, J. (2019). *What is the history of adoption*. Adoption.org https://adoption.org/what-is-the-history-of-adoption.
Kasza, L. (1996). *A mother for Choco*. Puffin Books.
Kim, J. R. (2021). Forever family is like a manufactured Hallmark idea: Adoption discontinuity experiences of intercountry adoptions. *Child Abuse and Neglect, 130*(12), 105184. https://doi.org/10.1016/j.chiabu.2021.105184
Kim, J. R., Lindley, J., Zhou, X., Lee, H., & Lee, R. (2024). Korean adoptees who adopt: Ethnic, racial and adoption socialization with second-generation adoptees. *Adoption Quarterly.*, 1. https://doi.org/10.1080/10926755.2024.2345051
Koh, E., Hanlon, R., Daughtery, L., & Lindner, A. (2022). *Adoption by the numbers*. National Council for Adoption.
Koskinen, M. G., & Book, M. L. (2019). Searching for the self: Adult international adoptees' narratives of their search for and Reunion with their birth families. *Adoption Quarterly, 22*(3), 219–246. https://doi.org/10.1080/10926755.2019.1627449
Kreider, R. M., & Cohen, P. N. (2009). Disability among internationally adopted children in the United States. *Pediatrics, 124*(5), 1311–1318. https://doi.org/10.1542/peds.2008-3206
Kupecky, R. M. & Keck, G. C. (2009). *Parenting the hurt child: Helping adoptive families heal and grow.* NavPress, imprint of Tyndale House Publishers, Inc.
Lee, R. M. (2003). The transracial adoption paradox: History, research, and counseling implications of cultural socialization. *The Counseling Psychologist, 31*(6), 711–744. https://doi.org/10.1177/0011808000003258087
Lifton, B. J. (2010). Ghosts in the adopted family. *Psychoanalytic Inquiry, 30*(1), 71–79. https://doi.org/10.1080/07351690903200176
Lifton, B. J. (2009). *Lost & found: The adoption experience (Third edition)*. University of Michigan Press.
Lifton, B. J. (1995). *Journey of the adopted self: A quest for wholeness*. Basic Books.
Liu, Y., & Hazier, R. J. (2015). What counselors and parents need to know. *The Professional Counselor, 5*(2), 238.
March, K. (1995). Perception of adoption as social stigma: Motivation for search and Reunion. *Journal of Marriage & the Family, 57*(3), 653–660. https://doi.org/10.2307/353920
Maskew, T. (2003). *Our own. Adopting and parenting the older child*. Snowcap Press, Imprint of V3 Graphics.
Melina, L. R. (1989). *Making sense of adoption: A parent's guidebook*. Harper Perennial.
Melina, L.R. (1998). Raising adopted children: Practical reassuring advice for every adoptive parent *(Revised edition)*. .
Melosh, B. (2002). *Strangers and kin: The American way of adoption*. Harvard University Press.

Mignot, J. F. (2015). Why is intercountry adoption declining worldwide? *Population and Societies, 519*(2), 1–4.

Montgomery, J. E., & Jordan, N. A. (2018). Racial-ethnic socialization and transnational adoptee outcomes: A systematic research synthesis. *Child and Adolescent Social Work Journal., 35*(6), 439–453. https://doi.org/10.1007/s10560-018-0541-9

Montgomery, M. & Powell, I. (2018). International adoptions have dropped 72 percent since 2005—Here's why. *The Conversation.* https://theconversation.com/international-adoptions-have-dropped-72-percent-since-2005-heres-why-91809

Parr, T. (2011). *We belong together: A book about adoption and families.* Little Brown Books for Young Readers.

Pavao, J. M. (2005). *The family of adoption: Completely revised and updated.* Beacon Press.

Pertman, A. (2011). *Adoption nation: How the adoption revolution is transforming our families—And America.* Harvard Common Press.

Post, B. (2010). *From fear to love: Parenting difficult adopted children.* Post Publishing.

Der Princess, L. (1928). *Old Buddha.* Dodd, Mead & Company.

Purvis, K., Cross, D. R., & Sunshine, W. L. (2007). *The connected child: Bring hope and healing to your adoptive family.* McGraw Hill.

Rampage, C., Eovaldi, M., Ma, C., & Weigel-Foy, C. (2011). Adoptive families. In F. Walsh (Ed.), *Normal family processes: Growing diversity and complexity* (4th ed., pp. 210–232). Guilford Press.

Richmond, M. (2008). *I wished for you: An adoption story.* Sourcebooks Jabberwocky.

Schwartz, L. L., & Kaslow, F. (2003). *Welcome home!: An international and nontraditional adoption reader.* (Haworth Marriage and the Family Series). Routledge.

Selman, P. (2009). The rise and fall of intercountry adoption in the 21st century. *International Social Work Journal, 52*(5), 575–594. https://doi.org/10.1177/0020872809337681

Seymore, M. L. (2015). *Openness in international adoption.* Columbia Human Rights Law Review. Texas A & M University School of Law.

Siegel, D. H. (2008). Adoption issues from a strengths perspective. *Social Work Today, 8*(4), 34.

Siegel, D. J. (2012). *The developing mind: How relationships and the brain interact to shape who we are* (2nd ed.). Guilford Press.

Smalley, B. K., & Schooler, J. E. (2015). *Telling the truth to your adopted or foster child: Making sense of the past.* Praeger Publishers.

Soares, J., Ralha, S., Fonseca, S. M., Prego, J., & Barboa-Ducharne, M. A. (2023). Why and how do parents decide to adopt? A study on motivations and the decision-making process in becoming an adoptive family. *Child & Family Social Work, 28*(3), 589–596. https://doi.org/10.1111/cfs.13001

Steinberg, G., & Hall, B. (2013). *Inside transracial adoption: Strength-based, cultural-sensitizing parenting strategies for inter-country or domestic adoptive families that don't match.* Jessica Kingsley.

Suter, E. A., & Ballard, R. L. (2009). "How much did you pay for her?": Decision-making criteria underlying adoptive parents' response to inappropriate remarks. *Journal of Family Communication., 9*(2), 107–125. https://doi.org/10.1080/15267430902773253

Tan, T. X., Camras, L. A., Deng, H., Zhang, M., & Lu, Z. (2012). Family stress, parenting styles, and behavioral adjustment in preschool-age adopted Chinese girls. *Early Childhood Research Quarterly, 27*(1), 128–136. https://doi.org/10.1016/j.ecresq.2011.04.002

Tan, T. X., Marfo, K., & Dedrick, R. F. (2010). Early developmental and psychosocial risks and longitudinal behavior adjustment outcomes for preschool-age girls adopted from China. *Journal of Applied Developmental Psychology, 31*(4), 306–314. https://doi.org/10.1016/j.appdev.2010.04.002

Tan, T. X., & Yi, Z. (2019). Is adoption equally beneficial to different aspects of youth's behavioral health? Findings from comparing adopted Chinese youth with non-adopted American and Chinese Youth. *Youth & Society, 53*(1), 153–169. https://doi.org/10.1177/0044118X19849742

Tessler, R., Tuan, M., & Shiao, J. S. (2011). The many faces of international adoption. *Contexts, 10*(4), 34–39. https://doi.org/10.1177/1536504211427866

Tieman, W., van der Ende, J., & Verhulst, F. C. (2008). Young adult international adoptees search for birth parents. *Journal of Family Psychology, 22*(5), 678–687. https://doi.org/10.1037/a0013172

van den Dries, L., Juffer, F., Van IJzendoorn, M., & Bakermans-Kranenburg, M. (2009). Fostering security? A meta-analysis of attachment in adopted children. *Children and Youth Services Review, 31*(3), 410–421. https://doi.org/10.1016/j.childyouth.2008.09.008

Verrier, N. (1993). *The primal wound: Understanding the adopted child.* Gateway Press.

Verrier, N. (2015). *Information for adoptees.* www.family-institute.org, http://nancyverrier.com/information-for-adoptees

Watkins, M., & Fisher, S. (1995). *Talking to young children about adoption.* Yale University Press.

Wilner, K. B. (2024). *Releasing toxic anger for women: Somatic practices & CBT skills to transform negative thoughts, soothe stress & stay true to yourself.* New Harbinger.

Wilner, K. B. (2020). The wounding womb, healing prenatal trauma. *International Body Psychotherapy Journal*, 20th Anniversary Issue, *19*(2), 56–63.

Karyne B. Wilner, MA, MA, PsyD, Clinical Psychologist, is Director of the Core Energetics Academy in Newtown, CT and on the faculty of the Institute of Core Energetics, founded by John C. Pierrakos, MD, who along with Alexander Lowen, MD, developed Bioenergetics. She has private practices in Bethel, CT and Newport, RI. Formerly Director of Counseling Services for Drexel University in Philadelphia and adjunct faculty member in the Graduate School for Holistic Counseling at Salve Regina University in Newport, RI, she was Assistant Director of the International Institute of Core Energetics headquartered in NYC (1995–2011). A national speaker and presenter, her published articles and book chapters include "The Wounding Wound: Healing Prenatal Trauma," The Case of the Broken Heart; A Modern Perspective," and "Releasing Toxic Anger for Women: Somatic Practices & CBT Skills to Transform Negative Thoughts, Soothe Stress & Stay True to Yourself."

Chapter 12
Summation and Epilogue

Florence W. Kaslow

Summation

This summation of what would be presented in each of the 12 chapters in the book is presented in the Foreword, where why this book was written, and the focus of each chapter is also contained. It also includes a highlighting of the issues covered by each author and the suggestions made to help resolve the problems and issues being discussed. These therefore do not need to be repeated here.

Epilogue

It is sincerely hoped that you have found reading and absorbing the material contained in the previous eleven chapters challenging, informative, and stimulating. Feel free to contact me or any of the contributing authors if you have any questions or comments.

Florence W. Kaslow, PhD, ABPP, is in private practice as an individual, couples and family psychologist and Family Business Consultant in West Palm Beach, FL. She has been a Professor at a Medical School in Philadelphia and a former Dean of a Psychology graduate school in Florida. She has guest lectured in over 50 countries, is the author or editor of 32 books, and a contributor to over 100 other books.

F. W. Kaslow (✉)
Kaslow Associates, Palm Beach Gardens, FL, USA

F. W. Kaslow (ed.), *Contemporary Issues in Individual, Couple, and Family Lives and Treatment*, https://doi.org/10.1007/978-3-031-90006-8_12

Index

A
Ancestry, 179
Attachment, 1, 3, 15, 30–32, 36, 132, 134, 140–142, 144, 158, 186, 187, 189, 191, 192

B
Business succession, 109

C
Children, 1–4, 6, 8–11, 13–22, 41–43, 46, 47, 51, 52, 54, 55, 57, 58, 60, 66, 98–100, 109, 113, 115–118, 120–124, 130, 131, 141, 152, 153, 156, 160–162, 165–173, 177–195
Concierge medicine, 72–74, 77
Consultants, xv, 115, 117–121, 125, 126, 175
Couple interventions, 133, 136, 151
Cultural considerations, 102–105

F
Family businesses, xv, 109–126
Family composition, 20
Family dynamics, 2, 9, 10, 14–18, 20–22, 83, 84, 93, 95, 96, 104, 114, 130–134, 193
Family interventions, 133
Family structures, 2–4, 7, 9–15, 19–22, 59, 132
Finances, 160, 165–175

G
Gender dynamics, 168
Grief and loss, 189, 193

I
Identity formation, 3–10
Intergenerational families, 42
International adoptions, 177–195
Internationally adopted children, 177, 181, 185–193, 195
Internet, 68, 151–157, 184
Interventional neurosurgery, 81–106

L
Loneliness, 5, 6, 8, 42, 44, 48

M
MDMA, 30–37
MDMA-assisted couple therapy, 32, 34–37
Multigenerational families, 109–126

N
Neuropsychology, 81–106
New lifestyle norms, 156–162

F. W. Kaslow (ed.), *Contemporary Issues in Individual, Couple, and Family Lives and Treatment*, https://doi.org/10.1007/978-3-031-90006-8

P
Patient-physician communication
Physician burnout, 67, 72, 74–75
Political differences, 130–143
Politics, 122, 129–134, 137–144, 152
Postpartum blues and postpartum depression, 51–59
Postpartum disorders, 51–61
Postpartum disorders and couples, 55–57
Postpartum family, 59
Postpartum psychosis, 52–57, 59, 60
Primary care, 63–77
Primary care practice models, 72
Psychedelic-assisted treatment, 32
Psychedelics, 29–37

R
Relational family dynamics, 81–106
Relationship trends, 151–162
Relocations, 165–175
Resilience, 2, 5, 6, 10–15, 18, 19, 21, 23, 75, 131
Retirement, 41, 43–48, 117, 161

S
Safe family environments, 10–11
Separation, 11, 161, 167, 189

T
Telehealth, 68–71

U
Uncoupling, 162

V
Virtual couples therapy

W
Women, 5, 19, 20, 43, 44, 51–54, 56, 58–61, 67, 73, 75, 113, 159, 165, 168, 171–174, 178, 179, 183

MIX
Papier aus verantwortungsvollen Quellen
Paper from responsible sources
FSC® C105338

If you have any concerns about our products,
you can contact us on
ProductSafety@springernature.com

In case Publisher is established outside the EU,
the EU authorized representative is:
Springer Nature Customer Service Center GmbH
Europaplatz 3, 69115 Heidelberg, Germany

Printed by Libri Plureos GmbH
in Hamburg, Germany